W9-ASG-060

Abdera

SCYTHIA

Cyzicus

PHRYGIA

Hellespont

Lemnos

Troy

ASIA MINOR

EA

Lesbos

LYDIA

Sardis

Chios

Ephesus

Samos

Meander R.

Icaria

Miletus

DODECANESE IS.

ADES

Delos

Paros Naxos

Calymne

Cos

Rhodes

Cnossus

* Mt. Ida

CLASSICAL GODS AND HEROES

CLASSICAL GODS

Myths as Told by
the Ancient Authors

BL 722
H45

176908

JUL 2 5 1973

AND HEROES

TRANSLATED AND INTRODUCED BY
RHODA A. HENDRICKS

FREDERICK UNGAR PUBLISHING CO. *New York*

Copyright © 1972 by Rhoda A. Hendricks
Printed in the United States of America
Library of Congress Catalog Card Number: 74-163140
ISBN: 0-8044-2376-8

*For
Stephen, Mary,
and
Hannah Sechrist*

Contents

Editor's Note

The primary purpose of this book is to present the myths of the Greeks and Romans in direct translation from the original words of the classical authors. When the ancients are allowed to recount their own myths in their own way a deeper appreciation of their literature and civilization is attained. At the same time the allusions to Greek and Roman mythology that appear so frequently in art, literature, music, and everyday vocabulary are made more meaningful.

The material selected for translation includes the more familiar myths and those which have had a profound influence on Western culture; it is also representative of a wide range of Greek and Roman sources of mythology. In an effort to preserve a balance between the exigencies of space and a proper treatment of each myth, omissions have been made, without the use of ellipses, when they do not interfere with the narrative and atmosphere of the story or detract from a feeling of continuity and smooth transition.

Except in the case of Pollux, less commonly known by his Greek name, Polydeuces, and some instances where names have been Latinized, the Greek names have been retained in the translations from Greek texts; and Roman names from Latin texts.

The Glossary is intended for ready identification of the names of those persons and places that occur in the translations. Most names that appear only once or twice and are identified when they are found in the text have not been included in the Glossary. Maps of the ancient Greek and Mediterranean areas for reference by the reader are provided as front and back endpapers.

Introduction

During the period of prehistory, before the dawn of recorded events, when man was limited to oral communication, the peoples of Hellas, the land we know as Greece, recounted to each other and to succeeding generations a variety of myths and legends. Some of these stories were told for pure entertainment, others were etiological in nature, and still others contained some germ of truth or fact from past or current history or about real personages. Whatever the purpose or theme, whether the tale was one of adventure or in explanation of natural phenomena, religious beliefs or customs, or was about a hero or legendary incident, or comprised more than one of these elements, it was handed down by word of mouth from person to person.

With the advent of writing, the corpus of mythology that had been developed by the Greeks naturally continued to be related orally, but it also tended to take on the character that was imposed upon it by the professional bards and the authors who utilized this rich storehouse of material. Changes and embellishments resulted from attempts to adapt the stories to special purposes or to reconcile the numerous divergencies that were the inevitable consequence of the heterogeneous origins of the myths.

Numerous other forces were at work as the myths went through varying stages of development. One such change was that of anthropomorphism, a process that began at an early period and was almost completed by about the eighth or seventh century B.C. The functions, attributes, and epithets of the deities were also subject to change. Poseidon, for example, was known in early times as a god of the depths of the earth and was, therefore, thought to cause earthquakes, thus giving him his epithet "earth-shaker." Later Poseidon became more exclusively a god of the sea. Political developments and struggles, periods of war or peace, migrations and colonization, new geographical or social concepts, and broader contacts brought about through trade were among the manifold influences that affected the myths.

In the hands of the Greek tragedians the myths were put to a new use. The subject matter of all but one of their extant tragedies was drawn from mythology, but it was not their purpose to present the myths per se, since their audiences were familiar with the details of the stories. Instead, by modification and adaptation the dramatist shaped a myth into a vehicle for the development of a psychological study of the characters of the play. The focus was not so much on the events of the drama as on the emotional impact resulting from the interaction of the characters as they were involved in these episodes.

In addition, as early as the sixth century B.C. in Greece more personal and emotional religions had begun to replace the traditional belief in the deities and in the mythology surrounding them. New rites and cults, such as the Eleusinian Mysteries and the Orphic cult, appeared and won wide followings.

The following authors are the sources for the translations in this book. Each played his part in the evolution and modification of the mythology with which he dealt.

Homer, the earliest of the extant Greek authors, was a wandering bard. Modern dating places him in the ninth century B.C., as did Herodotus. Dialectic and other linguistic evidence points to the Asiatic coast of the Aegean Sea as his probable birthplace. The composition of his two great epics—the *Iliad*, dealing with the final year of the Trojan War and the theme of the wrath of Achilles, and the *Odyssey*, telling of Odysseus' wanderings after the Trojan War and the events after his return to Ithaca—indicates that they were intended to be recited. The Homeric controversy is a ceaseless, academic pendulum questioning whether one man could have composed or recited such long poems and whether his name was in fact Homer. Whatever the answer, it is certain that the *Iliad* and the *Odyssey* were indebted to the past.

Hesiod's date is uncertain, but most evidence, including that of Herodotus, indicates that he was a contemporary of Homer or lived at a slightly later time. We have little knowledge of his life, but he tells us in his poetry that he lived the life of a farmer in Boeotia. *Works and Days*, a didactic poem in hexameters, describes agricultural activities and presents moral precepts, proverbs, and myths. The *Theogony*, also in hexameters, provides a mythological explanation of the creation of the universe and an account of the genealogy of the gods. The *Astronomy* has survived only in fragmentary form and its authenticity is doubtful.

The *Homeric Hymns,* poems in the epic manner and style of Homer, were composed by various bards or minstrels to be sung as a type of prelude before the recitation of passages from the *Iliad* or the *Odyssey.* The thirty-three poems of the *Homeric Hymns,* each of which is addressed to a deity, either summarize the accomplishments and attributes of the god or goddess invoked, or narrate a myth connected with the deity. Most of these poems were composed during the eighth and seventh centuries B.C., but a few are of a later date.

Pindar was born near Thebes toward the end of the sixth century B.C. He composed *Odes* to glorify the winners in the games of the four principal festivals of Greece—the Olympian, Pythian, Isthmian, and Nemean—using myths as background themes to elevate or support the material he was treating.

Sophocles lived in the fifth century B.C., the time when Athens was at her height and when the other great Greek tragedians, Aeschylus and Euripides, lived and wrote. Dramatic contests became an integral part of the festival of Dionysus at Athens, and they attracted keen competition among the dramatists. Sophocles won first place more than 20 times and second place in all the other contests he entered. Sophocles wrote over 120 tragedies before his death in 406 B.C. at the age of ninety, but only seven of these are extant. The titles or fragments of his other plays are all that have survived. Sophocles' best-known work, *Oedipus Tyrannus* (Oedipus the King), was held by Aristotle to measure up to all the requirements of a perfect tragedy.

Apollonius Rhodius (of Rhodes) lived in the third century B.C. and, for a time, he held the position of librarian at Alexandria. Later he went to live on Rhodes. Although Apollonius' epic, *Argonautica,* lacks imagination and true inspiration, some passages do show vivid descriptive powers and emotional depth.

Moschus was an Alexandrian poet of the second century B.C. who lived at Syracuse. He has left us only a handful of poems, but these are evidence that he was a capable poet.

Apollodorus' date is uncertain. He is generally placed in the second century B.C. or possibly later. Apollodorus was the author of an extensive compendium of Greek mythology, the *Bibliotheca*, or *Library*. Though it is a factual, often dull account, it contains much valuable information. Less than half of the *Library* is extant, but the material from the lost parts has been preserved in an *Epitome*.

Diodorus Siculus (of Sicily) lived in the first century B.C. and undertook the writing of a history of the world from the legendary beginnings to the Gallic War. This work, the *Bibliotheca historica*, or *Library*, is to a great extent a comprehensive compilation of the work of his predecessors, but Diodorus spent many years traveling, observing, and studying to prepare himself to execute his task effectively. A little over a third of his *Library* is extant.

Roman mythology is largely a mirror of Greek mythology. The Greeks had started on a program of planned colonization by about 800 B.C. As a result, Greek thought and culture entered Italy by way of the cities founded by the Greeks in southern Italy and Sicily, known as Magna Graecia. The colonies, naturally, kept their religious ties with the mother cities of Greece. When the Romans entered Italy they found there the religions of three groups of people: the Etruscans north of the Tiber River, the local Italian tribes of central Italy, and the Greeks of Magna Graecia. The Romans adopted and assimilated the deities of the Etruscans and Italians—deities that were not highly evolved and showed very little anthropomorphism—made some modifications of their own, and borrowed extensively from the mythology of the Greeks.

The Romans applied the myths, attributes, and epithets of the Greek deities to their own deities by a process of identification, and many of the Roman gods and goddesses became counterparts of those of the Greeks. Those deities the Romans did invent do not often show imagination and are, for the most part, in the Greek pattern. Following the Roman conquest of Greece in the second century B.C. the Roman writers imitated and followed the tradition of Greek literature. It should be remembered, however, that a change in focus and attitude toward mythology had taken place between the time of the Greek writers of the fourth and third centuries B.C. and the Roman writers, whose production came afterward.

Apuleius was born in northern Africa, probably in the latter half of the second century B.C. He lived in Carthage and traveled extensively. Apuleius' *Metamorphoses*, or *The Golden Ass*, is a fanciful novel that describes the numerous adventures of a certain Lucius who had been changed into an ass. Among the many stories contained in the *Metamorphoses* is that of Cupid and Psyche, for which Apuleius is the only extant source.

Catullus, one of the greatest of lyric poets, was born at Verona circa 84 B.C. and died circa 54 B.C. Although most of his poems are subjective, a number of them deal with mythological subjects. Catullus' poetry, especially the longer poems, shows his debt to the Alexandrian school of writers.

Vergil, the author of the *Aeneid*, lived from 70 to 19 B.C., during the period of transition between the Roman Republic and the Empire. To glorify Rome's past and future, Vergil wrote the story of the wandering of Aeneas and his followers after the Trojan War and of their arrival at last in Italy, thus linking the legendary founders of Rome with Trojan origins. Vergil drew on the *Iliad* and the *Odyssey* for his material and inspiration, but he made these and other sources his own by the manner in which he treated them and by his independence and originality. Although Vergil died before the *Aeneid* was in the perfected state he intended it to have, he left the world one of its finest literary treasures.

Ovid, who lived from 43 B.C. to 17 or 18 A.D., was educated for the law, but his real interest and talent lay in versification. To Ovid a myth had value only as a good tale to delight the imagination and to entertain. He has left us an extensive treatment of a vast number of Greek myths and a few of Roman origin, some of which are to be found in no other classical author. Most of the myths in the *Metamorphoses* describe some type of change in form and they cover the gamut of mythology from the creation of the world to the deification of Julius Caesar, making this a valuable source book.

Valerius Flaccus was a writer of the first century A.D. He died in 90 A.D. before his epic the *Argonautica* was finished. Like many other Roman authors, Valerius Flaccus was influenced by his Greek predecessors, but his work demonstrates that he had a keen insight and an imagination of his own.

Among the more important of those writers who did not deal primarily with mythological themes but whose works contain numerous and important references to the myths of the classical world are the Greeks Herodotus, Plato, Pausanias, and the Roman Horace. Their subjects, ranging from history, philosophy, travel and geography to lyric poetry, reveal their familiarity with mythology and the strong influence it had upon them.

Mention should be made, too, of the contribution of the scholiasts to our knowledge of mythology. Their textual criticism, clarification, and interpretation in the form of notes written in the margins of manuscripts they copied and studied furnish additional information and valuable commentary.

A number of the Greek myths are of Thracian or Asiatic origin and others belong to a pre-Hellenic or pre-Homeric period. Many of the myths are laid against the setting of the cities of Minoan and Mycenaean civilization—Cnossus, Mycenae, Tiryns, and Thebes. Some understanding of the history of the eastern Mediterranean area and significant events that influenced the inhabitants of Greece therefore forms a necessary background to a rounded picture of the mythology of those people.

While most of the Greek mainland was still in the Neolithic stage of development, Crete had become a center of advanced culture and Cnossus had attained a position of importance by about 2300 B.C. Factors in the development of this culture, known as Minoan, were a prosperous trade and close contact with neighboring lands, especially Egypt. The palace of Cnossus was destroyed by an earthquake in about 1700 B.C. and was rebuilt on an enlarged, grand scale. It is this extensive complex that is known as the palace of Minos. By about 1400 B.C., the power of the Minoans came to an abrupt end. There is strong evidence that the palace of Cnossus was burned at that time, possibly in connection with a flood following an earthquake. The fact that few bones have been found at the site suggests that the inhabitants fled from a natural disaster or were captured by invaders.

In the second millenium B.C., or perhaps even earlier, the indigenous non-Hellenic inhabitants of the Greek mainland were invaded by Indo-Europeans who migrated from the north. These Greek-speaking Hellenes settled mainly in Attica and the Peloponnesus, merging with the native Pelasgians and dominating them culturally and linguistically. One group pushed on across the Aegean Sea to Asia Minor, where the Hittites, their power fading, offered little resistance.

While the newcomers built their towns and cities—Tiryns, Mycenae, Argos, Athens, Thebes and others—and their fortresses and palaces, they increased in strength and reached a high level of civilization and prosperity under the influence of Minoan culture. They controlled the Aegean Sea and were strong enough to win the war they fought against the Trojans in about 1250 B.C. There is every indication that it was this Mycenaean civilization that gave birth to Greek mythology as we know it.

Around the middle of the twelfth century B.C., however, the rich culture of the Mycenaeans was overwhelmed by a new wave of invasion. This time the invaders, the Dorians, coming from the rugged northwest regions of Epirus and Thessaly, brought destruction with them and the Hellenes were forced to flee. Some took refuge in Athens, the only city to resist the attackers with success, but the vast majority were driven into Asia Minor by the continued advance of the Dorians, who occupied not only the mainland but also Crete and the Aegean Islands.

Following the Dorian invasions, Greece underwent a period of recovery that lasted several centuries. Finally, the Hellenic culture, which had been preserved in the settlements on the coast of Asia Minor, emerged and grew to dominate the Greek world once more, reaching its epitome in fifth-century Athens. It is this culture that is the fount of Western civilization.

The study of mythology took on another dimension with the birth of archaeology in the nineteenth century. Heinrich Schliemann, a German scholar equipped with a fortune and a knowledge of languages—both the result of his own determined efforts —went to Asia Minor in 1870 and, with a copy of Homer's *Iliad* at hand, discovered the site of ancient Troy. Thus he not only fulfilled his boyhood dream but also became the father of the

science of archaeology. Before his death in 1890, Schliemann
went on to unearth further evidence of the seeds of fact in the
mythology of the ancient Greeks as he carried on excavations at
Mycenae, Tiryns, Ithaca, and Orchomenus. In the following dec-
ade the English archaeologist Sir Arthur Evans was to demon-
strate that there had indeed been an extensive, elaborate palace at
Cnossus.

Since the time of Schliemann and Evans, continued excavation and research on the Greek mainland, Crete, the Aegean
Islands, Troy, and many other sites have shed further light on the
prehistory of that area. Archaeological evidence is no longer
limited to visible remains, such as the Acropolis of Athens, that
required little excavation, but now extends as deep as modern
methods can take the archaeologist's tools on the land and in the
sea. Archaeological research enlarges our comprehension of the
civilization the myths portray and presents us with representations of mythological subjects in the form of architectural sculpture, statuary, and vase and wall paintings. In a surprising number of instances, its findings corroborate the words of Homer,
Herodotus, Pausanias, and other writers of classical Greece.

Before the nineteenth century little or no attempt was made to
study the traditional mythology of the Greeks or to classify the
myths systematically. It was not until Christian A. Lobeck and
Karl O. Müller, who were contemporaries but worked separately
along similar lines, brought together the body of extant mythology and examined it with method and purpose, that mythological research evolved. By the end of the nineteenth century Max
Müller's work with Sanskrit gave impetus to comparative mythology, a study that was continued and developed by Andrew
Lang and others who followed him.

By tracing a single myth or a group or cycle of myths from
their earliest appearance many details can be observed and com-
pared. Geographical and historical information becomes apparent, as do evidences of adjustments, additions, and omissions
that crept in over the centuries as different writers handled the
material in various parts of the Mediterranean world. Exegesis
of this kind also brings out some chronological testimony that

enables the scholar to formulate reasonable speculations about the causes underlying the modifications.

The mythologist is aided in his examination of the literary evidence left by the ancient Greek and Roman writers not only by archaeological research but by countless scholars in other related disciplines. The linguist, geographer, anthropologist, artist, architect, paleographer, and many others all contribute to our ever widening understanding of classical mythology.

THE MAJOR DEITIES

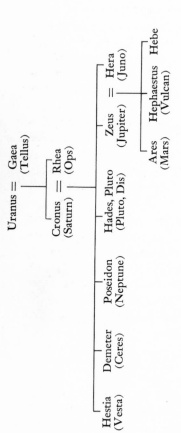

Uranus = Gaea
(Tellus)

Cronus = Rhea
(Saturn)   (Ops)

Hestia   Demeter   Poseidon   Hades, Pluto   Zeus   =   Hera
(Vesta)   (Ceres)   (Neptune)   (Pluto, Dis)   (Jupiter)   (Juno)

Ares   Hephaestus   Hebe
(Mars)   (Vulcan)

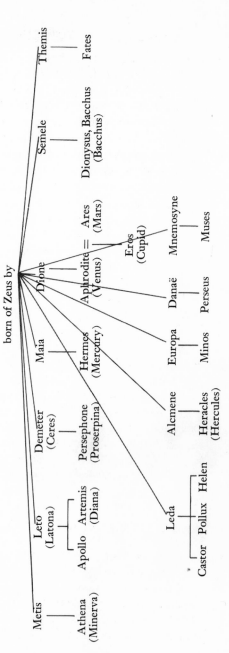

born of Zeus by

Metis   Leto   Demeter   Maia   Dione   Aphrodite = Ares   Semele   Themis
         (Latona) (Ceres)   (Venus)   (Mars)

Athena   Apollo Artemis   Persephone   Hermes   Eros   Dionysus, Bacchus   Fates
(Minerva)   (Diana)   (Proserpina) (Mercury)   (Cupid)   (Bacchus)

         Leda   Alcmene   Europa   Danaë   Mnemosyne

Castor Pollux Helen   Heracles   Minos   Perseus   Muses
                        (Hercules)

The Creation

The mysteries related to the beginnings of things, and especially to the origin of the universe, have always presented themselves to man as challenging questions. Various versions of the creation appeared at different periods in ancient times, but in all of them Chaos, or infinite space, was the first to come into being and was generally accepted as the earliest state of the universe. Later, the name Chaos was applied to the lower world, the kingdom of darkness, and also to the god of that world.

In comparing the two following accounts of the creation, it can be seen that Ovid's, written about eight centuries after Hesiod's, is a more objective description, relating the creation of natural phenomena in a straightforward manner without an effort to personify. Hesiod's role was that of a trailblazer, while Ovid's was that of a storyteller or narrator.

Hesiod presented an explanation of the separation of heaven (Uranus) and earth (Gaea) as a natural and irreversible phenomenon. He described Eros (love) as an elemental force and one of the earliest gods to come into being. In later mythology Eros was the son of Aphrodite, goddess of love. Ovid's version not only bears more resemblance to that found in the Book of Genesis but also selects one of the gods, an unnamed god, as the creator who brought order to the universe out of Chaos.

As told in Greek verse by Hesiod

FIRST OF all Chaos came into being, and then Gaea, the broad Earth, the ever certain support of all the deathless gods who dwell on the summit of snowy Olympus, and also dark Tartarus in the innermost part of the broad-pathed earth, and also Eros, the fairest of the immortal gods, who relaxes the limbs and overpowers the resolution and thoughtful determination in the hearts of all the gods and all mankind.

From Chaos came both Erebus and Nyx, the black Night, and of Nyx there were born Aether and Hemera, the Day, whom she bore to Erebus in a union of love. And Gaea first of all brought forth an equal to herself, Uranus, the starry Heaven, to cover her about on all sides and to be an ever certain dwelling place for the blessed gods.

Gaea also brought forth far-reaching Hills, the pleasant homes of the goddess Nymphs, who dwell in the wooded valleys of the hills. Without the delights of love, she also gave birth to the barren sea, Pontus, with his swelling waves. But later she lay with Uranus and bore deep-eddying Oceanus, Hyperion, and Iapetus, also Theia and Rhea, and Themis and Mnemosyne, and gold-crowned Phoebe and lovely Tethys. After them the youngest was born, the wily Cronus, the most dreadful of her children, and he hated his vigorous father.

In addition, she gave birth to the Cyclopes, who possess mighty hearts, Brontes and Steropes and also strong-minded Arges, who gave thunder to Zeus and forged the thunderbolt. They were like the gods in all other respects, but a single eye was set in the middle of their foreheads. They were given the name Cyclopes, because indeed one round eye was set in their foreheads. Strength and force and craftiness were in their deeds.

Three other sons were also born of Gaea and Uranus, huge and strong Cottus and Briareus and Gyges, overpowering offspring. A hundred arms rose from their shoulders, and each one had fifty heads growing out of his shoulders, set upon sturdy limbs, and the physical strength in their great frames was mighty and dreadful. They were the most terrible of the children born of Gaea and Uranus, and they were hated by their father from the beginning. As soon as each one of them was born he would hide him away in the depths of the earth and would not allow him to return to the daylight.

Uranus delighted in his evil deed, but Gaea groaned within because she was filled with distress, and she planned an evil and deceitful trick. She quickly created gray steel, forged a great sickle, and explained her plan to her beloved sons. She spoke, encouraging them, but she was grieved at heart. "My children, offspring of a sinful father, if you have the will, we shall make your father pay for this wicked outrage, for he was the first to devise shameful acts." So she spoke, but terror seized them all, and not one of them uttered a sound. Great Cronus, however, took courage and spoke these words in answer to his beloved mother:

"Mother, I shall in truth take it upon myself to accomplish this deed, since I have no feeling for my father, who bears an evil name, for he plotted shameless deeds from the first." So he spoke, and Gaea was greatly delighted in her heart. She concealed him in an ambush and placed in his hands a sickle with sharp, jagged teeth and laid before him the whole plot.

Then mighty Uranus came, bringing the night with him, and he lay over Gaea with the longing of love, spreading out at full length, and his son stretched out his left hand from the ambush, grasping the huge jagged sickle in his right hand, and quickly cut the genitals from his father's body and cast them behind him.

They did not fall from his hands in vain, for Gaea received kindly all the drops of blood that fell from them. As time rolled on she bore the mighty Erinyes and the huge Giants, shining with armor, and the Nymphs, whom they call Meliae throughout the boundless earth.

As soon as Cronus cut off the organs with the steel and threw them from the land into the swelling sea, they were carried off on the surface of the water, and a white foam from the immortal flesh rose up around them, and within the foam a maiden came into being. First she was carried close to holy Cythera, and then from there she came to seagirt Cyprus. She stepped forth as a beautiful goddess, and all about her, grass grew up beneath her delicate feet. The gods and men call her Aphrodite, and also the foam-born goddess and fair-crowned Cytherea, because she arose from the foam near Cythera, and Cyprus-born, because she was born on wave-washed Cyprus.

And Eros walked beside her, and lovely Desire followed her from the first, when she was born and when she entered the assembly of the gods. She had this honor from the beginning, and this was the destiny allotted to her among men and the immortal gods—the conversations of young maidens, and smiles, deceptions and sweet delight, love and affection, and gentleness.

From *Theogony*, 116–206

As told in Latin verse by Ovid

BEFORE THE sea and lands and the sky that covers everything existed, the appearance of nature in the entire universe was the same. This has been called Chaos, an unformed mass without order, and it was not anything except an inactive weight and the inharmonious seeds of things gathered in one place and loosely joined together. Up to that time, there was no Titan [the sun] spreading light over the world, and Phoebe [the moon] did not rise with new crescent horns, nor did the earth hang balanced by its own weight in the air flowing around it, nor had Amphitrite [the sea] stretched out her arms along the long borders of the land.

And although there was in existence not only land but sea and air, nevertheless the land was not firm, the water could not be swum in, the air lacked light. Nothing kept its proper shape.

One of the gods, or a quiet kindly nature, broke up this disorder, for he separated the lands from the sky and the seas from the lands and divided the clear sky from the dense air. After he had freed them and had removed them from the blind mass, he bound each element he had separated in its proper place in harmonious peace.

When this god, whichever of the gods it was, had divided the mass of Chaos and arranged it in order and had gathered each part into separate elements, he first of all collected the earth into the shape of a great sphere, so that it would be the same on all sides. Then he commanded the seas to pour forth in all directions and to swell before the swift winds and to encircle the earth and surround its shores.

He also created fountains and vast pools and lakes, and he hemmed in the flowing rivers with sloping banks. And he ordered the fields to spread forth, the valleys to settle down, the forests to be covered with leaves, and the stony mountains to rise up.

Hanging above these was the air, which is as much heavier than the weight of fire as water is lighter in weight than earth. He commanded the clouds to take their positions there, and also the mists, as well as the thunder that would shake the minds of men, and the winds that, with the thunderbolts, bring cold and chill.

He had hardly separated all these things and set them within definite limits when the stars, which for a long time had been held hidden below a dense fog, began to glow throughout the whole sky. And so that no region might be without its appropriate living beings, the stars and the forms of the gods occupied the sky, the waters fell to the shining fish as their dwelling place, the earth took on the wild animals, and the light air received the birds.

There still was lacking a being more venerable than animals such as these, one with greater powers of thought and reasoning who might be master over all other living creatures. Thus man was created, and although the other animals look down upon the earth, the creator of all things gave man an uplifted countenance and caused him to look to the sky and raise his upturned face toward the stars.

From *Metamorphoses* I, 5–86

The Birth of Zeus

Uranus (Heaven) and Gaea (Earth) were the parents of the Titans, six brothers and six sisters. Gaea, who took things into her own hands on more than one occasion, stirred up the Titans against their father. The result was that the Titans overthrew Uranus and made Cronus, their youngest brother, ruler. Cronus then married his sister Rhea.

Cronus and Rhea became the parents of six of the major Greek deities—Zeus, Hera, Hades, Poseidon, Demeter, and Hestia. Zeus, in turn, was the father of the other great gods and goddesses of Greek mythology—Athena, Apollo, Artemis, Ares, Hephaestus, Hermes, Dionysus, and, in Homer and most later accounts, Aphrodite.

Although Homer names Zeus as the oldest child of Cronus and Rhea, in the following account by Hesiod and in later mythology he is the youngest. Non-Greek, atypical elements in the myth of the birth of Zeus indicate that it was of pre-Hellenic, possibly Minoan, origin. The stone that Cronus swallowed and disgorged became the sacred stone at Delphi, known as the omphalos, *because it was believed to mark the center or "navel" of the earth.*

As told in Greek verse by Hesiod

RHEA WAS joined in wedlock to Cronus and bore to him glorious children; Hestia, Demeter, Hera with sandals of gold, mighty Hades, who dwells in his home below the earth and has a heart without pity, and loud-sounding Poseidon, the earth-shaker, and wise Zeus, the father of both gods and men, by whose thunder the broad earth is made to tremble.

Great Cronus swallowed these children as soon as each one came forth from his mother's womb, having this purpose in mind; that not any other one of the illustrious gods should have the honor of being king among the immortals. For he had learned from Gaea and starry Uranus that it was fated that even though he was powerful he would be overpowered by his own son, through the plans of mighty Zeus. For this reason he did not keep a blind watch, but lay in wait and swallowed each infant, while unceasing grief held Rhea in sorrow.

But when she was on the point of giving birth to Zeus, the father of gods and men, she turned in prayer to her dear parents, Gaea and starry Uranus, to contrive some plan with her so that she might bear the dear child without his knowledge, and that vengeance might be taken on the father for the children whom the mighty and crafty Cronus had swallowed. They in truth heard the plea of their beloved daughter and helped her, and they told her also what was fated to happen in regard to Cronus the king and his stout-hearted son.

Then they sent her to the fertile land of Crete, when she was about to give birth to the youngest of her children, great Zeus. Mighty Gaea took him willingly from her in broad Crete to nourish and rear. There Gaea carried him in her arms and hid him in a deep cave below the depths of the sacred earth on heavily wooded Mount Aegeum. She put into the arms of Cronus, the earlier king of the gods and the mighty son of Heaven, a great stone wrapped in swaddling clothes. Thereupon, lifting it up in his hands he put it down into his stomach, merciless as he was. He did not realize in his heart that his son, undefeated and carefree, had been left alive in place of the stone, and that his own son was soon destined to overpower him by an act of force and to keep him from his honors, reigning over the immortal gods himself.

As time rolled on, great Cronus, because he was tricked by the plans of Gaea, brought his offspring forth again, vomiting up first the stone he had swallowed last. Then Zeus set the stone firmly in the broad earth at sacred Pytho* below the valleys of Parnassus, to be a sign from heaven from that time on, a thing

---

* An early name for Delphi associated with Python, the serpent that guarded the sacred shrine there and that was killed by Apollo.

of wonder to mortal men. He also freed from their bonds his father's brothers, the sons of Uranus, whom his father foolishly had bound fast. They remembered to show gratitude for his kindness and gave him thunder and the blazing thunderbolt and lightning. Trusting in these, he rules over mortals and immortals.

From *Theogony*, 453–506

Zeus and the Titans

The Titans, six sons and six daughters of Uranus and Gaea, were a generation older than Zeus, son of the Titans Cronus and Rhea. The following account of the power struggle between the Titans and the Olympians, children of Cronus and Rhea, gave Hesiod an opportunity to describe Tartarus and the gloom of the lower world. Most of the Titans sided with Zeus, and Zeus cast those who opposed him into Tartarus, with the exception of Atlas.

The Olympian gods defeated the Titans with the aid of the Hecatonchires, hundred-handed giants named Briareus, Cottus and Gyges (or Gyes). Zeus was also aided by Styx, the daughter of the Titans Oceanus and Tethys.

As told in Greek verse by Hesiod

As soon as their father, Uranus, became angry in his heart with Briareus and Cottus and Gyges, he bound them in strong bonds because he despised their arrogant manhood and their appearance and size, and he forced them to dwell below the broad-pathed earth at the edge of the world, grieving deeply for a long time and holding great sorrow in their hearts.

But the immortal gods whom fair-heaired Rhea bore in wedlock to Cronus, at the bidding of Gaea, brought the three back again to the light; for she told them everything from beginning to end, explaining that with the three sons of Uranus they would win victory and a splendid achievement. For the Titan gods and those gods who were born of Cronus had been fighting a heartbreaking war for a long time. They struggled against each other in mighty combat, the illustrious Titans going into battle from lofty Othrys, while the gods whom fair-haired Rhea bore in wedlock to Cronus fought from Olympus.

Thus they held heartbreaking anger against each other and had been fighting without ceasing for ten long years. Nor was there any end to the bitter struggle, but the outcome of the war was hanging in the balance.

But when Zeus had furnished Briareus and Cottus and Gyges with all that was needed—nectar and ambrosia, the things that the very gods themselves eat—the manly spirit grew strong within the breasts of all three of them.

Then the father of both men and gods spoke to them: "Listen to me, splendid children of Gaea and Uranus, so that I may tell you what my heart bids me say. For the Titan gods and those who are born of Cronus have already been fighting for a very long time against each other to win a great victory. Now show your great power and invincible strength by opposing the Titans in fierce combat."

Thus he spoke, and blameless Cottus answered him: "Divine Zeus, you speak of things that are not unknown to us. It was because of your thoughtful planning that we came back again from the gloomy land of darkness and returned once more from cruel bondage, O king, son of Cronus. Now, therefore, with firm resolution and prudent planning we shall fight to defend your power in fierce combat, contending with the Titans in a violent struggle."

Thus he spoke, and the gods approved when they heard his words, and their hearts longed for war even more than they had before. Then they all, both the females and the males, stirred up battle that day; the Titan gods and those who were born of Cronus, and also those mighty and powerful ones whom Zeus released from Erebus below the earth and brought back to the light. They had a hundred arms rising from their shoulders, and each had fifty heads growing out of his shoulders, set upon sturdy limbs.

These three indeed took their stand against the Titans in grim combat, holding enormous rocks in their powerful hands. The Titans, opposing them, quickly strengthened their ranks, and both sides at the same time displayed the mighty force of their hands. The boundless sea echoed and reechoed terribly, and the earth resounded loudly. The broad heaven groaned as it was shaken, and lofty Olympus quivered on its foundations under the onslaught of the immortal gods. A heavy trembling reached dark Tartarus, as did the loud sound of their feet and their mighty weapons in the indescribable attack, when they hurled their dread missiles against each other. And the shouts of both sides rose to the starry heavens as they clashed with a great war cry.

Then Zeus no longer held his spirit in check; now his heart was filled with rage and he displayed all his power. He came from heaven and from Olympus hurling his lightning bolts without pause. The life-giving earth resounded all about with flames, and the great forest crackled on all sides with fire. All the earth throbbed with heat, and the streams of Oceanus and the barren sea were seething. The heat surrounded the earthbound Titans, and unspeakable flames reached up to the upper air, and the bright light of the flashing lightning took the sight from their eyes. A dreadful burning heat took possession of Chaos, and it seemed as if the earth and vast heaven above had come together, so great was the din as the gods opposed each other in strife. The terrible sound of fearful combat rose up, and acts of courage were displayed.

Until the end of the battle they faced each other and fought without ceasing in a fierce struggle. And among those in the front Cottus and Briareus and Gyges stirred up bitter fighting, for they hurled three hundred rocks from their sturdy hands, one after another, covered the Titans with their missiles, and sent them beneath the broad earth. Then, when they had overpowered them by force, even though they [the Titans] were full of spirit, they bound them in heavy chains as far down below the earth as heaven is above the earth—for that is the distance from earth to dark Tartarus. A bronze anvil falling for nine nights and nine days from heaven would reach the earth on the tenth, and, in turn, a bronze anvil falling for nine nights and nine days from earth would reach Tartarus on the tenth.

Around Tartarus stretches a wall of bronze, and night spreads about it in three rows, and, moreover, above it grow the roots of the earth and of the barren sea. In that place the Titan gods have been hidden by the plan of Zeus the cloud-gatherer under the gloomy darkness in a dank region at the extreme edge of the vast earth. There is no way out for them, for Poseidon placed on it gates of bronze, and a wall surrounds it on all sides. There Gyges and Cottus and great-hearted Briareus dwell, the faithful guardians of aegis-bearing Zeus.*

And there in order are the sources and ends of the dark earth and murky Tartarus and the barren sea and starry heaven, all dreadfully dark and dank, hated even by the gods. There the terrible home of dark Night stands covered over with murky clouds. Standing in front of this, Atlas, the son of Iapetus, holds up the wide heaven on his head and untiring hands without moving, where Night and Day come quite close, addressing each other in greeting as they cross the great bronze threshold. While one is coming down inside and the other is going out through the door, the house does not keep them both inside at the same time. But one is always outside the house and moves over the earth while the other is, in turn, inside the house and waits until the hour of her own journey arrives. One holds full-seeing light for men on earth, while the other, deadly Night, covered by a murky cloud, holds in her arms Sleep, the brother of Death.

There also the children of black Night have their homes; Sleep and Death, terrible gods. Never does the shining Sun look upon them with his rays, either as he goes forth into heaven or as he returns from heaven. Of these, the former, Sleep, lingers over the earth and the broad surface of the sea and is gentle and kind to men, but the other has a heart of iron, and the spirit of bronze within his breast is pitiless, and he holds fast to whatever man he has seized and is hated even by the immortal gods.

There, in the front, the echoing chambers of the god of the lower world, mighty Hades, and his wife, dread Persephone, stand, and a terrible dog guards the entrance; a dog without pity, and he has an evil habit. He welcomes those who enter with his tail wagging and his ears erect, but does not allow anyone to go out again, for he lies in wait and chews up whomever he finds leaving the gates.

And in that place dwells the goddess hated by the immortal gods, dread Styx, the eldest daughter of Oceanus, who flows back

---

* The aegis was an attribute of Zeus and Athena. In early times, the aegis represented the clouds and storms; later, a protective covering—generally a goatskin, breastplate or shield. Hephaestus made the aegis of Zeus. Athena's aegis had the head of the Gorgon Medusa at the center.

into himself. She dwells apart from the gods in a splendid house overarched with huge rocks and supported all around by silver columns reaching toward heaven. Seldom does swift-footed Iris come to her with a message over the wide surface of the sea. When discord and strife appear among the immortal gods, however, and when any one of those who dwell on Olympus has spoken falsely, then Zeus sends Iris to bring the mighty oath of the gods from afar in a golden pitcher, the renowned chill water that runs down from a steep and lofty rock.*

Deep below the spacious earth a branch of Oceanus flows out of the holy stream through the dark night and runs out from the rock, a great sorrow to the gods. Indeed, whichever one of the immortal gods who hold the summit of snowy Olympus is revealed as having broken his oath—the oath he has sworn by pouring a libation of this water—will lie breathless until a full year has passed. Never does he touch ambrosia and nectar, but he lies on a couch without breathing or speaking, and he is shrouded in a deep and sound sleep. But after he has passed a full year in sickness, another and more severe difficulty follows. For nine years he is deprived of the company of the gods and does not ever take part in their councils or in their feasts. But in the tenth year he again joins in the assemblies of the immortal gods who have their dwellings on Olympus. Indeed, it was ordained by the gods that the oath sworn on the imperishable and primeval water of Styx be of such a kind.

And there in order are the sources and ends of the dark earth, and murky Tartarus and the barren sea and starry heaven, all dreadfully dark and dank, hated even by the gods. There, also, are gleaming entrance gates and an immovable threshold of bronze. And over this threshold and apart from all the gods the Titans live, on the other side of gloomy Chaos. But the splendid allies of loud-thundering Zeus—Cottus and Gyges—dwell in homes on the bottom of Oceanus. And, indeed, since Briareus was brave, Poseidon the heavy-sounding earth-shaker made him his son-in-law and gave him his daughter in marriage.

From *Theogony*, 617–819

* When Zeus was attacked by the Titans, Styx went to his aid. Zeus, therefore, raised Styx to Olympus and declared that the oaths sworn by Styx should be inviolable.

Pandora

Prometheus, whose name means "forethought" or "fore-thinker," and Epimetheus, "afterthought" or "afterthinker," were sons of the Titan Iapetus. It was because Zeus wanted to punish Prometheus in particular and mankind in general—Prometheus had stolen fire from the gods for man—that the first woman appeared on earth. She was called Pandora, a name meaning "all gifts."

As told in Greek verse by Hesiod

THE GODS keep the means of livelihood hidden from mankind. Indeed Zeus concealed it from men, for he was angered in his heart because the crafty Prometheus had deceived him. For that reason he brought about sorrowful misery for mankind.

Zeus hid fire, but Prometheus, the brave son of Iapetus, stole it back from him in a hollow stalk of the fennel plant without being seen by Zeus who delights in thunder. But soon Zeus the cloud-gatherer spoke to him in anger:

"Son of Iapetus, crafty above all others in schemes, you rejoice that you have stolen fire and deceived me, but this will be a great sorrow to you yourself and to all men in the future. For, in return for the theft of fire, I shall give mankind an evil over which everyone may rejoice in his heart, but he will lovingly embrace his own destruction at the same time."

As he finished speaking, the father of men and gods laughed aloud. Then he commanded famous Hephaestus to mix earth with water without delay and to put into the mixture the voice and strength of a human and to create the shape of a fair and lovely young maiden like the immortal goddesses in appearance. He also bade Athena teach her handicrafts and how to weave a web with artistic skill, and directed golden Aphrodite to shed grace upon her, and longing and cares that bring pain and weariness to soul and body. He also instructed the guide Hermes to put into her both a shameless heart and a deceitful disposition.

Thus he commanded them, and they obeyed their king, Zeus the son of Cronus. Immediately the famous lame god fashioned from clay the likeness of a fine maiden according to the instructions of Cronus' son. Then the bright-eyed goddess Athena adorned her with clothes, and the divine Graces and queenly Persuasion placed necklaces of gold around her neck, and the fair-haired Hours set upon her head a crown of spring flowers. Next the guide Hermes wove into her falsehoods and crafty words and a deceitful disposition according to the will of loud-thundering Zeus, and then the messenger of the gods gave her a voice. He named this woman Pandora, because all those who had their homes on Olympus presented her with a gift, each one a source of misery to mortal men.

When he had completed this utterly unavoidable snare, the father sent renowned Hermes, the swift messenger of the gods, to take it as a gift to Epimetheus. Epimetheus was not mindful of what Prometheus had told him when he had warned him never to accept a gift from Olympian Zeus but to send it back so that it might not in any way turn out to be an evil to mortals. Instead, he accepted the gift and then, after he already had the evil thing, he remembered the warning.

For before this the tribes of men had lived on earth apart from evils and without the hardships of toil and grievous sicknesses. But the woman lifted up the great cover of the jar of gifts with her hands, and they were scattered everywhere. Thus she brought about sorrowful misery for mankind. Hope alone remained there inside her unshatterable home under the rim of the jar and did not fly out, for before she could come forth the lid of the jar caught and held her, according to the will of aegis-bearing Zeus the cloud-gatherer.

But numberless miseries wander about among men, for the earth as well as the sea is full of evils. Sicknesses of their own accord come constantly to mankind both by day and by night, bringing evils to mortals in silence, since wise Zeus took away their voices. Thus there is no way at all to escape the will of Zeus.

From *Works and Days,* 42–105

The Ages of Mankind

After the creation of the universe came the creation of the gods and of man. Hesiod and Ovid both described the early periods of man's life on earth in accounts that parallel each other in most respects. The Roman version, however, gives only four Ages, while Hesiod gives five races of man, putting a race or Age of Heroes between the Ages of Bronze and Iron. This is indicative of the important role of the heroes in Greek thought and mythology. Hesiod's emphasis is on mankind himself, whereas Ovid's is on periods of time.

Ovid describes the Golden Age as the time when Saturn was upon the earth. Saturn, an Italian god of agriculture, was identified by the Romans with the Greek god Cronus. Jupiter, the chief Roman god and god of the sky, identified with Zeus by the Romans, was Saturn's son.

As told in Greek verse by Hesiod

IF YOU wish, I shall sum up another story for you well and skillfully, telling how the gods and mortal men arose from the same origin.

First of all the immortal gods who have their homes on Olympus created a golden race of mortal men, who lived in the time of Cronus, when he was king in heaven. They lived just like gods, carefree in heart, aloof and apart from toil and sorrow. Wretched old age did not come to them, but, ever strong in legs and arms, they enjoyed themselves with feasts, separated from all evils. They had all good things, for a fruitful earth of its own accord brought forth plentiful and abundant fruit, and they lived happily and peacefully, blessed with many riches. They were wealthy in cattle and were loved by the gods.

But when the earth had covered this race, those who have

their homes on Olympus created a second race, a race of silver that was inferior by far, resembling the golden race neither in stature nor in mind. For a hundred years a child was cared for close to his mother's side, playing like a helpless babe in his home. But when at last children grew into manhood and reached the measure of man's estate, they lived for a very short time, coming to grief because of their folly. For they were not able to refrain from violence and wrong among themselves, nor were they willing to do service to the immortal gods or to offer sacrifice to the gods on the altars, as it is the custom for men to do in their homes. Then indeed Zeus the son of Cronus was angry with them, because they did not honor the gods who dwell on Olympus.

But when the earth had covered this race also, Zeus the father created a third race of human beings, a race of bronze, not at all resembling the silver race, but both fearful and strong, taking part in the sorrowful acts of war and deeds of violence. They did not eat any bread, but they had hearts of steel, these unbending men. Great was their bodily strength, and their arms were invincible. Their weapons were of bronze, their houses were of bronze, and their tools were of bronze. When these people were destroyed by their own hands, they passed to the dark abode of icy Hades and oblivion.

But when the earth had covered this race also, Zeus the son of Cronus created even another race, the fourth upon the fruitful earth, a race that was more righteous and militant, a godlike race of heroes who are called demigods. These were our ancestors throughout the boundless earth.

Ugly war and terrible battles destroyed these people, bringing some to their deaths when they were fighting for the flocks of Oedipus before the seven gates of Thebes in the land of Cadmus,* and others when they had been carried in ships across the vast expanses of the deep sea to Troy because of beautiful Helen.

---

* Cadmus, son of King Agenor of Tyre, following instructions from the oracle at Delphi, founded the city of Cadmea, later called Thebes. The sons of Oedipus—Eteocles and Polynices—fought for the kingship of Thebes and killed each other in single combat. This is the subject of Aeschylus' play *The Seven Against Thebes.*

There, in truth, death engulfed them, but father Zeus the son of
Cronus caused others to settle at the ends of the earth, giving
them a life and dwelling place apart from mankind. They dwell
far from the immortal gods, and Cronus is king over them. And
they live with carefree hearts on the isles of the blessed beside
the deep-eddying Ocean, blessed heroes for whom the fruitful
earth bears honey-sweet fruit, which indeed blooms three times a
year.

I wish, therefore, that I did not live among the men of the
fifth race, but had either died earlier or had been born later. For
now there is in fact a race of iron, and men never find an end to
toil and hardship by day or destruction by night. And the gods
will bestow upon them grievous suffering, but they will nevertheless also have some good fortune mingled with the bad. Zeus
will also destroy this race of mortal men.

From Works and Days, 106–180

As told in Latin verse by Ovid

THE FIRST age of mankind was a Golden Age, which, with no
one to give punishment, of its own free will cherished what was
right and good. There was no punishment and no fear, but men
lived in safety without judges. Mortals knew no shores but their
own; not yet did protective ditches surround cities. There were
no helmets, no swords. Without the need for soldiers, nations
lived in pleasant peace, free from care. The earth gave forth all
things of her own accord, and mankind, content with foods
created without labor, picked the fruit of the trees and the mountain strawberries and the cornel-cherries and mulberries clinging
to the wild thickets and acorns that fell from the spreading oak
of Jupiter.

Spring was eternal, and the gentle breezes caressed the flowers,
all springing forth without seed, with clear warm air. Soon, also,
the unplowed earth was rich with grain, and the fields, always
fertile, were white with the heavy beards of corn. Then rivers of
milk, then streams of nectar flowed forth, and golden honey
dripped from the blossoming trees.

After Saturn had fallen to the shadowy lower world and the earth was under the rule of Jupiter, the Silver Age followed, peopled by men of less worth than gold but of greater value than tawny bronze. Jupiter shortened the length of springtime, and through winter and summer and a changeable autumn and a short spring he completed a year of four seasons. Then for the first time the scorched air glowed with parching heat and ice hung frozen by the winds. Then first, mankind lived in houses. Before that time, their homes had been caves and dense shrubs and branches bound with bark. Then first, seeds of grain, the gift of Ceres, were sown in long furrows, and young bullocks groaned under the burden of their yokes.

After that came the third age of mankind, the Age of Bronze, with a race harsher in nature and quicker to take up rough weapons, but nevertheless not wicked people.

The last was the Age of Iron, a harsh one. Immediately all sins and crimes broke forth in this age of baser metal, and shame and truth and faith fled. In place of them there came frauds and tricks and plots, also force and an evil love of profit.

Sailors raised their sails before the winds, but they were not yet familiar with them, and ships, which but recently were pines standing on lofty mountain slopes, sped over unknown waves. And the surveyors carefully marked out with long boundaries the ground, which up to then had belonged to everyone just as did the light of the sun and the air.

And now harmful iron, and gold more harmful than iron, had appeared, and war, which fights with both, sprang up and flourished, clattering weapons in its bloody hand. Men lived by plundering. Friends were not safe from friends, nor relatives from relatives, and even brotherly love was rare.

Respect lay conquered, and the maiden Astraea, the last of the deities, left the earth, now stained with slaughter.

And, lest lofty heaven might be less troubled than the earth, they say the Giants attacked the kingdom of the immortals and piled up mountains on top of each other, reaching to the lofty stars.

Then the father all-powerful, hurling a thunderbolt, shattered Olympus and struck Pelion from its position above Ossa. They say that when the fearful bodies of these mountains lay destroyed, Earth, their mother, bathed in the gore of her offspring, gave life to their warm blood and, lest there might be no remaining trace of her children, transformed it into the shape of humans. But even that race of men was scornful of the gods and very eager for cruel slaughter, and was impetuous.

From *Metamorphoses* I, 89–162

The Council of the Gods

In the Iron Age, when man had grown evil and scornful of the gods, the deities abandoned the earth. Even Astraea, a deity representing justice, had fled from earthbound mortals. This was the situation when Jupiter, whom the Romans identified with the Greek god Zeus, decided to act.

As told in Latin verse by Ovid

WHEN JUPITER, Saturn's son, looked down from his lofty throne and saw this, he groaned and quickly called the gods to a council. No excuse delayed them when they had been summoned.

There is a lofty highway, seen plainly in a clear sky. Its name is the Milky Way, well-known for its splendid brilliance. This is the road the gods travel to the kingdom and royal palace of great Jupiter, the thunderer. On the right and left, the halls of the renowned gods, seen through the open doorways, are crowded. The less important gods live in different places. On the Milky Way the powerful and glorious deities have placed their dwelling places.

Then, when the gods had seated themselves in the marble chamber, Jupiter himself, sitting on a raised throne and leaning upon his ivory scepter, shook the terror-bringing hair of his head three and four times, the hair with which he moved the earth, the sea, the stars.

Then he spoke angrily, in this manner: "Now, wherever Nereus, god of the sea, surrounds the whole world with sound, I must destroy the mortal race. I swear this by the rivers flowing below the earth in the grove of the Styx. All other ways have been tried already, but the incurable matter must be cut out with a sword, lest the uninfected part be contaminated. I have demigods, I have rustic deities, nymphs and fauns and satyrs, and sylvan gods dwelling in the mountains. Since we have not yet glorified them with the honor of heaven, certainly we should allow them to continue to live in the lands we have given them."

All the gods trembled and, with burning eagerness, demanded to know who had dared such evil deeds. After Jupiter raised his voice and hand to quiet their murmurings, all held their silence.

As soon as the commotion, suppressed by the authority of the king of gods, had ceased, Jupiter again broke the silence with these words: "Fear not, for man has indeed been punished. Wherever the earth stretches out, there savage Fury holds rule. One might think mankind had taken an oath to follow crime. Let them all pay the penalty they deserve to receive as quickly as possible. Thus I have resolved."

Some spoke out in approval of Jupiter's words and added encouragement to his anger. Others were satisfied with silent agreement. They all, however, felt grief over the sacrifice of the human race. They asked what sort of world it would be without mortals, they wondered who would place incense on the altars, and inquired whether Jupiter was preparing to hand the earth over to the wild animals to plunder. As they asked these questions, the king of the gods—for all things are his concern—would not permit them to be disturbed, and so he promised a race different from the first, people of wonderful origin.

And at that moment Jupiter was about to cast his thunderbolts onto the whole earth, but he was fearful that by chance the sacred heaven might be kindled into flames from so much fire and the length of the sky might be burned. The thunderbolts forged by the hands of the Cyclopes were placed aside. A different sort of punishment seemed suitable—to send down rainstorms from the whole sky and destroy the human race beneath its deluge.

From *Metamorphoses* I, 163–261

The Flood

Man's degeneration, his neglect of the gods during the Iron Age, and the evils brought by Prometheus and Pandora so angered Jupiter, the Roman counterpart of Zeus, that he had announced to the gods his intention to destroy the race. Since he did not want to endanger the heavens by hurling the fire of his thunderbolt, Jupiter decided on the use of water, the province of his brother Neptune, whom the Romans identified with Poseidon.

As told in Latin verse by Ovid

WITHOUT DELAY Jupiter enclosed Aquilo, the north wind, in the cave of Aeolus, and also imprisoned whatever breezes cause the gathered storm clouds to scatter; but he set free Notus, the south wind. Notus flew forth with rain-soaked wings, his dreadful face covered in a pitch-black cloud. His beard was heavy with rain, water poured down from his white hair, storm clouds clung to his forehead, his wings and clothing dripped with moisture. And when he pressed on the overhanging clouds with his broad hand, thunder pealed forth, and the heavy clouds poured forth rain from the skies.

Iris, the messenger of Juno, clothed in many colors, drew up water and carried it to the clouds as nourishment. The growing grain was leveled to the ground, and the crops the farmers prayed for lay in ruins, and the labor of the long year was lost and useless.

Nor was Jupiter's anger content with the power of his own storms, but Neptune, his brother, aided him with additional waves. The ruler of the sea called together the rivers. After they had entered the palace of their king, he said, "It is not fitting to urge you on with a long explanation now. Simply pour

33

forth all your strength. This is what is needed. Open your caves and, when the dams have been broken, give full rein to your river waters!"

Thus Neptune commanded them. They returned to their abodes, opened wide the sources of their fountains, and rolled down to the sea in unbridled flow.

Neptune himself struck the earth with his trident and it trembled, and, by its motion, it lay open wide paths for the waters. The overflowing rivers rushed through the open fields and carried with them both trees and, at the same time, animals and humans and even temples and their sacred chambers and statues. If any house remained standing and was able to resist the great flood without being thrown down, nevertheless the water rose higher than the roof, covering it, and the towers, buried under the whirling waters, lay hidden. And now the water and the land had nothing to distinguish them. All things were sea, but the sea had no shores.

In one place, someone escaped up a hillside; in another direction, a man sat in a small boat and pulled on the oars where he had been plowing not long before. One man sailed above his crops or the top of his farmhouse now submerged in water, while another discovered fish in the top of an elm tree. The Nereids were amazed at the groves and cities and houses below the water, and the dolphins swam through forests and rubbed against lofty branches and struck against oak trees, shaking them. Wolves swam among sheep. The water carried along golden-colored lions; the waves bore tigers with them. His lightning strength was of no use to the boar, his swift legs were of no help to the deer as they were swept away by the tide. The birds, wandering and searching long for a perch on which to light, fell into the sea when their wings were exhausted. The boundless flooding of the sea had buried the hills, and strange waves were breaking against the mountaintops. Most creatures were drowned in the flood. A long starvation from lack of food overcame those whom the water spared.

From *Metamorphoses* I, 262–312

Deucalion and Pyrrha

Floods were not an uncommon occurrence in the Greek world, an area of earthquake, and tradition recounts a number of them. There is some scientific evidence that a flood of unusual and destructive size may have occurred some time near the middle of the fourteenth century B.C. In any case, the story of the flood described here as taking place at the end of the Iron Age of prehistory made an excellent tale to hand down through the generations.

The sole survivors of the great flood, as related in the following passage, were Deucalion and Pyrrha, he the son of Prometheus and she the daughter of Epimetheus. One of their sons was Hellen, who gave his name to the Hellenes, the early Greeks, and who, through his sons and grandsons, was the eponymous ancestor of the Aeolian, Ionian, and Dorian tribes of Greece.

As told in Latin verse by Ovid

PHOCIS, STANDING between the territory of Boeotia and Thessaly, was a fertile land, while it was land, but at that time it was part of the sea and was a wide surface of unexpected waters. There, a lofty mountain, Parnassus by name, reached toward the stars with its two peaks, and clouds hung above its summit. When Deucalion and his wife, carried in their small boat, landed there—for water had covered all other things—they paid honor to the nymphs and the deities of the mountain and to the goddess, the prophetess Themis, who at that time was the oracle of Apollo. There was not anyone better than Deucalion or a man more devoted to justice, or any woman more god-fearing than his wife.

When Jupiter saw that the world had become a lake of flowing waters and that only one man was still alive out of so many thousands and that but one woman had survived from so many thousands, both of them innocent and both worshipers of the gods, he dispersed the clouds. And, when the storm had been blown away by the north wind, he disclosed the land to the sky and the heavens to the earth. The anger of the sea ceased.

Now the sea had a shore, the riverbeds held the full rivers, the waters subsided, and the hills were seen coming forth. The earth rose to sight, the land increased as the waves decreased, and at long last the forests showed their uncovered treetops, bearing the slime that was left behind in the leaves.

The world had been restored. After he saw that it was empty and that deep silence hung over the deserted lands, with tears rising in his eyes Deucalion spoke to Pyrrha thus: "O sister, O wife, O only woman left alive, out of all the lands that the setting and rising sun looks upon, we two are the sum total. The sea holds all the others. Now the human race rests in the two of us. Thus it seemed fitting to the gods; and we remain as the examples of mankind."

Thus he spoke and they wept. It seemed best to pray to the divine power and to seek help through sacred prophecies.

As they reached the steps of the temple, both fell forward on the ground and kissed the cold stone, trembling, and spoke thus: "If deities, won over by proper prayers, are ever moved, if the anger of the gods can be turned away, tell us, Themis, by what means the damage to our race might be repaired, and bring help, most kind goddess, to our ruined condition."

The goddess was moved and gave them this oracular response: "Go from this temple and veil your heads and loosen the garments you wear. Then throw the bones of your great mother behind your backs!"

For a long time they stood amazed. Pyrrha first broke the silence with her voice and refused to obey the orders of the goddess. Then, her lips trembling, she begged the goddess to pardon her, because she was afraid to injure the spirit of her dead mother by casting her bones behind her.

Meanwhile, they repeated the words the oracle had spoken, words obscure with hidden meanings, and pondered them and discussed them together.

Then Deucalion, the son of Prometheus, soothed his wife

Pyrrha, daughter of Epimetheus, with comforting words, saying, "Either my ingenuity deceives me or—oracles are just and advise no wrong deed!—the earth is our great mother. I believe the stones in the body of the earth are called bones. We are ordered to throw these behind our backs."

Although Pyrrha was moved by her husband's interpretation of the oracle, her hope nevertheless wavered. They both distrusted the advice from heaven so much. But what would be the harm in trying?

They left the temple. They veiled their heads, loosened their garments, and threw the stones behind them as they had been ordered. The stones—who would believe this unless the great age of the story served as evidence?—began to lay aside their cold stiffness and to soften gradually and, when they had become soft, to take form. Soon, when they grew larger and their nature became less harsh, a certain human shape, still not clear, could be seen, but it was very much like rough figures beginning to be carved from marble and not well-defined.

Then in a short time, by the divine will of the gods, the stones thrown from the man's hands took on the appearance of men, and women were created again from those stones thrown by the woman. This is the reason we are a tough race, a race that endures hard work, ever showing evidence of the origin of our being. The earth, of its own accord, brought forth other animals of different forms.

Damp warmth brings all things to life. When, therefore, the earth, covered with mud from the recent flood, grew warm again from the nourishing heat of the sky's sunlight, she put forth countless kinds of living things. Some she brought back in their ancient forms, some she created as new and unfamiliar shapes.

From *Metamorphoses* I, 313–437

The Birth of Athena

Because Zeus had come to power by overthrowing his father, Cronus, who had in turn overthrown his own father, Uranus, he knew only too well how easily he might be displaced if a son were born to his first wife, Metis. Here we see the stratagem he employed to avoid his fate as a father.

The birth of Athena was the subject of the sculpture on the east pediment of the Parthenon. According to Pindar and others, Athena was brought forth by the stroke of an ax delivered on Zeus' head by Hephaestus. Athena was sometimes called Tritogeneia, but there is no real etymological connection between this epithet and Lake Tritonis, which Hesiod records as her birthplace.

Metis was the personification of wisdom and counsel. Thus Zeus, by his actions as they are recounted here, took to himself additional wisdom, giving an allegorical cast to this myth. In time, Athena herself came to represent wisdom personified.

Athena was her father's favorite child. Among her attributes were her helmet and aegis, her shield with the Gorgon's head, indicative of the active role she was to play in war as a protective deity, especially of the city bearing her name. The olive tree and the owl were also attributes of Athena, whom the Romans identified with the goddess Minerva.

Unfortunately this part of Hesiod's text is quite fragmentary.

As told in Greek verse by Hesiod

ZEUS, THE king of the gods, first made the Titan Metis his wife, and in truth she was very wise. But Zeus deceived Metis, the fair-haired daughter of Oceanus and Tethys, even though she was full of wisdom, for, before she was to bear the bright-eyed goddess Athena, he grasped Metis in his hands and swallowed her, following the advice of Gaea and starry Uranus.

They had devised this plan so that no one other than Zeus might hold the royal power over the eternal gods. For it was decreed by fate that very thoughtful children would be born from Metis, and the first to be born would be the bright-eyed maiden Athena, who would have strength and wisdom equal to her father's, but that after her first-born Metis was to bear a son who would be dauntless in spirit and would become king of gods and men. Zeus, therefore, swallowed Metis so that that goddess might bring about both good and evil for him.

Metis, however, soon conceived Pallas Athena. And, furthermore, Metis, the mother of Athena, who was even wiser than the gods and mortal men, remained concealed within the innermost parts of Zeus. There the goddess Athena received from her father the aegis, with which she surpassed in strength all the other immortal gods who have their dwellings on Olympus. And the father of men and gods brought her into the world, bearing the aegis and clad in the armor of war, from out of his head on the shores of Lake Tritonis.

From *Theogony*, 886–929

The Muses

The Muses, the personification of knowledge and the arts, especially literature, dance and music, were the nine daughters of Zeus and Mnemosyne, memory personified. They were associated with Mount Helicon in Boeotia, where a temple and statues were erected to them, and with Mount Parnassus, where the Castalian Spring, still visible today, was held sacred to Apollo and to the Muses.

Hesiod's account and description of the Muses was the one generally followed by the writers of antiquity. It was not until Roman times that the following functions were assigned to them, and even then there was some variation in both their names and their attributes: Calliope, epic poetry; Clio, history; Euterpe, flutes and lyric poetry; Thalia, comedy and pastoral poetry; Melpomene, tragedy; Terpsichore, dance; Erato, love poetry; Polyhymnia, sacred poetry; and Urania, astronomy.

As told in Greek verse by Hesiod

LET US begin to tell of the Muses, who delight the heart of their father Zeus on Olympus with their songs, singing with blended voices of the things that are and will be and were before this. The sweet music flows from their lips effortlessly, and the home of their father Zeus, the loud-thundering one, is filled with joy as their gentle voices are heard afar, and the summit of snowy Olympus and the homes of the immortal gods echo with the sound.

Singing out in divine tones, the Muses first of all celebrate in song the beginnings of the revered race of the gods whom Earth and spacious Heaven brought forth, and also the gods, the givers of fine things, whom they bore in turn. Then the goddesses sing next of Zeus, the father of gods and men, as they begin their song and bring their singing to an end, telling how he is the mightiest of the gods and the most powerful. Then again, as they sing of the race of men and of the mighty giants they delight the heart of Zeus on Olympus, these Olympian Muses, the daughters of aegis-bearing Zeus.

Mnemosyne gave birth to them in Pieria, and they bring a forgetfulness of evils and rest from cares. Not far from the highest peak of snowy Olympus, she brought forth nine daughters, who are very much alike, whose hearts are devoted to song, and who have carefree spirits. In that place are their bright dancing circles and lovely homes. The Graces dwell beside them, and with melodious voices they celebrate in song the laws of all and the noble customs of the immortal gods. Then they went to Olympus, rejoicing in their sweet voices, with divine singing. The dark earth resounded around them as they sang, and a pleasing sound arose beneath their feet as they approached their father.

Such things, then, are celebrated in song by the Muses, who have their homes upon Olympus; nine daughters born of mighty Zeus—Clio and Euterpe and Thalia and Melpomene and Terpsichore and Erato and Polyhymnia and Urania and Calliope, who is the most outstanding of all of them, for she accompanies noble princes.

From Theogony, 36–80

Demeter

Demeter and Persephone, mother and daughter, almost always appear together in Greek mythology, and they were worshiped together. Demeter, the Roman Ceres, was the goddess of corn and the fruits of the earth. Persephone, whose Latin name was Proserpina, a corruption, was called Kore, meaning "Maiden." The Homeric Hymn *that follows contains the earliest appearance of the myth of Demeter and Persephone in extant literature.*

Eleusis, about twelve miles west of Athens, was the site of the Eleusinian Mysteries, religious rites celebrated in honor of Demeter and Persephone as late as the fourth century A.D. *There was a sanctuary at Eleusis as early as the seventh century* B.C. *and the cult was extremely sacred to the Greeks. The two goddesses were worshiped in connection with the planting and harvesting of corn, the rotation of the seasons, and the mythological seasonal appearance of Persephone on earth and her return to the kingdom of Hades. The rites were secret and known only to the initiated, but what literary evidence we have points to their connection with immortality, life and death in nature and man, and resurrection.*

Excavations at Eleusis have brought to light extensive remains, including the Propylaea and a large square hall that was supported by columns and contained rock-hewn seats for the worshipers. During the Persian Wars the sanctuary was destroyed, but it was rebuilt under Pericles. Building was continued at the site by the Romans.

As told in Greek verse in the
Homeric Hymns

TO DEMETER

I BEGIN to sing of Demeter, a stately goddess, of her and her daughter, Persephone, a girl with slim ankles, whom Hades

42

snatched away after she had been granted to him by loud-thundering Zeus, who sees afar.

At a distance from Demeter, the goddess who bestows rich fruits, Persephone was playing with the fair daughters of Oceanus and was gathering flowers in a grassy meadow—roses and crocuses and lovely violets as well as irises and hyacinths. There too was the narcissus, a marvelously bright and fresh flower, which Earth brought forth at the will of Zeus as a snare for the girl, who was like a flower bud herself.

She was astonished indeed and stretched out both her hands to pick the delightfully beautiful blossom, but the broad earth opened wide, and the king of the dead, driving his immortal horses, rushed upon her. He snatched her up into his golden chariot, even though she resisted him, and carried her off weeping.

Then she cried out in a loud voice, calling upon her father, Zeus the son of Cronus, for help. Not any one of the immortal gods or mortal men heard her cries, but while the peaks of the mountains and the depths of the sea echoed with her deathless voice her revered mother heard her.

Piercing grief grasped her heart, and she flew like a lone vulture over the dry land and over the flowing sea, seeking her daughter. But not any one of the gods or mortal men was able to tell her the truth, none of the birds of omen came to her with true reports.

Then for nine days queenly Demeter roamed up and down the earth, grieving so much that she did not touch any ambrosia or a sweet drink of nectar. But when the tenth light-bringing dawn came, Hecate met her and spoke to her. Then Demeter, the daughter of Rhea, went with her swiftly, carrying a blazing torch in each hand.

Thus they came to Helios, the guardian of both gods and men, and stood before his horses, and the goddess among goddesses asked his aid: "Helios, I heard the loud cry of my daughter coming through the barren air as if she were being carried away by force, but I did not see her with my eyes. But—for you look down with your sunbeams upon all the earth and sea—tell me truly about my beloved child. If you have seen her anywhere, tell me which one of the gods or mortal men has snatched her off."

Then Helios, the son of Hyperion, replied, "Queen Demeter, daughter of Rhea, you will learn the truth, for I have respect for you and pity you greatly in your grief. Not any other one of the immortal gods is to blame but Zeus the cloud-gatherer, who gave her to Hades to be called his wife. So he seized her and carried her off to the lower world of darkness."

Then distress even more painful and fierce than before filled Demeter's heart. Thereafter she was so angry with Zeus the son of Cronus that she abandoned the assembly of the gods and lofty Olympus and went instead among the cities and fertile fields of men, disguising her appearance. Not any of the men or women recognized her when they saw her, until she came near the house of Celeus, who was at that time king of Eleusis.

Grieving in her heart, she sat down by the roadside in a shady spot close to the Maiden Well, looking like an old woman full of years, such as are the nurses of the children of kings and the housekeepers in their echoing palaces. The daughters of Celeus saw her there when they came to draw water and carry it in bronze pitchers back to their father's house. There were four girls, resembling goddesses. They did not recognize her, but as they stood near they addressed her with winged words:

"Who are you and from what place do you come, old woman? Why, pray, do you stay away from the city and not come near the houses? There are women in the shady halls of the homes there, aged as you are, and others younger, who would treat you kindly in both word and deed."

Thus they spoke, and the queenly goddess answered them, saying, "Hail, dear children, whoever you are. I shall tell you, for it is not improper to answer truly what you ask. Doso is my name, for my revered mother gave it to me. Just recently I came across the wide surface of the sea from Crete, but against my will. Then they put in at Thoricus in their swift ship and, dashing off in secret across the dark countryside, I escaped from my insolent captors, so that they would not carry me across the sea without ransom to sell me for a price.

"And so I wandered about and came here, and I have no idea what land this is or what people live here. But have pity on me, young maidens, and tell me plainly to what man and woman's house I may go, so I may work for them willingly and perform those tasks that belong to an elderly woman."

Thus the goddess spoke, and immediately the maiden Callidice, the most beautiful of the daughters of Celeus, answered her: "Good woman, we mortals of necessity endure with patience whatever the gods give us, even while we suffer, for they are far more powerful than we are. But if you wish, wait here while we go back to our father's house and talk over all this in detail with our mother, Metaneira, so that she may urge you to come to our house instead of seeking out the houses of others."

When she had spoken thus, the goddess nodded her head in agreement, and the maidens filled their shining pitchers with water and carried them off happily. In a short time they reached their father's spacious house and quickly related to their mother all they had seen and heard. She then urged them to go quickly and summon the woman to come to the house to be employed indefinitely. They found the noble goddess near the roadside where they had left her only a short time before and led her to their father's house.

They went through the entrance hall to the place where their revered mother was sitting near a pillar of an inner portico, holding her young son on her lap. Her daughters ran over to her, but the goddess stood still at the threshold, and she filled the doorway with a divine radiance.

Reverence and wonder and pale fear seized Metaneira, and, rising from her couch, she urged her to sit down. Then thoughtful Iambe set a well-made seat before her and threw a silver-white fleece over it. For a long time she sat on the stool grieving in silence and did not greet anyone either by word or action, until thoughtful Iambe, cheering her up with many jests, induced the holy lady to smile and laugh and to show a cheerful heart.

Then Metaneira began to speak: "Hail, lady—for I believe you are not born of lowly but of noble parents. We mortals of necessity bear patiently whatever the gods give us, for a yoke is placed upon our necks. Now, however, since you have come here, accept whatever I have. Take this child of mine and be a nurse to him for me, and, if you take care of him until he reaches young manhood, any woman who sees you will easily envy you, so great a reward shall I give you for his upbringing."

Then Demeter answered her, saying, "And to you, lady, all hail, and may the gods grant you good fortune. I shall be glad indeed to take the boy, as you bid me, and I shall take good care of him." When she had spoken thus, she took the boy in her immortal arms, and his mother rejoiced in her heart.

Thus the goddess nursed Demophoön, the fine son of Celeus and Metaneira, in the palace. He grew like a young god, but did not eat food or drink milk, for by day Demeter anointed him with ambrosia as though he were the child of a god, and at night she concealed him like a firebrand in the depths of a fire without the knowledge of his dear parents.

It caused great wonder to them that he was developing so quickly, for he was like the gods in appearance. And the goddess indeed would have made him both ageless and immortal if Metaneira, in her thoughtlessness, had not watched from her chamber at night and seen this. Because she was afraid for her son, she wept as she spoke winged words to him: "Demophoön, my son, the stranger buries you in deep fire, causing me sorrow and grievous concern."

Thus she spoke, grieving, and the goddess heard her. Then beautiful Demeter, because she was angry with her, took the dear child from the fire with her immortal hands and let him drop to the ground, and then said to Metaneira, "You, in your foolishness, have made a mistake that can not be rectified, for I would have made your beloved son deathless and ageless for all his days, and I would have given him undying honor. But now he has no way of escaping evils and death.

"Indeed, I am Demeter, who is held in honor and who brings the greatest help and pleasure to the immortal gods and to mortal men. But come now, let all the people erect a great temple and an altar below it for me, building it upon a prominent hill beneath the city and the lofty city wall. I myself shall instruct you in my sacred rites so that you may then carry them out with reverence and thus appease my heart."

Immediately Metaneira's knees grew weak, and she became speechless for a long time, and she did not remember to lift her son from the floor. But his sisters heard his pitiful crying and gathered around him and treated him with loving care. His heart was not comforted, however, for he now had nurses who were much less skillful.

Quivering with fear, they spent the whole night trying to appease the glorious goddess, but as soon as dawn appeared they told Celeus everything exactly as the goddess, the lovely-crowned Demeter, had ordained. Then he summoned the people to an assembly to bid them erect a fine temple to fair-haired Demeter and an altar on a prominent hill. They carried out his commands with haste and did as he bid them do. And the child grew like a god. Moreover, when they had finished and ceased their labor, all the people returned to their homes.

Golden-haired Demeter, however, remained there far away from all the blessed gods, wasting away with longing for her daughter. Then she brought about a very terrible and dreadful year for mankind upon the earth. The soil did not send forth seeds at all because Demeter kept them hidden. The oxen pulled many curved plows in the fields, but in vain; in vain much white barley was scattered upon the ground.

Thus, therefore, she would have completely destroyed the race of man with painful famine, and she would have deprived those who dwell on Olympus of their glorious privilege of gifts of honor and sacrifices, if Zeus had not been anxious about this and pondered it in his heart. First he called forth Iris, with wings of gold, to summon Demeter, and she obeyed Zeus, the cloud-wrapped son of Cronus, flying off on swift feet.

She came to the city of Eleusis, found Demeter in her temple, and addressed her, speaking winged words: "Demeter, father Zeus, who has undying wisdom, summons you to come among the host of the gods who live forever. Come, therefore, and let my message from Zeus not be brought in vain."

But the goddess's heart was not swayed. Then Zeus the father sent all the blessed gods to her in turn, and they came, one following another, summoning her. But she firmly spurned all their attempts, for she declared she would not set foot on sweet-smelling Olympus or bring forth fruit from the earth before she looked upon her fair daughter again with her own eyes.

Indeed, when loud-thundering Zeus, who sees afar, heard this, he sent Hermes the slayer of Argus to Erebus, so that he might persuade Hades with gentle words to allow him to lead chaste Persephone forth from the misty land of darkness to the light and the gods above—to do this in order that her mother might behold her with her own eyes and cease her bitter anger. Hermes did not refuse to obey, but quickly sped down to the depths of the earth. He came upon the king of the world of darkness in his palace, with his shy wife seated beside him—but very unwillingly, because she longed for her mother. Then the mighty slayer of Argus stood near and said:

"Dark-haired Hades, master over the dead, father Zeus has ordered me to lead forth noble Persephone from Erebus to the gods above, so that her mother may see her, since she is planning a violent deed; namely, to cause the weak tribes of earthborn men to waste away by keeping the seeds of things hidden beneath the soil. Now she is nursing her bitter anger and does not mingle with the gods."

Thus he spoke, and the lord of those beneath the earth smiled sadly and did not refuse to obey the command of Zeus the king, but quickly addressed the thoughtful Persephone, saying, "Go, Persephone, to your dark-veiled mother, and keep a kindly spirit and feeling toward me in your heart and do not be too downhearted. I shall not be an unsuitable husband for you—I, who am Zeus' own brother. Moreover, while you are here you will have the highest honors among the immortal gods."

So he spoke to her, and wise Persephone was delighted and quickly jumped up for joy. But he, indeed, in secret, gave her the seed of the sweet pomegranate* to eat, protecting his own interests so that she would not stay there with the revered dark-veiled Demeter all the time. Then Aïdoneus, ruler over many, prepared his deathless horses and golden chariot, and she mounted the chariot, and beside her, Hermes the strong slayer of Argus took the reins and whip in his hands and drove off. Soon he came to a stop in front of the temple in which fair-crowned Demeter had been staying.

---

* The pomegranate was the food of the dead, and those who had eaten of it could not be freed from the land of the dead.

As soon as Demeter saw them she rushed out, while Persephone, when she saw her mother, jumped down from the chariot to run to her and, throwing her arms around her neck, embraced her. While she was still holding her beloved child in her arms, Demeter's heart was filled with sudden fear, and she questioned her at once: "You did not taste any food, did you, my daughter, when you were in the kingdom below? Speak up and do not conceal anything, so we may both know. For then indeed you will return from hateful Hades and live with me and your father, the cloud-wrapped son of Cronus, and be held in honor by all the immortal gods.

"If, however, you did touch food, you must return again to the depths of the earth to live for one third of each year, and live here with me and the other immortal gods for two seasons of the year. When the sweet-smelling earth comes into bloom with all kinds of blossoms in the springtime, then you will come forth from the gloomy land of darkness as a great marvel for the gods and mortal men to behold."

Beautiful Persephone then spoke to her mother in reply: "To you, mother, I shall tell the truth about everything. When Hermes, the swift messenger, came to lead me forth from Erebus so you might look on me with your own eyes and bring an end to your wrath and terrible anger against the immortal gods, I immediately jumped up with joy. Hades, however, in secret, fed me the seed of a pomegranate, a sweet food, bringing me by force to taste it reluctantly."

Thus for a long time they lightened each other's spirits sympathetically and embraced lovingly. Their hearts ceased their grieving as they received joy and gave it in turn. Then brightly-veiled Hecate came toward them and embraced the chaste daughter of Demeter many times. From then on the lady Hecate became her attendant and companion.

Then loud-thundering Zeus, who sees afar, sent a messenger to them, fine-haired Rhea, so that she might bring dark-veiled Demeter back to the host of the gods, promising to give her those honors that she might choose for herself among the immortal gods. He agreed, also, that her daughter should in truth spend a third part of the revolving year in the gloomy land of darkness, but that she should spend two seasons of the year with her mother and the other immortal gods. Thus he ordained it.

The goddess Demeter did not refuse to obey the commands of Zeus, but at once sent forth fruit from the fertile soil. Then all the broad earth was heavily laden with leaves and blossoms.

From *Homeric Hymns* II, 1–473

Atlas

Atlas, a Titan and the brother of Prometheus and Epimetheus, had taken part in the battle of the Titans, thus incurring Zeus' anger. Zeus punished the other Titans by hurling them into Tartarus, but reserved a different punishment for Atlas.

In later accounts, Atlas is said to be the father of the Hesperides and to live at the western extremity of northern Africa, giving his name to the mountains there. Atlas was generally considered to be the father of the Pleiades, one of whom, Maia, was the mother of Hermes.

As told in Greek verse by Hesiod

IAPETUS TOOK as his wife a maiden with beautiful ankles, Clymene, the daughter of Oceanus, and she bore a son to him, the stout-hearted Atlas.

Atlas, standing at the ends of the earth before the clear-voiced Hesperides, holds up the wide vault of the sky with his untiring head and arms by the force of his mighty strength—for the wise counselor Zeus gave this destiny to him by lot.

From *Theogony*, 507–520

GLORIOUS ATLAS was the father of the Pleiades, whose stars are these: lovely Taygete and dark-eyed Electra and Alcyone and noble Asterope and Celaeno and Maia and Merope.

Astronomy 1

Daphne and Apollo

Apollo's loves were many, but he was not always a successful lover. The following account by Ovid tells of one of Apollo's failures in love, this one with Daphne, the daughter of the river god Peneus.

The Greek word daphne *means "laurel" or "bay tree." The laurel was sacred to Apollo, who wore a laurel wreath, and became the prize presented to the victors in the Pythian Games, games held at Delphi every four years in honor of Apollo and his victory there over the serpent Python.*

As told in Latin verse by Ovid

THE FIRST love of Phoebus Apollo was Daphne, daughter of the river god Peneus. Not blind chance but the fierce anger of Cupid gave her to him.

Delian Apollo had seen Cupid when he was bending his bow with its string drawn tight and had said, "Why are you concerned, playful boy, with powerful weapons? Such weapons are suitable only for my shoulders. I am the one who is able to give sure wounds to the wild animals, my enemies. See to it that you are content to kindle the little flames of love with your torch and do not try to claim a skill for which I am famous."

Venus' son Cupid answered him thus: "It may be that your arrow pierces all things, but mine shall pierce you, and by as much as all things living are of less worth than divine power, by that much is your glory of less value than mine."

Thus Cupid spoke and, lifting himself through the air on fluttering wings, he quickly came to rest on the shady heights of Mount Parnassus and drew forth from his quiver, full of arrows, two darts of different purpose. One drives love away, the other brings love. The arrow that causes love to be kindled is golden and its sharp point is shining bright; the arrow that causes love to flee is blunt and has lead under its shaft. The god Cupid shot the latter dart into the nymph Daphne, daughter of Peneus, but with the former he pierced the bones and struck the marrow of Apollo.

At once Apollo felt love, but Daphne fled the mention of love and found pleasure in the remote parts of the forests. Many men sought after Daphne, but she, avoiding all her suitors and shunning the sight and thought of men, wandered over the pathless groves and had no care for Hymen, or Amor, or marriage.

Often her father would say, "Daughter, you ought to give me a son-in-law." Often he would say, "Daughter, you ought to give me grandsons." She, throwing her arms around her father's neck, would say coaxingly, "Dearest father, grant me that I enjoy perpetual maidenhood. Diana's father has already granted this to her." He, in truth, gave in to her pleading, but Daphne's beauty did not allow it to be as she wished, for her charm was stronger than her hope.

Phoebus Apollo loved Daphne when first he saw her, and he longed to wed her. What he longed for he hoped for, and his own prophecies deceived him. And just as hedges are inflamed by torches that by chance a traveler has either thrown too close or has left behind even at daybreak, so the god was caught up by the flames of love, so his whole heart was set on fire and nourished his unreturned love by hoping.

He saw her eyes twinkling with light like the stars; he saw her lips, but it was not enough only to see them. She fled from him, however, more swiftly than a light breeze, and she did not tarry even when he called out to her thus: "O nymph, I beg you, daughter of Peneus, pray stop. I am not pursuing you as an enemy. O nymph, wait. Thus a lamb flees from a wolf, thus a deer from a lion, thus doves with trembling wing flee from an eagle, each trying to escape its enemy. But it is love that is the reason for my pursuit.

"Run more slowly, I beseech you, and check your flight. I shall run more slowly myself. Only ask who is the one who loves you. I am not a man of the mountains, I am not a shepherd.

You know not, heedless girl, you know not from whom you flee and that is why you seek to escape.

"Jupiter is my father. Through me, what will be and what has been and what is are all revealed; through me, songs are sung in harmony to the lyre. My arrow is indeed certain, but one arrow more certain than mine has carried a wound into my heart, free of love until now. The art of healing is my discovery and I am called the Healer throughout the world, and the power of herbs is subject to me. Alas for me that love is not curable by any herbs and that the arts that benefit all men are of no use to their master!"

Just as he was about to say more, Daphne ran on in frightened flight and left him alone with his words unfinished. Even then she seemed lovely, and her beauty was increased by her running.

But she did not run far, for the young god could no longer bear to waste his words of endearment, and, as his very love drove him on, he followed after her in pursuit at full speed. Just as a Gallic hound when he sees a hare in an open field, and the hound runs on swift foot after his prey while the hare seeks safety, so were the god and the maiden—he swift with hope, she with fear. He, however, sustained on the wings of love as he pursued her, was the swifter one and denied her any rest.

When her strength was exhausted and she was overcome by the fatigue of her swift flight, Daphne, seeing the waters of the river Peneus, cried out, "Bring me help, Father! If you hold any power as a river god, destroy my beauty, which has made me too pleasing, by changing it!"

She had hardly finished her prayer when a heavy numbness filled her limbs, and her soft body was encircled by thin bark, her hair changed to leaves, her arms to branches. Her feet, just a moment ago so swift, clung to the ground in dull roots, and her head turned into a treetop. Her beauty alone remained unchanged.

Phoebus Apollo loved her even in this shape and said to her, "At least, since you cannot be my wife, you will indeed be my tree. My hair, my lyre, my quiver will always bear you, O laurel, as adornment. You will crown Roman generals when

joyful voices celebrate their triumphs and the Capitoline Hill*
beholds their long processions. And as my head is always young
with uncut locks, may you always keep the beauty of your leaves
everlastingly green."

From *Metamorphoses* I, 452–565

* The triumphal processions passed along the Sacred Way through the
Roman Forum and up the Capitoline Hill to the temple of Jupiter Optimus
Maximus at its summit.

Io

Io, the granddaughter of Oceanus and daughter of King Ina-
chus of Argos, was a priestess of Juno, whom the Romans iden-
tified with the Greek goddess Hera.

When Io was fleeing before the Furies she crossed the strait
between Europe and Asia. This strait was said to have been
named the Bosporus, or "Oxford," after Io, from the Greek
words bous—*"ox" or "cow"—and* porus—*"river ford," or "strait."*
The following account also explains how Mercury, identified by
the Romans with the Greek god Hermes, gained his epithet "the
Argus-slayer."

Io came to be identified with the Egyptian goddess Isis. Her
son by Jupiter, the Roman counterpart of Zeus, was called
Epaphus. Among his descendants were Cadmus, Europa, Phoe-
nix, Aegyptus, and Danaus. He is thus linked with Thebes, Crete,
Phoenicia, Egypt, and the Argives.

As told in Latin verse by Ovid

THERE IS in Thessaly a valley closed in by wooded hills on all
sides. They call this the Vale of Tempe. Through this valley the
river Peneus pours forth from the foot of Pindus and rolls out
its foaming spray. This is the dwelling, this the home, this the
deep-set source of the mighty river. Here, seated in a cave of
hanging rock, Peneus makes laws for his waters and the nymphs
who dwell beneath. To that place there came the rivers of his
native land—though they knew not whether to rejoice or com-
miserate with Daphne's father, Peneus—and soon the other
rivers also came. Inachus alone failed to come, for he remained
hidden in the depths of his cave, grieving in wretched sorrow for
Io, his daughter, believing she was lost. He knew not whether
she still knew the joy of life or had taken her place among the
dead—but nowhere could he find her.

It happened that Jupiter had seen the girl walking near her father's stream and had said to her, "O maiden, worthy of Jupiter and one to make some husband happy, go into the shade of the cool woods while the heat of the noonday sun is overhead. But if you fear to go alone where the wild animals have their haunts, you shall walk in safety through the deepest woods, protected by a god. Nor am I an ordinary god; but I am he who holds the mighty scepter of heaven in my hand, I am the one who hurls the flying thunderbolt. Do not run from me—" for she had turned in flight. She had already run across the fields of Lerna and wooded Lyrcea when the god overtook the fleeing girl and her modesty, covering all in a thick overspreading cloud.

Shortly, Juno looked down upon Argos and noticed with surprise that newly formed clouds had given the appearance of night below a bright sky, realizing that they were neither river mists nor fog rising from the earth. Then she looked about to find where her husband was—for she knew well his deceptions, so often discovered before this. When she could not find him in the heavens, she thought, "Either I am mistaken or I am being deceived," and, slipping down from heaven's height to earth, she commanded the clouds to scatter.

But Jupiter had sensed his wife's coming, and he had changed Io into a white heifer—even as a cow she was beautiful. Juno admired the heifer's appearance, although unwillingly, and asked whose she was and where she came from, just as if she didn't know the truth. Jupiter lied in reply, saying she was brought forth from the earth, and Juno then asked for her as a gift. What could he do? It was cruel to give away his love, but not to give the gift would bring suspicion.

Even when she had been presented with her rival, the goddess did not lose all suspicion—for she feared what Jupiter might do and was anxious about his deceits—until she had turned her over to Argus to guard. Argus' head was covered with a hundred eyes, which took their rest two by two in turn, while the others stayed awake and kept watch. Wherever he stood he watched Io, keeping Io before his eyes even when he was turned away from her. By day he permitted her to graze, but when the sun was below the vast earth he tied her up with a halter about her

humbled neck. When she tried to stretch out her arms in supplication to Argus, she had no arms. When she tried to utter a word
of complaint, she made a mooing sound, a sound that frightened
her—she was afraid of her own voice.

Jupiter, ruler of the gods, could endure the distressful plight of
Io no longer, and he, therefore, called his son Mercury, child of
the bright Pleiad [Maia], and instructed him to bring about the
death of Argus. Straightway Mercury put his winged sandals
upon his feet, took his sleep-bringing wand in his hand, and put
on his cap. Then he jumped down from the heavens to earth and
laid aside his cap and wings. He kept his wand, however, and
with it he drove a herd of goats along the byways of the countryside as though he were a shepherd, and as he walked he played
a tune on his pipes of reeds. Argus, while he guarded Io, was
captivated by the sweet sound and called, "Whoever you are,
come sit with me on this rock, for there is no better grass for
your flock anywhere."

Mercury sat down by Argus and passed the time of day by
talking of many things, and he tried to lull the watchful eyes to
sleep with the music of his reed pipe. Argus, however, fought
against the temptation of sleep, and, even though some succumbed to slumber, he still kept watch with the rest of his eyes.
Then he asked how the shepherd's pipe, newly invented at that
time, had been discovered.

Then Mercury said in reply, "There was one of the hamadryads, who dwell upon the shady mountainsides of Arcadia,
who was especially attractive. The other nymphs called her
Syrinx. Not once but many times she fled from the attentions of
the satyrs and the gods who inhabit the fertile countryside and
shady woods. In her way of life and cherished maidenhood, she
imitated the Delian goddess, and she could indeed be taken for
Diana.

"Once when she was returning from Mount Lycaeus, Pan
saw her and began to speak——" Mercury had yet to relate the
words and to tell how the nymph, scorning Pan's entreaties, had
fled from him through untrodden ways until she came to a quiet
river and had begged her sister nymphs of the waters to change
her shape, and how Pan, when he thought he had caught Syrinx

at last, had held only marsh reeds instead, and how, when he had breathed a sigh, the breath of his sigh moving over the reeds had brought forth a soft sound like the low tone of his complaint. Enchanted by the charming sweetness of this new form of music, the god had cried out, "This meeting between us will be a lasting union." And thus the shepherd's pipes were made by joining reeds of varying lengths together with wax, and they took their name from that of the girl.

Just as Mercury was about to continue his tale he saw that all the eyes of Argus were closed in sleep. He checked his words at once and put Argus into a deep slumber by touching the heavy eyelids gently with his wand. Losing no time, Mercury struck the nodding head across the neck with his sword and sent it hurtling down the cliff. Argus, you now lie dead, and the darkness of one final night has fallen upon the light of a hundred eyes.

Juno took the eyes of Argus and set them among the tail-feathers of her bird, the peacock, where they shine like starry jewels. Then, filled with anger, she at once sent one of the dread Furies against Io to bring terror into her heart and pursue her as she fled in fear over all the wide earth. When at last she reached the Nile, she fell to her knees at the river's edge and lifted up her head—for that alone she could raise—toward the stars of heaven, and by groaning and weeping and sorrowful mooing she sent forth her complaints to Jupiter and begged for an end to her misery.

Then Jupiter, putting his arms around Juno's neck, pleaded with his wife to put an end to her revenge at last, saying, "Do not be afraid for the future, for Io will never again cause you sorrow." And he swore the oath by the waters of Styx. The goddess was won over, and Io regained her former shape and was as she had been before. Not a trace of the heifer remained except for the whiteness of her skin, and the nymph stood erect at last.

From *Metamorphoses* I, 568–745

Phaëthon

In Greek mythology Phaëthon was the son of Helios, the sun god, and in Ovid's account he is called the son of Phoebus, since the Romans identified Phoebus with Helios.

The ancients believed that the sun, moon, and larger planets traveled along one narrow path in the sky. They divided the sky into twelve parts, each representing one month and given the name of a constellation, or "sign of the zodiac."

As told in Latin verse by Ovid

To Io there was born of mighty Jupiter a son, Epaphus, who had as his friend a youth of the same age and disposition, the child of the Sun, named Phaëthon. Once, when Phaëthon was speaking with pride and declared boastfully that Phoebus was his father, Epaphus could not bear it and said, "What a fool you are! You believe everything your mother tells you, and you are puffed up with a false idea of your father."

Phaëthon grew red and held back his anger in shame, then went to Clymene, his mother, with Epaphus' insult, saying, "I am ashamed that this insult could have been spoken but could not be denied. But may you, if I am really born of divine origin, give me proof of such high birth and declare me to be born of heaven."

Clymene, moved by the entreaty of Phaëthon or by anger at the charge against her, raised her arms to the sky and, looking toward the light of the sun, answered, "I swear by this brilliance and his gleaming rays; I swear to you that you are the son of this Sun, whom you behold; that you were born of this Sun, who governs the world. It is not a difficult task, however, for you to learn to know your father's house. The dwelling from which he rises is quite close to our land. If your spirit moves you thus, go there and ask him your questions." Phaëthon jumped up happily at his mother's words and had already reached the heavens in his thoughts. Then he crossed his own land, Ethiopia, and India, lying beneath the sun, and came quickly to his father's dwelling. The palace of the Sun was built with lofty columns, a dwelling bright with gleaming gold and flaming bronze. Shining ivory covered the gables above and the double doors of the entrance shone with polished silver. The skill of their workmanship was even more artistic than the material. For Vulcan had engraved upon them the waters that encircle the earth in their midst, the lands of the world, and the sky above the circle of the earth. The waters are filled with sea-dark gods, the land with men and cities, forests and wild animals, and rivers, and nymphs and other deities of the countryside. Above all this there was depicted the scene of the shining sky—six signs of the zodiac on the doors on the right, six signs on the left.

When Phaëthon, Clymene's son, had reached the entrance doors by the steep path and had entered the house of the one he questioned as his father, he went before his father and faced him. But he stood still some distance from him, for he could not endure the brilliance any closer. Phoebus, dressed in a purple robe, was seated on a throne that sparkled with glittering emeralds. On his right and left were Day and Month and Year and Century, and the Hours, standing at equal distances. Early Spring stood there, crowned with a wreath of flowers; and naked Summer, bearing a garland of corn; and Autumn, stained with the newly trampled grapes; and icy Winter, bristling with white hair.

The Sun, seated in their midst, looked at the boy and asked, "What is the reason for your coming? What are you looking for in this citadel, Phaëthon—you, a son no father should deny?" The youth replied, "O light shared by all the great universe, Phoebus my father, if you grant me the right to use this name, give me proof, father, by which I may be known as your true son and remove this doubt from my mind."

Then his father took off his sparkling crown of light and asked the boy to come nearer. He embraced his son, saying, "You are worthy to be called my son and Clymene has told you the truth about your birth. And so that you may have no doubt at all, ask whatever favor you wish, so that you may receive it from me."

He had scarcely spoken when the boy asked for his father's chariot and the right to drive his winged horses for one day. Then his father regretted his promise. Shaking his shining head three and four times, he said, "Your words prove that mine were spoken rashly. I wish that I might take back my promise. I confess that this is the one favor, my son, I would deny you. But let me try to dissuade you, since your wish is not a safe one. Your fate is mortal; what you seek to do is not for mortals. In your ignorance you would attempt even more than can be achieved by the gods, even the ruler of vast Olympus.

"The first part of the path is steep and the horses can make their way up it only with difficulty, though it is morning and they are fresh. In mid-heaven the road is very high, and it often brings fear to me to look down on the sea and lands from there, and my heart trembles with terror. The last part of the way is precipitous and demands a firm control. Then even Tethys herself, who receives me in her deep waters below, fears I may fall headlong into the sea. Beware, my son, lest I be the donor of a fatal gift to you. While there is still time, change your request. I prove myself to be your father by my fatherly fears. You will suffer no denial, but I beg you not to ask this one thing. Do, I beg you, choose more wisely."

His father finished his warnings, but Phaëthon disagreed with his words and pressed his request, burning with eagerness to mount the chariot. Phoebus, therefore, when he had delayed as long as he could, led the youth to the lofty chariot, a gift from Vulcan. The axle was of gold, the pole was golden, of gold the rims of the wheels, and the circle of spokes was silver. Across the yoke, topaz and other gems reflected bright lights from the rays of the sun.

Behold, wakeful Aurora in the reddening east has flung wide her purple gates, and her halls are filled with a rosy glow. The stars flee, and Lucifer follows at the end of their ranks, the last to leave his outpost in the sky. When Phoebus saw him leave and saw the world growing red, and saw the thin horns of the waning moon disappearing from view, he ordered the swift

Hours to yoke the horses. The goddesses quickly obeyed his command and led the steeds from their lofty stalls, breathing fire and well-fed with ambrosia, and harnessed up their clinking bridles.

Then the father anointed his son's face with sacred ointment and made it able to endure the scorching flames. Then he set on his head his shining crown, sighing deeply from a heart foreboding sorrow, and said, "If you can, obey at least these warnings of your father. Spare the whip, my son, and use the reins with force. Do not take the route straight across the five zones of the sky. A path cuts obliquely in a wide curve and, confined to three zones, keeps away from both the deep southern and far northern heavens. Let this be your route. You will see the clear tracks of my wheels.

"And so that both the sky and the earth may receive equal heat, do not go too low; but do not set your course at the height of the heavens. If you go too high, you will burn up the roof of the sky; if too low, the earth. You will travel most safely in the middle. The rest I entrust to Fortune* and I pray she may aid you and guide you better than you take care for yourself. While I have been speaking, dewy night has touched the goal on the western shores and we may delay no longer. We are summoned. But let me be the one to give light to the world, light for you to look at in safety."

But the boy had already taken possession of the swift chariot, and, standing tall, he rejoiced as he took the reins in his hands. And then he thanked his father for his gift, a gift unwillingly given.

After Tethys, unaware of the fate of her grandson, pushed back the bars and they were given the freedom of the measureless sky, the horses flew on their way and broke through the clouds in their path with flying feet. And, borne on wings, they passed by the east winds, which rise up from the same region. But their burden was light and not enough for the horses of the Sun to feel, and the yoke lacked its usual weight.

* Fortune, or destiny, was worshiped by the Romans in the form of the goddess Fortuna.

As soon as they sensed this, the four-horse team bolted and left the well-trodden path and no longer kept to their former course. Phaëthon was terrified with panic. He did not know how to manage the reins entrusted to him or which was the right road, and, even if he had known, he could not control the horses. Then for the first time the cold Bears grew warm from the sun's rays and tried, but in vain, to dip themselves in the forbidden sea. And the Serpent, which lies next to the icy pole—until then sluggish with cold and not harmful to anyone—grew hot and became frenzied from the fire.

When, in truth, the unfortunate Phaëthon looked down from the summit of the heavens upon the lands lying spread out far, far below, he grew pale, and his knees shook with sudden fear, and darkness came over his eyes in spite of the strong light. Now he wishes he had never touched his father's horses; now he is sorry he has learned of his true birth; now he regrets he was given what he begged for. Now he is being carried along just like a ship driven before a gale.

What is he to do? Much of the sky is behind him, but more is still before him. He measures both in his mind. At times he looks ahead toward the west—which he was fated never to reach —at times he looks back toward the east, but not knowing what to do, he is dazed. He neither drops the reins nor has the strength to hold them, and he does not even know the names of the horses.

At length, robbed of his senses and chilled with fear, Phaëthon dropped the reins. As soon as the horses felt the reins fall across their backs, they left their course and, with no one curbing them, wandered over unfamiliar regions of the air, going wherever impulse led them. They rushed in all directions without aim and ran against the stars set high in the sky and dragged the chariot along through untraveled byways. Now they make for the top of the heavens, now they plunge headlong down steep paths in a region nearer to earth. Luna wondered at her brother's horses running lower than her own, and the scorched clouds were smoking. The earth was swept up by flames, all the highest parts first, and was split with cracks and dried up as it lost all its moisture. The fields were burned white with ashes, the trees and their leaves were destroyed by the flames, and the dry grain furnished fuel for its own fire. But these were small losses, for great cities perished, and the flames turned whole nations and their people to ashes. The forests and the mountains together were ablaze.

Then, in truth, Phaëthon looked down upon a world in flames in all directions, and he could not bear the intense heat, for the air he breathed was like the hot blast of a vast furnace as he felt the chariot growing hot around him. No longer could he endure the ashes and the flying sparks, and he was wrapped up in hot, thick smoke, so that he knew not where he was going or where he was, covered as he was by pitch-black darkness, but was carried along at the will of the winged steeds.

It is thought that at that time, because the blood was drawn to the surface of the body, the skin of the people of Ethiopia turned black. Then, also, Libya was made a desert, when her moisture disappeared in the dry heat. The Nile, terrified, fled to the end of the earth and hid his head. It still lies hidden, and the seven mouths are arid and filled with dust, seven river beds without a river. The same fate dried up the rivers of the west as well —the Rhine and the Rhone and the Po, and even the Tiber, to which supremacy over the world had been promised.

Everywhere the earth was split apart, and light penetrated into Tartarus through the cracks, bringing terror to the ruler of the lower world and his queen. The sea, too, shrank up, and what had only recently been deep sea waters now became a field of dry sand. And the mountains that the sea's surface had covered stood forth and joined the scattered Cyclades. The fish dove to the ocean's depths, and the dolphins did not dare to leap into the air as they always had. The rumor is that Nereus himself and Doris, too, with all their daughters hid themselves in their caves. Three times Neptune ventured to raise his arms and shining head above the water's surface, and three times he retreated, unable to endure the blazing air.

The Earth was no longer able to bear the heat and withdrew into herself and into the caverns near to the land of the dead. But the father all-powerful—calling on the gods, and calling especially on the one who had given up his chariot, to witness that, unless he brought help, everything would be consumed in utter destruction—went up to the summit of the lofty citadel from where he was accustomed to spread the clouds over the wide earth, and from where he shook his thunder and hurled his darting thunderbolts. But now he had no clouds that he could spread over the earth, nor had he rain to send down from the heavens. He thundered and, balancing it in his right hand, aimed a bolt of lightning at the charioteer and cast him with one stroke from life and from the chariot. He had quenched the fire with a fiercer fire.

The horses reared up, tore the harness from their backs and left the broken reins behind. But Phaëthon, his fiery hair ravaged by flames, was thrown headlong and fell through the air, leaving a long train of fire, just as a star is sometimes seen falling from a clear sky. Eridanus received him as he came to earth, far from his native land in a remote part of the world, and bathed his burning face. The naiads of Hesperia placed his body, still smoking with the flames of the forked thunderbolt, in a tomb and carved a stone with this inscription:

Here lies Phaëthon, who drove his father's chariot.
Great was his attempt, greater still his daring.

From *Metamorphoses* I, 748–779 and II, 1–328

Europa

The two following versions of the rape of Europa illustrate the similarities and differences that appeared between one telling of a myth and another. The first was written in Greek in the second century B.C., and the second was written in Latin over a century later. The myth emphasizes the connection between Zeus and Crete, his birthplace, and also the importance of the bull in Cretan mythology. Ovid, of course, used the names Jupiter and Mercury, since the Romans identified those gods with the Greek gods Zeus and Hermes.

Although Homer made Europa the daughter of Phoenix, a tradition followed by Moschus, in most later accounts she was the daughter of King Agenor of Tyre (or of Sidon), the son of Poseidon; Phoenix was her brother. When Phoenix became king, his country was renamed Phoenicia. Europa was worshiped in Crete as the mother of Minos and Rhadamanthus, both of whom were judges in the lower world after their deaths.

As told in Greek verse by Moschus

EUROPA ONCE had an unpleasant dream. It was almost dawn, when the maiden Europa, daughter of Phoenix, dreamed that two continents, one near and one far, struggled to win possession of her. They appeared to her in the shape of women, one bearing the look of a woman from another country, the other resembling those of her own land.

Europa jumped from her bed with her heart pounding in fear, for she had seen the dream as though it were reality. She sat for a long time in silence, and even then, now wide-awake, she saw the two women before her eyes. Finally the maiden spoke out in terror, asking, "Which one of the heavenly beings sent such apparitions upon me? What was the meaning of the dream that came to me as I lay in sweet slumber? Who was the strange woman I saw in my sleep?"

With that, she went in search of her friends, girls her equals in age and high birth. She quickly found them, carrying baskets on their arms and walking toward the meadows near the sea to enjoy the roses growing there and to listen to the roar of the waves. Europa carried a golden basket, a wondrous basket, the fine work of Hephaestus, skillfully wrought with many sparkling scenes.

When the maidens reached the blossoming meadows, they filled their hearts with joy over one flower and another. But not for long was Europa to enjoy the flowers, for as soon as Zeus the son of Cronus saw her there, his heart was struck by a swift arrow of the goddess of love, which alone has the power to conquer Zeus. Then he, wishing both to escape from Hera's jealous anger and to deceive the tender heart of the maiden, changed himself into a bull.

Thus he came into the meadow and did not frighten the maidens when he appeared, but instead they all had the desire to draw near and to touch the lovely animal. And he went and stood before the innocent Europa and licked her cheek, casting a spell of enchantment upon that maiden, and she gave him a kiss. At that, the bull lowed sweetly and sank to his knees at her feet, looking up at Europa and turning his head toward his broad back to entice her.

Thus the maiden called out to the others: "Come here, dear friends, and let us climb on this bull's back for fun, for certainly he will carry us all on his wide back. He looks so friendly, kind, and gentle—not at all like the other bulls—and seems to have a temperament like that of a man, lacking only speech."

And so she took her seat upon his back, smiling, and the others were just about to follow her, when suddenly the bull, now that he had gained the one he wanted, made off with her, charging toward the sea. She turned and cried out, holding out her arms to her dear friends, but they could not reach her. And when he came to the shore of the sea, the bull continued on over the broad expanse of waves with his hoofs as dry as a dolphin's fins, and the sea grew calm before Zeus as he went. But Europa, in truth, was keeping her seat on his back by grasping a horn of the bull with one hand while she held the folds of her skirts above the water with the other.

When she had been carried far away from the land of her ancestors, and no wave-washed shoreline or mountain height could be seen—only the sky above and the boundless sea below—Europa looked about timidly and cried out, "Where are you taking me, god-bull, and who are you in truth? For indeed you must be a god, since what you are doing is the accomplishment of a god. As dolphins do not roam over the land, so bulls do not travel the seas, but you move across land and sea alike. O Poseidon the earth-shaker, guardian of the sea, come to my aid with your kindness and guide me."

Thus she spoke, and the wide-horned bull answered her, saying, "Be of good courage, dear maiden, and do not fear the sea's waves. I, in truth, am Zeus, although to all appearances I seem to be a bull—for I am able to take on any shape I wish. Love for you has led me to cross the sea in the form of a bull, and presently Crete, who nursed and reared me, will receive you kindly. There you will have your wedding, and from our marriage there will be born famous sons, who will bear the scepter as rulers of those who dwell upon the earth." So he spoke, and those things he told of were indeed accomplished.

From *Bucolica* II, 1–162

As told in Latin verse by Ovid

MERCURY'S FATHER spoke to him in secret—although he did not admit the reason was his new love—saying, "My son, my trusted messenger, go quickly, slipping down to the earth in your swift flight, and come to land at the place that sees your mother's star [Maia] in the Pleiades on its left—the natives call it Sidon by name. When you reach this place, drive toward the shore of the sea the king's cattle, which you will find grazing on the mountainside."

No sooner had Jupiter spoken than, just as he had commanded, the cattle were herded down from the mountain toward the shore, where the daughter of the king was in the habit of playing with Tyrian girls as her companions.

Royal dignity and love do not suit each other well and do not remain together long. The father and king of the gods, who brandishes the three-pronged lightning in his right hand and shakes the world by his nod, therefore, set aside his royal scepter and assumed the shape of a bull. He then mingled with the cattle and, handsome in appearance, lowed as he walked about here and there on the tender new grass. He was as white as snow that has not been touched by a footprint or melted by the rainy wind from the south. His neck was broad with muscles, and though small, his horns might have been formed by a sculptor's art, so clear and bright were they, catching the light like pearls.

His expression was not menacing, nor would his eyes cause fear, but his whole appearance suggested peace. Agenor's daughter, Europa, looked at him in wonder, thinking how handsome he was, how unmenacing. But, although he seemed gentle, she was afraid to touch him at first. Soon, however, she went up to him and held out some flowers before his snowy lips. He rejoiced in his love and caressed her hands with kisses. And now he prances and jumps about in the grass, now he lies down and rolls in the golden sand.

Then, as her fear was overcome little by little, he allowed himself to be patted and let her wreathe his horns with garlands of fresh flowers. She had even dared to climb onto his back, unaware of who the bull really was, when the god began to move gradually away from the land and the dry shore. He left the marks of his hoofs—imprints not his own—at the water's edge, then waded out farther and soon carried off his prize in flight over the deep sea. Europa paled with fear as she looked over her shoulder at the receding coastline, and she clutched a horn with one hand and braced the other on his back, while her clothing fluttered behind her in the wind.

And then the god, laying aside the disguise of a bull,* revealed his true identity and carried her to the land of Crete.

From *Metamorphoses* II, 836–875 and III, 1–2

* According to Eratosthenes, a scholar of the third century B.C., the bull that carried Europa to Crete was placed in the heavens as the constellation Taurus.

Arachne

Arachne, a maiden skilled at weaving, bore a name meaning "spider's web" or "spider." Ovid tells the story of Arachne with an appreciation of the art of weaving.

Athena, too, was a maiden, the maiden goddess, as her epithet Parthenos, the Greek word for "virgin," or "maiden," indicates. The contest between Athena and Poseidon that resulted in Athena becoming the guardian and patroness of Athens was the subject of the sculpture on the west pediment of Athena's temple, the Parthenon. Athena was also known as Athena Nike and was often depicted holding a small statue of Victory in her hand. Nike, the goddess and personification of victory, was identified with Pallas Athena in her capacity as a goddess connected with war. The charming little temple of Athena Nike dominates the western slope of the Acropolis.

As told in Latin verse by Ovid

PALLAS ATHENA said to herself, "To praise is not enough. Let me be praised indeed for myself, and let me not allow my divine majesty to be scorned without punishment." Then she turned her thoughts to the fate of Arachne of Maeonia, who she had heard would not admit to her superiority in the art of weaving.

Arachne was not famous for the place where she was born nor for the origin of her family, but for her skill. Her father used to dip the wool for her in Phocaean purple.* Her mother had died, but she had been of the same lowly birth as her husband. Their daughter, however, had made her name famous throughout the cities of Lydia because of her skill, even though she came from a humble home and lived in the village of Hypaepa.

---

* Phocaea was a town on the coast of Lydia near which the shellfish murex, the source of purple dye, could be found.

Not only was her finished work a joy to behold, but it was a pleasure also to watch her while she worked, such grace and dexterity did she have. Whether she was winding the raw wool into a new ball, or was guiding it with her fingers, or was twisting the smooth spindle with the light touch of her thumb, or was embroidering with her needle, you would have known she had been taught by Pallas. She herself denied this, however, and, because she was offended at the idea of a teacher, even one so great, she declared, "Let her compete with me. There is nothing I would not give up if I should be surpassed."

Pallas assumed the shape of an old woman, put false gray hair on her temples, and supported her feeble legs by leaning on a staff. Then she addressed the girl thus: "Everything about old age is not to be scorned, for experience comes with the ripening years. Do not spurn my advice. You may seek to win the greatest fame among mortals for your skillful work with wool, but show your deference to the goddess and beg her forgiveness for your proud words, thoughtless girl, with a prayer of supplication. She will pardon you if you ask."

But Arachne looked at her fiercely, dropped the threads she was spinning, and answered the disguised Pallas with these words: "You come here feeble in mind and worn out with old age, and your trouble is that you have lived too long. Let your daughter-in-law, or your daughter if you have one, listen to you. I have wisdom enough to take care of myself. Why doesn't the goddess come herself? Why does she avoid a contest?"

Then the goddess declared, "She has come!" And she threw off the disguise of the old woman and revealed herself as Pallas. The nymphs and the women of Phrygia worshiped her divinity, but the girl alone was not afraid, although she did jump in surprise, and a sudden blush spread over her face and quickly disappeared. But she stood firm in her determination, and, in her confidence and eagerness for victory, she rushed headlong toward her fate.

Without delay they both set up their looms and stretched the fine warp over them. The threads were fastened to the beams, and reeds separated the threads of the warp. Then the woof was woven in by the pointed shuttles, which their quick fingers tossed between the threads, and each time the shuttle passed through the threads of the warp the notched teeth of the reed beat the thread of the woof firmly into place.

They both work quickly, moving their experienced arms and hands skillfully, and their eagerness makes light of their labor. They weave in threads dyed purple in the bronze kettles of Tyre and lighter hues with subtle gradations of tone. They also interweave fine threads of gold, tracing out an ancient story in their weaving.

Pallas depicts the Acropolis, the citadel of Cecrops,* and the ancient contest over the name of the city. The twelve gods and goddesses are seated in solemn majesty on lofty thrones with Jupiter in their midst. She distinguishes each of the deities with his own distinct appearance. The figure of Jupiter is regal. The god of the sea stands and strikes the solid rock with his long trident, and from the midst of the break in the rock, sea water sprang forth, and by this pledge he laid claim to the city as his own.

And to herself Pallas gives a shield, as well as a spear with a sharp point, and also a helmet for her head, and her breast is protected by the aegis. She depicts the earth, where it was struck by her spear, sending forth a young gray-green olive tree laden with fruit, and the gods watch with wonder as Victory comes at the end. She wove around her piece a border of olive, the token of peace, and thus she finished her work and completed her weaving with her own tree.

Arachne depicts Europa deceived by Jupiter in the disguise of the bull. You would think the bull real, the water real. Europa seems to be looking at the land she has left behind and to be calling to her companions, and she appears to be afraid of the touch of the leaping waves and to be pulling back her timid feet. She added, also, scenes showing how Jupiter tricked Danaë as a shower of gold, Aegina as a fire, and Mnemosyne as a shepherd.

---

* Cecrops, the legendary first king of Athens, was half man and half serpent. It was during his reign that Athena and Poseidon contested for the control of Athens. Poseidon struck the Acropolis with his trident, causing salt water to gush forth. Athena's gift, the olive tree, was judged to be the more valuable one, and the city was awarded to her.

She also pictured you, Neptune, changed into a fierce bull, with the maiden of Aeolia.* The very gentle golden-haired mother of grain [Ceres] experienced you in the form of a horse; the snake-haired mother [Medusa] of the winged horse [Pegasus] experienced you in the form of a bird. To all of these figures Arachne gives their own likenesses and their own proper settings. In one place she shows Phoebus in the disguise of a farmer. She pictures, also, how Saturn in the form of a horse became the father of the centaur Chiron. The edge of her weaving, surrounded by a narrow border, is made up of flowers and intertwining ivy.

Pallas could not find fault with her work, nor could Envy criticize it. The fair-haired maiden goddess was filled with pain by Arachne's success and ripped the tapestry with its scenes of the crimes of the gods. Then, as she was holding a shuttle of boxwood in her hand, she struck Arachne over the head with it three and four times. The ill-fated girl could not bear it and tied a noose about her proud neck. Pallas, pitying her, lifted her up as she hung there, saying, "Live indeed, but live hanging, impudent girl. And let this same form of punishment—for do not think the future will be free of penalty—be imposed on all your family and all its descendants to come."

Then, as she turned to depart, Pallas sprinkled over Arachne the juice of Hecate's herb. And at once, touched by the poisonous drug, her hair fell out, and with it her nose and ears fell off, and her head became very small. Her whole body, also, shrank and was small. Her slender fingers were fixed to her side in the shape of legs and all else became the belly, from which she spins her thread. Thus, as a spider, she carries on forever her ancient skill at weaving.

From *Metamorphoses* VI, 3–145

* Arne, daughter of King Aeolus of Thessaly, a descendant of Deucalion and Pyrrha, became the mother by Neptune of twin sons, Aeolus, ruler of the winds, and Boeotus, ancestor of the Boeotians.

Tantalus

Tantalus was said to be the son of Zeus or of Tmolus, a deity of Lydia. Most of the various myths about him deal with his sins, especially his pride, and the penalties he suffered in consequence. According to Homer and numerous other authors, Tantalus was punished in the lower world by being made to stand in water with fruit trees overhead; but the water receded when he tried to quench his thirst, and the wind blew the fruit out of reach when he tried to satisfy his hunger.

In the following account, Pindar rejects the story that Tantalus invited the gods to a banquet and served his son Pelops to them as a dish to test their ability to recognize human flesh.

The Peloponnesus, meaning "island of Pelops," received its name from Tantalus' son.

As told in Greek verse by Pindar

PELOPS, SON of Tantalus, I shall celebrate your fate not as those who have gone before me. When your father summoned the gods to a well-ordered banquet at his beloved Sipylus, in repayment for feasts he had had with them, then Poseidon, the god with the gleaming trident, his heart filled with a desire for you, seized you and carried you off in his chariot of gold to the lofty dwelling of Zeus, he who is honored afar—where at a later time Ganymede was also brought to perform the same service for Zeus.

When you disappeared and could not be found, and men looking everywhere did not restore you to your mother, then some one of your jealous neighbors secretly started the tale that they cut up your limbs with a knife and plunged them into boiling water, and then divided up the pieces of your flesh, and the gods ate them as the last course of their feast. But I am not

75

one to call any of the blessed gods a glutton. I refrain from that. Most often one who speaks evil reaps no gain.

If the gods who watch over Olympus ever honored a mortal, that man was indeed Tantalus. He could not, however, hide his pride in these great blessings, and because of his insolence he brought upon himself a harsh punishment; namely, a huge stone, which the father of the gods hung over him and which he is always struggling to keep from falling on his head. Thus he knows no happiness.

His life, therefore, is beyond his own control and full of pain, with a fourth punishment in addition to three others, because he stole the nectar and ambrosia—by which they had made him immortal—from the gods and gave them to his friends. If any man hopes to escape the notice of the gods in anything he does, he is mistaken. For that reason, therefore, the immortals again cast forth Tantalus' son among the short-lived race of mortals.

From *Olympian Odes* I, 36–66

Niobe

In many ways Niobe was like her father, Tantalus, who had so little feeling for his son, Pelops, that (according to some accounts) he did not mind serving him to the gods at a banquet. Niobe thought about her children too much, but, like her father, she was overproud.

Leto was the mother of the twin deities Apollo and Artemis. Ovid uses Leto's Roman name, Latona, and the name Diana for the Roman counterpart of the Greek goddess Artemis.

Pausanias, a writer of the second century A.D., said that on Mount Sipylus in Lydia, a region associated with both Tantalus and Niobe, he had seen the stone that was the result of Niobe's metamorphosis.

As told in Latin verse by Ovid

BEFORE HER own marriage Niobe had known Arachne, but she did not, however, heed the warning of that girl's punishment to respect the gods and address them with humility. Niobe had many reasons to be proud, but nothing pleased her as much as her children, and she would have been called the most fortunate of mothers, if she had not viewed herself as such. For Manto, the daughter of Tiresias, who had knowledge of coming events, had proclaimed, under divine inspiration, as she passed through the streets: "Women of Thebes, gather at Latona's temple and offer her and her two children sacred incense and your prayers, and bind your hair with laurel. Thus Latona, through me, commands."

The Theban women obeyed and wreathed their temples with laurel and burned incense at the altars and spoke their words of prayer. But behold! Niobe came, accompanied by a great throng and outstanding in her Phrygian garments interwoven with gold.

She stood still and, standing erect, looked around proudly as she asked, "What madness makes you consider gods you have merely heard about more highly than those you have seen? Why is it Latona who is worshiped at the altars, while my divine majesty receives no incense?

"My father is Tantalus, the only man permitted to share the food of the gods; a sister of the Pleiades is my mother; mighty Atlas, who supports the axis of the heavens on his shoulders, is my grandfather; my other grandfather is Jupiter, and I am proud that he is also my father-in-law. The people of Phrygia look up to me with reverence. My beauty is worthy of a goddess, and, in addition, I have seven daughters and seven sons, and I shall soon have sons-in-law and daughters-in-law.

"Latona gave birth to two children on Delos, only one seventh of the number of my children. I am blessed—for who can deny it? And I shall always be blessed—who can doubt it? The wealth of my blessings has made me safe, and I am above the reach of Fortune's harm. Come now, this is enough. Make haste and remove the laurel wreaths from your heads." They took off the wreaths and left the sacred rites unfinished, although they continued to worship the goddess Latona as best they could in silent devotion.

The goddess was greatly offended and spoke to her twin children, Diana and Apollo, on the summit of Mount Cynthus thus: "Behold, I your mother am proud that you are my children, and I shall be second to no other goddess but Juno alone. Now even my divinity is being questioned, and, unless you, my children, help me, I shall be denied worship at my altars forevermore. This is not the only reason for my distress, for this offspring of Tantalus has added insult to injury by daring to call you inferior to her own children." Then Phoebus cried, "Stop! Further complaint would only delay her punishment." And Phoebe agreed with her twin. At once, slipping down quickly through the sky, they came to earth at Thebes, the cloud-covered citadel of Cadmus.

There was a wide, flat field near the city walls, where several of Amphion's seven sons, clad in Tyrian purple, were riding their sturdy steeds, bright with gold bridles. One of them, Ismenus, his mother's first-born, who was riding around the course on his foaming stallion, cried aloud, exclaiming "Woe is me!" as an arrow pierced his breast, and the reins fell from his hands in death. Next, Sipylus, when he heard the whir of arrows piercing the quiet air, gave rein to his horse. But just then he caught the direct hit of an arrow and fell headlong to the ground.

Unlucky Phaedimus and his brother Tantalus, bearer of his grandfather's name, were engaged, as youths do, in a wrestling match. Even as they were locked together breast to breast in their struggle, one swift arrow pierced them both, and they groaned together, fell together, twisted in pain, and with one final glance, died together. Alphenor, seeing it happen, beat his breast in grief as he ran toward them to lift up their bodies, but while he was bent on this dutiful act, he too fell dead, for Delian Apollo pierced his breast with a fatal shaft. But a single wound did not fell young Damasichthon. He was struck just below the knee, where the leg is vulnerable, and while he struggled to pull out the deadly arrow, another pierced his throat. The last was Ilioneus, who lifted his arms in prayer, crying, "O gods, all the gods, spare me." Apollo was moved by his plea, but he could not then call back his arrow.

Rumor of evil, the grief of the people, and the tears of her friends told Niobe of the disaster. She was dazed and angry at what the gods had dared and at their great power. Their father Amphion ended both his life and his grief by driving a dagger through his heart. Oh, how changed was this Niobe from that Niobe who had driven the people away from Latona's altar but a short time ago! Walking proudly through the city, she had been the envy of her friends; now even her enemies could pity her.

Niobe bent over the bodies of her sons, now cold in death, showering them with kisses. Then, raising her arms toward the heavens, she cried, "Feed, cruel Latona, on my grief, feast your heart on my sorrow! Exult and triumph over your victory! But why do I say victory? Even in my misery I have more left to me than you have in your glory. Even after so many deaths I am the victor!"

As she spoke the twang of the bowstring rang out, bringing

terror. The sisters, with their hair flowing and dressed in black, were standing where their brothers lay in death. One, as she pulled the arrow from his flesh, fell dying while she tried to kiss her brother's lips. A second, endeavoring to console her mother in her misery, suddenly fell silent and doubled up with a hidden wound. One sank down as she tried in vain to escape; another fell dead upon her sister. One tried to hide; another stood there trembling. When six had been taken by death, suffering various sorts of wounds, only one remained alive. Then the mother, shielding this last child with her body and covering her with her cloak, cried out, "Leave this one for me, leave me the youngest one! I pray you, leave the smallest, leave one!" But even as she prayed, the one she prayed to save fell dead.

Childless now, Niobe slumped down among her lifeless sons and daughters and her husband, turned to stone in her grief. The breeze did not even stir her hair; her face was white and bloodless; her unseeing eyes stared straight ahead; there was no life in her form. Yet she continued to weep, and then, caught up in the eddy of a whirlwind, she was carried back to her native land. There on a mountaintop, she weeps but never moves, and even now her tears roll down from the marble statue that was Niobe.

From *Metamorphoses* VI, 148–312

Dionysus

Dionysus, the god of the fruits of the trees and the vine, was a wandering god who taught men throughout the Mediterranean world to plant the vine—a staple of life in ancient as well as modern times in that area. The worship of Dionysus was, therefore, widespread. Dionysus was the son of Zeus and—according to Hesiod and those following him—Semele. He was thus the only major deity to have a mortal parent. He was associated especially with Thrace, Phrygia, and Thebes, the city founded by Cadmus, his maternal grandfather.

The bringer of pleasure, joy and merriment, Dionysus is represented in art with vines and grapes, or ivy. He was attended by a retinue of satyrs and other followers. His worshipers were called bacchantes or maenads. Dionysus was also known as Bacchus, the name by which the Romans called him.

As told in Greek verse in the
Homeric Hymns

TO DIONYSUS

I SHALL tell about Dionysus, the son of glorious Semele, recalling how he appeared on a cliff above a beach of the barren sea, looking like a young man in the first bloom of youth. His fine dark hair was thick upon his head, and he wore a purple mantle over his sturdy shoulders. Soon a well-fitted ship came sailing swiftly over the wine-dark sea, manned by Tyrrhenian pirates looking for plunder, for an evil fate drove them on.

As soon as they saw him they nodded to each other in agreement and quickly reached the shore. They seized him without delay and took him aboard their ship, rejoicing in their hearts, for indeed he seemed to be a son of one of the kings cherished by Zeus. And they tried to bind him fast with strong chains, but the chains did not hold him. The chains loosened and fell away from his hands and feet, and he stayed there with his deep blue eyes smiling.

The helmsman realized the truth at once and called out to his companions, saying, "Foolhardy men, what god have you seized and bound, what powerful god? Indeed the ship, well-built as it is, is not strong enough to carry him. For this must be Zeus or Apollo of the silver bow, or Poseidon, since he is not like mortal men but resembles the gods who have their homes on Olympus. Come now, let us set him ashore on the dark beach at once. Do not set hands on him, lest he become angry and let loose upon us gale winds and severe storms."

Thus he spoke, and the captain rebuked him with harsh words: "Foolish man, take heed of the wind, quickly set to and hoist the sails. The others will take care of this man. He is, I believe, headed for Egypt or Cyprus, or for the Hyperboreans or even farther away. And in time he will tell us about his friends and all his possessions and his relatives, since fate has sent him to us."

As he finished speaking he ordered the sails to be hoisted, and the wind swelled the sails. But soon wondrous sights appeared before them. First of all, indeed, sweet and fragrant wine flowed gurgling over the black ship, sending up an ambrosial scent, and astonishment struck all the sailors as they watched it. Then, too, a vine stretched itself out on one side and the other, across the top of the sail, and hanging down from it were many clusters of grapes. Around the mast dark ivy, luxuriant with blossoms and a full growth of fruit, entwined itself, and all the oarlocks also were wreathed with garlands.

When the men saw this, they then directly urged the helmsman to bring the ship to land. But then the god turned into a lion right there on the bow of their ship and gave a loud roar. And then he created a shaggy bear, which stood on its haunches to attack. At the same time, the lion was eying them fiercely from the lofty prow. The men fled in fear to the stern of the ship and gathered in panic around the helmsman, who kept a level head. But when the lion suddenly sprang at the captain and pounced upon him, all the sailors jumped overboard as one man into the glistening sea to escape this violent death they had witnessed. Then they were changed into dolphins, but the god took pity on the helmsman and brought him joy as he spoke to him, saying, "Be of good cheer, for you have gladdened my heart. I am far-crying Dionysus, whom my mother Semele, the daughter of Cadmus, bore to Zeus in a union of love."

From *Homeric Hymns* VII, 1–57

Hermes and Apollo

Hermes was the son of Zeus and Maia, the daughter of Atlas. The messenger of Zeus and the other gods, he was also the god of travelers, crossroads, and thieves. Born in Arcadia, he was worshiped especially by the shepherds there. Hermes is depicted in art as a herald with winged sandals and a staff or wand. Mercury, his Roman counterpart, was a god of trade and commerce.

Apollo, the son of Zeus and Leto, was an adult when his half brother Hermes was born. Apollo and his twin sister, Artemis, were born on Delos. Delphi was also sacred to Apollo, and his oracle there was the most famous of the Greek world. Apollo was god of music, poetry, and dance, and it was he who taught the Muses. As the god of prophecy, Apollo had insight and knowledge that gave him an advantage over his younger brother.

As told in Greek verse in the
Homeric Hymns

TO HERMES

SING, MUSE, of Hermes, the son of Zeus and Maia; guardian of Cyllene and Arcadia, a land rich in flocks; the luck-bringing messenger of the gods; whom Maia, a fair-haired nymph, bore to Zeus in a union of love. A shy creature was she, and she avoided the assembly of the blessed gods, living in a shady cavern.

There she gave birth to her son, a wanderer, a crafty flatterer, a cattle thief, a bringer of dreams, who was destined to display glorious deeds among the immortal gods in a short time. Born at the break of day, at midday he played on the lyre and in the evening he stole the cattle of far-shooting Apollo.

On the day on which queenly Maia gave birth to him, Hermes did not lie still long in his sacred cradle, but rose up quickly and went in search of the cattle of Apollo. As he crossed the threshold of the high-vaulted cavern, he found a tortoise there, which brought him immense happiness. Hermes, in truth, was the first to shape the tortoise into an instrument of song.

Picking up the tortoise with both hands, he went back into the cave with the lovely plaything. Then he cut it open and scooped out the meat from the shell with a chisel of gray iron. Glorious Hermes planned both song and action at the same time. When he had cut stalks of reed to size, he pierced the shell and fastened them across the back of the tortoise. Next, he stretched oxhide around it to act as a sounding box and attached horns to it. Then he joined the two horns by a bridge, from which he strung seven strings of catgut.

When he had finished it, holding the lovely instrument, he tried out the strings by plucking each in turn with a plectrum, and it gave forth wondrous sounds beneath his hands. The god sang sweetly of Zeus the son of Cronus and beautifully-sandaled Maia, telling in song about his own glorious birth. But even as he was singing, his heart was longing for other things. Taking the hollow lyre in his hands, he put it in his sacred cradle and went out from the sweet-smelling cavern, for he was hungry for meat.

As Helios was sinking below the earth down into Oceanus with his horses and chariot, Hermes came running to the shadowy hills of Pieria, where the immortal cattle of the blessed gods were pastured and grazing in the lovely green meadows. Then the son of Maia, the sharp-sighted slayer of Argus, cut fifty loud-bellowing head of cattle from the herd. He drove them backward over sandy places so that their tracks turned back. He also quickly made sandals beside the sandy shore of the sea, weaving them together in a wondrous fashion, a marvelous invention, and bound them securely to his feet.

Glorious Hermes drove the fine herd of cattle along through many shadowy hills and resounding ravines and flower-covered fields. Soon his dark ally, the night, was coming to an end, and the dawn was fast approaching when the strong son of Zeus herded the broad-browed cattle of Phoebus Apollo to the Alpheus River. Then, when he had fed the loud-bellowing cattle well and had penned them all together in a shelter, he sought to find a way of making fire. He took a strong branch of laurel and rubbed it against another held tightly in his hand, and warm smoke came forth. Thus Hermes was the first to kindle fire by rubbing two sticks together. Then, taking a bunch of dry kindling, he piled it deep in a pit in the ground and the flame grew bright.

Then, while the mighty strength of glorious Hephaestus kept the fire burning, Hermes pulled two cows with twisted horns up to the fire. He threw both of them to the ground, bent their necks back, and slit their throats. Going from task to task, he cut off the rich flesh, roasted it on spits of wood, and stretched the hides out across a rock. Then Hermes—he who is joyous of heart—next pulled the roasted meat from the fire, placed it on a flat stone, and divided it into twelve portions, making each one perfectly even. Then glorious Hermes longed for the sacred meat, for the sweet scent tempted him, but his proud spirit did not permit him to touch the sacrificial flesh.*

When, however, the god had done all that needed to be done, he threw his sandals into the deep-eddying Alpheus, then extinguished the coals and covered over the black ashes with sand, spending the remainder of the night at this task, while the gentle light of Selene shone upon him. Then he returned quickly to the splendid hills of Cyllene; nor did any one meet him on the long journey, not any one of the blessed gods or mortal men, nor did any dogs bark. And the son of Zeus, the luck-bringer Hermes, made his way like the autumn breeze into the cave and entered the splendid inner chamber, moving with soft step. Then glorious Hermes quickly lay down in his cradle, covering himself with his swaddling clothes like a newborn child.

Eos, the light of dawn, was rising out of deep-flowing Oceanus as Apollo came to Onchestus, the very lovely grove sacred to loud-roaring Poseidon. In that place Apollo found an old man pasturing his flock beside a path and spoke to him: "Hail, old man of grassy Onchestus. I have come here from Pieria seeking my cattle, all cows, all with twisting horns. They wandered off,

---

* Because Hermes was himself one of the twelve deities, it was not right for him to partake of the sacrificial meat.

just as the sun was setting, from the grassy meadow and away from their sweet pasture. Tell me now, old man full of years, if you have seen anyone making his way along here with these animals."

The old man spoke to him in reply, saying, "O friend, indeed it is difficult to recount all that one has seen with his eyes, for many travelers pass by this way and it is hard to remember each one. But I was digging in my vineyard all day until the time of sunset, and I thought—but I do not know with certainty—I saw a child, whoever he was, passing along here with some cattle with fine horns—an infant, and he had a staff. He was herding them backward, and he kept their heads facing him."

Apollo quickly went on his way when he heard this, and when he saw a bird of omen with a wide wingspread [an eagle], he realized immediately that the thief was the son of Zeus. In haste, therefore, the lord Apollo went on to sacred Pylos in search of his lumbering cattle, and his broad shoulders were covered by a dark cloud. He came to the hills of Cyllene, covered with forests, and the deeply shaded cavern of rock in which the divine nymph gave birth to the child of Zeus the son of Cronus. Then far-shooting Apollo quickly crossed the stony threshold and went down into the murky cavern.

When the son of Zeus and Maia saw that far-shooting Apollo was enraged over his cattle, he huddled down into his fragrant swaddling clothes, drawing his head and arms and feet up in a ball, just like a freshly bathed infant ready for sweet sleep—although he was indeed awake, and he held his lyre close to his side. But Apollo, the son of Zeus and Leto, was not unaware of the lovely mountain nymph and her dear son, even though he was a small child and dressed in swaddling clothes. Then, when the son of Leto had looked into the innermost parts of the great dwelling place, he spoke to glorious Hermes with these words:

"O child, lying there in your cradle, tell me quickly where my cattle are, for we shall quarrel with each other unless you do. Indeed, I shall take you and hurl you into murky Tartarus, into the terrible land of darkness, and neither your mother nor your father will set you free or bring you back to the light, but you will continue to wander about below the earth."

Hermes answered him with a crafty answer: "Son of Leto, what are these harsh words you have spoken? Have you come here in search of farm cattle? I have not seen them, nor have I heard anything about them. I am not one such as a herder of cattle, a strong man. And certainly it would be a great wonder among the immortal gods if an infant child should go through the entranceway of the house with cattle from the fields. I was born only yesterday and my feet are tender, the ground rough beneath them. But, if you wish, I shall take an oath by my father's head and swear that I myself am not the culprit and that I have not seen anyone who is the thief of your cattle."

Then Phoebus Apollo picked up the child, but the strong slayer of Argus devised a plan and sent forth an omen, a long-suffering sound from deep in his stomach, and sneezed. When Apollo heard this he let glorious Hermes fall from his arms to the ground and spoke, mocking him: "Be of good cheer, little infant, son of Zeus and Maia, for I shall soon find the stalwart herd of cattle by this omen, and you indeed will now lead the way."

When Apollo had spoken thus, Hermes of Cyllene jumped up in haste and started out at once. Then he walked quickly along the sandy shore, and the son of Zeus and Leto followed behind. In a short time these splendid children of Zeus came to the summit of sweet-smelling Olympus, even to their father, the son of Cronus. Then Hermes and Apollo, lord of the silver bow, stood before the throne of Zeus in supplication, and Zeus the thunderer questioned his glorious son as he spoke these words to him: "Phoebus, from what place have you carried off this fine captive, a newborn infant? This is a serious matter that has been brought before the assembly of the gods."

Then the lord Apollo answered, saying, "O father, I found this child, this robber, in the hills of Cyllene at the end of a long journey. After he stole my cattle from the meadow, he proceeded to drive them off at eventide along the shore of the loud-roaring sea, going directly to sandy Pylos. Then, when he had quietly put them in an enclosure and had returned by a devious route, taking now this path, now that, he lay down in his cradle, pretending to be as quiet as the dark night in the darkness of a dusky cave."

Then Hermes, in turn, related a different tale, addressing the son of Cronus, king of all the gods: "Zeus, our father, I shall tell you the truth, since I am without sin and know not how to lie. He came to our home looking for his lumbering cattle this morning, just as the sun was rising, and commanded me in great anger to tell him about his cattle, and he threatened to cast me into broad Tartarus. I was born only yesterday, and indeed he himself knows that, nor am I a strong man like a cattle thief. Moreover, you know yourself that I am not the culprit, and I shall take a mighty oath that I am blameless."

Zeus indeed laughed aloud when he heard his crafty child deny so well and skillfully any knowledge of the cattle. And he ordered them both to have one purpose in mind and to search together, with Hermes the guide leading the way and pointing out the place where he had hidden away the stalwart herd of cattle. Then the son of Cronus nodded his head, and splendid Hermes obeyed, for the will of aegis-bearing Zeus easily prevailed upon him.

The two very splendid sons of Zeus, therefore, hurried off together to sandy Pylos and came to the ford in the Alpheus River and the fields and the high, vaulted barn where the animals were penned up. Then the son of Leto at once questioned glorious Hermes: "How were you strong enough, crafty one, to slaughter two cows, when you are only a newborn babe? Indeed I myself marvel at the strength you will have in the future."

Then the strong slayer of Argus very easily bent the son of glorious Leto to his will, even though Apollo was stout-hearted. Taking his lyre in his left hand, he tried out the strings by plucking each in turn with the plectrum, and it gave forth wondrous sounds beneath his hands. Phoebus Apollo laughed with delight as the lovely sound of the sweet music went straight to his heart, and a joyous longing for the instrument overcame his heart while he listened. Then the son of Maia, playing beautifully on his lyre, sang of the immortal gods and the dark earth, telling how they came into being at the beginning and how each was allotted his share. And he honored Mnemosyne, the mother of the Muses, first in song, for she was his protector.

Then Apollo addressed winged words to him: "Sacrificer of

cattle, this music is worth as much as fifty cows. And I think, therefore, our dispute will be settled peacefully; for this fresh sound I hear is wondrous and such as I believe not any man or any one of the immortal gods who have their homes on Olympus has ever heard, except for you, son of Zeus and Maia. I admire, son of Zeus, the beauty of your playing on the lyre. And now, because you are, in truth, so clever, even though you are little, honor among the immortal gods will be bestowed on you, on both you and your mother. I speak the truth; for indeed I swear by this bow of dogwood that I shall make you a glorious and blessed leader among the immortal gods and that I shall grant you splendid gifts, and I shall keep my word to you."

And Hermes answered him shrewdly: "I, in truth, do not object at all that you learn this art of mine, since I wish to be kind to you in thought and speech. Indeed, Zeus the counselor loves you—as it is very right he should—and has bestowed on you glorious gifts. For they say that from the divine voice of Zeus you have learned the power of prophecy and all his decrees. But now, in truth, since you have set your heart on playing the lyre, sing to it and play on it and give yourself pleasure by accepting it from me. And may you, my friend, give me glory in return. Take the lyre without fear, therefore, to the bounteous feast and to the charming dance and joyful merrymaking to be a delight both by night and by day, splendid son of Zeus."

As he said this, he handed him the lyre, and Phoebus Apollo accepted it gladly. Then he put a splendid whip into Hermes' hand as a gift, making him the protector of cattle. The son of Maia took it with delight, as the noble son of Leto, the lord far-shooting Apollo, taking the lyre in his left hand, tried out the strings by plucking each in turn. The instrument sent forth sweet music beneath his fingers, and the god sang beautifully in accompaniment.

From *Homeric Hymns* IV, 1–502

Pan

As in the preceding Homeric Hymn, Hermes *was believed to have been born in Arcadia, a pastoral region where goats and sheep were raised, and that area was especially sacred to him. Pan, a minor deity associated chiefly with Arcadia, was generally said to be the son of Hermes, but in some accounts he is the son of Zeus. Various names are given for his mother.*

Because of the loneliness in the woods at night, Pan was thought to arouse sudden fear and terror, giving us the word "panic." According to Herodotus, the Greeks believed it was Pan who put panic into the Persians during the Battle of Marathon, 490 B.C., causing them to flee. He was, therefore, held in honor by the Athenians.

As told in Greek verse in the
Homeric Hymns

TO PAN

MUSE, TELL me of the beloved son of Hermes, Pan, the goat-footed god with two horns, who loves noise and who roams up and down through the woodlands with choruses of nymphs. The nymphs dance along the steep ledges of rock calling out to Pan, the shepherd god, the bright-haired and disheveled one. All the snow-covered ridges and mountain summits and rocky peaks are allotted to him.

Often Pan runs about through the gleaming lofty mountains; often he dashes along slaying wild animals on the mountain slopes, keen of sight. Then at evening time he makes a loud sound as he makes his way back from the chase, playing a sweet song on his shepherd's pipe of reed. With him at that time are the clear-singing mountain nymphs, dancing with quick feet as they sing beside a spring of dark water, and Echo moans on the summits of the mountains. And the god, here and there amid the band of dancers, or sometimes moving slowly into their midst, dances with quick feet. On his back he wears the skin of a tawny lynx, while he finds delight in clear-toned songs in a soft, grassy meadow where the crocuses and fragrant hyacinths are in bloom everywhere throughout the grass.

They sing of the blessed gods and lofty Olympus and tell of Hermes, the one who brings help, relating that he is the swift messenger of all the gods and also that he came to Arcadia—a land with many springs, the mother of flocks—where there is a precinct sacred to him. For in that place the god Hermes once shepherded flocks of shaggy sheep for a mortal man because a longing to marry the daughter of Dryops came to him and grew strong within him. Thus the happy marriage was consecrated, and she bore Hermes a fine son, indeed marvelous to behold—goat-footed, with two horns on his head, fond of noise, laughing sweetly.

At once the luck-bringer Hermes took him in his arms and went swiftly to the dwelling place of the immortal gods with his infant son wrapped in the thick warm skins of mountain hares. All the immortal gods rejoiced in their hearts, and above all Bacchic Dionysus. And they named the child Pan, because he delighted the hearts of all.

From *Homeric Hymns* XIX, 1–47

Echo and Narcissus

Echo was a wood nymph favored by Diana, the goddess whom the Romans identified with Artemis. Echo generally appears in mythology in connection with Pan, as she does in the preceding account. Juno, the Roman counterpart of the goddess Hera, was jealous of the many loves of her husband, Jupiter, the Roman counterpart of the Greek god Zeus.

As told in Latin verse by Ovid

Tiresias, who had widespread fame throughout the cities of Boeotia, gave blameless answers to those who came for his advice. The first to make a test of the truth of his utterances was the nymph Liriope, who had borne a son whom she named Narcissus. When she consulted Tiresias, asking whether her child would live to see a ripe old age, the prophet answered, "If he never knows himself."

For a long time the words of the prophet seemed empty, but what happened finally proved them true. For when Narcissus reached his sixteenth year and seemed still a boy but yet a young man, many youths, many maidens sought his affection. But in his slender form there was such chill pride that none of the youths, none of the maidens touched his feelings.

One day, while he was driving a startled deer into his nets, there stood watching him a nymph who had a resounding voice and could neither be quiet when anyone spoke nor speak herself until someone spoke to her—Echo by name. At that time Echo had a body, not just a voice alone, but yet, although garrulous, she had no other use for speech than she now has—that is, out of many words she could only repeat the last words. Juno had brought this about, because often, when she could have taken Jupiter with the nymphs by surprise on the mountainsides, Echo cleverly delayed the goddess by lengthy conversation until the nymphs had run away.

When Echo saw Narcissus wandering through the secluded countryside and felt love grow warm within her, she followed him in secret. And the longer she followed him, the more she was set afire by the nearness of her love's flame. Oh, how often she longed to approach him with gentle words and to call to him with a sweet prayer! Her nature denied her this, nor would it allow her to begin; but she was willing to wait for the sounds that she was able to imitate with her own voice.

By chance the youth, separated from his companions, had called out, "Is anyone here?" and "Here," Echo called back. He was amazed and, looking about in all directions, shouted in a loud voice, "Come." "Come," she shouted back to him. He looked back, and again, when he saw no one, he asked, "Why do you run away from me?" and heard in answer the same words he had spoken. He stood still, confused by the sound of the answering voice, and said, "Here let us meet," and Echo, who would never reply to another sound more willingly, replied, "Let us meet." Then, to fortify her words, she came out from the woods in the hope that she might throw her arms around his neck in a loving embrace. But he ran from her, and as he ran he cried, "Take your hands away, do not try to embrace me. May I die before you hold me in your power." And she answered only, "Hold me in your power."

Thus Echo, scorned, hid herself in the woods and concealed her face in shame among the leaves, living from then on in deserted caves. But yet her love clung to her heart and grew on the food of her sorrow, while her sleepless grief consumed her mournful body. A wasting thinness wrinkled her skin, and all her body fluids disappeared into the air. Only her voice and bones were left. At the last, her voice alone remained, for they say her bones turned into stones. Now she keeps herself hidden in the forest and is no longer seen on the hills but is heard by all. There is only a voice, a living voice.

So Narcissus had played with Echo, so he had made sport of other nymphs of the waters and mountains, so he had mocked the gatherings of men, until finally one of the youths raised his hands toward the heavens, praying, "So may he love himself, so may he fail to win what he loves." And Nemesis heard his prayer.

There was a pool, clear and silvery with shining waters, where neither shepherds nor mountain goats nor cattle came; which no bird or beast disturbed, or even a branch falling from a tree. Around it the grass, nourished by its waters, grew thick. Here Narcissus, tired from the hunt and heat and lured by the beauty of the setting and the pool, sank down to refresh himself. As he quenched his thirst, another thirst grew in its place, for as he drank he was engulfed by the beauty of his own image. He fell in love with an image without reality, and he mistook for reality what was only an image.

Narcissus was held spellbound by himself and lay there motionless in a fixed position like a statue of Parian marble, gazing into his own eyes, twin stars, and at his hair, godlike hair, such as the hair of Bacchus or Apollo. He gazed at his youthful cheeks, the ivory tones upon his neck, the beauty of his face, the rosy glow upon his snow-white skin, and he admired all that he saw, all that, in fact, made him admirable. Foolishly he longed for himself and he who was filled with desire was the very one he desired, while he sought he was sought, while he inflamed the mirrored vision with love he was in turn set on fire by love.

No desire for food, no desire for rest could move him from that place, but, lying flat upon the shady grass, he feasted his hungry eyes on the reflection there before him. Then, rising up a little and holding his arms out toward the trees about him, he cried, "Has anyone ever had a crueler love than mine? What I behold enthralls me, but the enchanting sight escapes my reach. Yet only a sheer covering of water separates us. You would think we could touch each other when so little stands between. Whoever you are, rise up and come here to me. Why, splendid youth, do you slip away from me? Where do you disappear to when I reach out?"

No longer could he endure his plight, but as tawny wax melts away in the soft glow of heat, as frost dissolves in the warmth of the morning sun, so Narcissus, pining with love, wasted away and was gradually consumed by the fire of love buried within him. No more is his rosy coloring touched with white, no more is there youthful strength and life in his appearance, but recently so handsome, no more is he the same youth Echo loved.

But when she saw him then, though she could not forget her anger, she felt pity for him, and as often as the young man in his misery cried, "Alas," she repeated, "Alas." As he continued to gaze into the water, now so familiar to him, he spoke his last words: "Alas, beloved boy, loved in vain," and all about him nature echoed his words. When he spoke his final "Farewell," "Farewell," said Echo.

Narcissus laid his weary head upon the green grass as death closed the eyes that wondered at the beauty of the sight that held them. And when he had been received below in the land of the dead, he still gazed at his image in the Stygian waters. The naiads beat their breasts in mourning for their brother; so, too, the dryads grieved, and Echo repeated the sounds of their sorrow. Then they got ready his funeral pyre, the waving torches, and his bier, but nowhere was his body to be found. Where his body had lain, they found a yellow flower circled with white petals.

From *Metamorphoses* III, 339–510

Perseus and Andromeda

Perseus was the son of Zeus and Danaë, to whom Zeus had appeared as a shower of gold. When Polydectes, king of Seriphos (one of the Cyclades Islands in the Aegean), was pursuing Danaë with unwelcome attentions, he sent Perseus off to get the head of Medusa. Perseus accomplished his mission and was returning to Seriphos when he came upon Andromeda.

Cassiopeia, Andromeda's mother and the wife of King Cepheus of Ethiopia, had claimed to be more beautiful than the Nereids. At the request of the Nereids, Poseidon sent a flood and a sea monster against the Ethiopians. The oracle of the Egyptian god Ammon, located in the Libyan desert, told Cepheus he could be rid of the plague if Andromeda were fastened to a rock as prey for the sea monster.

As told in Latin verse by Ovid

AEOLUS, KING of the winds, had closed the winds up in their eternal prison and bright Lucifer, the morning star that urges on all men to their work, had risen in the sky. Perseus bound wings to both heels, buckled on his curving sword, and took to the air, flying swiftly on winged feet.

He came into sight of the land of the Ethiopians, people ruled by Cepheus, where Ammon had unjustly ordered Andromeda to pay a penalty she did not deserve because of her mother's boasting words. When Perseus first saw her tied by the arms to a rocky cliff, motionless, had it not been for wisps of hair stirring in the gentle breeze and her eyes streaming with tears, he could have believed she was a statue of marble. Unknowingly he breathed the fire of love, and, amazed at her great beauty, he almost forgot to beat his wings in the air.

Then, as Perseus came to land close to her, he said, "Oh, you should not be wearing those chains, but you should be bound instead by the ties that link eager lovers together. Tell me your name and what land you come from and why you are chained." At first she was silent and, being a shy girl, did not dare to speak to a man. But when he kept on urging her, she told him her name and the name of her country and how her mother had boasted about her beauty.

Before she finished speaking, there came a roar from the waves and a monster appeared, advancing threateningly over the vast sea. The girl screamed. Her father and mother were at her side, both wretched, both helpless and weeping. Then the stranger said, "There will be time enough for weeping later, but there is only a little time in which to help her. If I ask for this girl as Perseus the son of Jupiter or as Perseus the slayer of the snake-haired Gorgon, I would indeed be preferred above all others as your son-in-law, and now, if only the gods will favor me, I shall try to add my helpfulness to my other qualities. That she be mine, if she is rescued by my courage, is the only condition I make." Her parents accepted the bargain—for who would hesitate to accept? —and promised him also a kingdom as her dowry.

Behold! Just as a swift ship plows through the waves with its pointed prow, so the monster approached, breaking the water on either side by the force of its breast. He was only as far from the cliff as a Balearic sling can throw its lead shot,* when suddenly Perseus, jumping up from the ground, rose up high into the clouds. When he saw Perseus' shadow on the top of the water, the beast lunged at it fiercely. Then, like one of Jupiter's eagles, Perseus swooped headlong through the clear sky and attacked the sea monster in the back, plunging his sword to the hilt in its right shoulder.

Gravely wounded, the monster reared up into the air, dived into the waters, then turned like a wild boar. The hero escaped the creature's hungry jaws by the speed of his wings, and, where an opening was afforded, he struck with the curved sword at its back, heavy with barnacles, at its sides, at its tail, until his wings

---

* The men of the Balearic Islands were noted for their skill with the sling, a weapon that made them excellent warriors.

were wet and heavy with the spray. Perseus, not daring to trust in his sodden wings any longer, saw a rock whose tip stood out when the waters were still but which was covered by rough waves. Leaning on this and holding to the top of the rock with his left hand, he drove his sword into the monster three and four times.

Then the shores rang with applause, and the shouting rang through the homes of the gods above. Cassiopeia and Cepheus, her husband, rejoiced and greeted their son-in-law as the savior and mainstay of their house. And the girl, now freed from her chains, came forward, the prize and reason for his deed of daring.

Lest the rough sand scratch the snaky Gorgon's head, Perseus makes a soft spot on the ground with leaves and seaweed on which to set down the head of Medusa. The fresh stems of the weeds and the still living, thirsty marrow drink in the monster's power and become hard with rigid branches and foliage. Even now coral has the same nature, so that it stiffens upon contact with the air, and what is a weed below the sea's surface becomes stone above the water.

From *Metamorphoses* IV, 663–752

Bellerophon and Pegasus

When Medusa was slain by Perseus, the winged horse Pegasus, a son of Poseidon, was born from her blood. It was said that Pegasus flew at once to the acropolis of Corinth.

The reference to Bellerophon as "son of Aeolus" carries his genealogy back to his grandfather, Sisyphus, who was the son of Aeolus, the grandson of Deucalion and Pyrrha. Iobates, king of Lycia in Asia Minor, sent Bellerophon against the monster Chimaera in response to a request by King Proteus of Argos that Bellerophon be killed, for Proteus believed that Bellerophon was attracted to his wife. When Bellerophon took on this task, a seer advised him to go to Corinth and sleep there.

As told in Greek verse by Pindar

WHEN BELLEROPHON was having difficulty in his attempt to harness Pegasus—the son of the snake-covered Gorgon Medusa—at the spring of Pirene in Corinth, the maiden goddess Pallas brought him a golden bridle. Then what had been his dream became a reality as she said, "Are you asleep, princely son of Aeolus? Come now, take this charm to tame your steed and, after you have sacrificed a white bull, take it to your grandfather, Poseidon the horse tamer."

Pallas, the maiden with the dark aegis, seemed to speak these words to him while he was sleeping in the night, and he sprang to his feet. Then he picked up the wonderful gift lying beside him and went off happily to find Polyidus, the seer of Corinth, and told him all that had happened—how he had gone to sleep at night on the altar of the goddess, according to the advice of the seer, and how the daughter of Zeus the thunderer had brought him the golden bridle.

Then Polyidus urged Bellerophon to carry out the instructions of his dream at once, and he told him that, after he had made the sacrifice to Poseidon, he was to erect an altar to Pallas Athena the lover of horses. Then, in truth, the valiant Bellerophon caught the winged horse by slipping the bridle over his head and setting the bit gently in his mouth.

Bellerophon mounted the steed and rode off at once to attack the Amazons, the army of women archers, from his solitary perch in the air on the back of flying Pegasus. He also killed the Chimaera, a monster breathing fire. Now Pegasus has been given his place in the ancient stalls of Zeus on Olympus.

From *Olympian Odes* XIII, 63–92

Daedalus

The Greek adjective daidalos *means "cunningly wrought" or "skillfully worked." To the Greeks, Daedalus was a cunning, clever artificer who was taught by Athena to be skilled in handicrafts. He was highly esteemed in Greece, especially at Athens, as a master craftsman, artist, architect, and inventor. Daedalus was said to have been descended from Erechtheus, a legendary king of Athens.*

In the light of modern archaeology, the labyrinth referred to in the following account probably included the entire palace of King Minos at Cnossus. The palace was excavated under the direction of Sir Arthur Evans and consists of a vast complex of rooms and corridors. The word labrys *means "double ax." The double ax had religious significance during the Minoan period and was also used as architectural adornment and mason's mark in the palace at Cnossus.*

As told in Greek prose by Diodorus Siculus

Daedalus was by birth an Athenian and was one of those who were called Erechthids,* for he was the son of Metion, whose father was Eupalamus, son of Erechtheus. He was very talented, surpassing all others, and was most active in carpentry, the fashioning of statues, and working in stone.

Daedalus was the discoverer of many inventions that were helpful in his craft, and he constructed wonderful buildings in many parts of the civilized world. In the carving of statues he so far surpassed all men that later generations told the story about him that his sculpture had the quality of being lifelike. For they seemed able to see and to walk and, in general, to give the appearance of a complete human being, so that one might think the

* -d- or -id- affixed to a proper name means "son (or daughter) of" or "descendant of." Compare, Nereus: Nereids.

102

images were living figures. He was the first to give eyes to statues and represent the legs standing apart and also to fashion the arms extended forward, so that he was naturally admired by everyone—for the artists before him had carved their statues with the eyes closed and also with the arms held straight down and fixed to the sides.

Even though Daedalus was greatly admired because of his fine workmanship, he fled from his native country when he was condemned for murder on the following grounds.

The son of Daedalus' sister, named Talos, was trained in the home of Daedalus from the time he was a boy. Since he was more talented than his instructor, he invented the potter's wheel, and when he happened upon a serpent's jawbone and sawed through a small piece of wood with it, he began to imitate the sharpness of the teeth. As a result, when he shaped a saw out of iron and sawed the pieces of wood for his work with it, he was said to have discovered something very useful to the carpenter's trade. Because he also invented a tool for drawing a circle and other clever instruments, he won a reputation of great honor.

Daedalus, however—because he was envious of the young man and realized that his fame would surpass that of his instructor by far—killed him treacherously. And when someone happened to see him burying the boy and asked him what he was burying, he told him he was burying a serpent. Someone might wonder at the strange coincidence—that it happened that the murder was discovered through the same animal from which the invention of the saw came. When he was accused and found guilty of the murder by the court of the Areopagus,* Daedalus first fled to one of the villages in Attica, whose inhabitants were named for him and called Daedalidae.

After that Daedalus escaped to Crete, and, because he was admired on account of the skill of his work, he became a friend of Minos, the king. According to the myth that has been handed down, before this time Minos had customarily dedicated to Poseidon each year the best of the newborn bulls and had sacrificed it

---

* The Areopagus, or "Hill of Ares," was the low hill to the west of the Acropolis where a court met to try cases of homicide, intentional injury, and arson.

to the god. But when there was born an outstandingly fine bull, he sacrificed another bull that was one of the inferior ones. Because Poseidon, as a result, was angered with Minos, he made Minos' wife, Pasiphaë, fall in love with the bull and give birth to the Minotaur, famous in legend.

They say that the Minotaur was a monster of double form and that the upper part of its body down as far as the shoulders had the form of a bull, but that the rest had the form of a man. It is said that Daedalus built a labyrinth in which this monster could be confined and that it had winding passages that were hard for those who were not used to them to find their way in. In the labyrinth in which it was kept, the Minotaur devoured the seven boys and seven girls sent from Athens.*

They say that Daedalus, when he learned about the threats of Minos because he had aided Pasiphaë, feared the king's anger and sailed away from Crete with the help of Pasiphaë, who gave him the boat for his flight. He and his son Icarus, who escaped with him, came to a certain island far out in the sea, and when Icarus was jumping carelessly toward the land he fell into the sea and drowned. The sea was named the Icarian Sea after him, and the island was named Icaria. After Daedalus sailed away from this island, he landed on Sicily near the place where Cocalus ruled as king. The king took Daedalus into his service and, because of his cleverness and reputation, made him his good friend.

Some, however, give a different version of the myth—that Daedalus stayed longer in Crete and was hidden by Pasiphaë, and that when Minos the king wished to bring punishment on Daedalus but was not able to find him, he had all the boats on the island searched and proclaimed that he would give a large reward to the one who found Daedalus.

Then Daedalus, because he despaired of escape by boat, cleverly constructed wings fashioned in a marvelous manner and wonderfully held together by wax. When he had fastened these to his son's body and his own, he spread out his wings and escaped out over the sea surrounding the island of Crete.

Icarus, flying high because of his youthful recklessness, fell into

* Minos exacted this yearly tribute from the Athenians because he blamed King Aegeus for the death of his son, Androgeus, who was killed in Attica.

the sea because the wax that fastened the feathers together melted from the sun. But Daedalus, on the other hand, flying near the sea and getting his wings wet, luckily arrived safely in Sicily.

From *Bibliotheca historica* IV, 76, 1–77, 9

As told in Latin verse by Ovid

DAEDALUS, MEANWHILE, hating Crete and his long exile, and influenced by a longing for his native land, sought escape but was hemmed in by the sea.

"Though King Minos may block me off by land and sea," he said, "at least the sky indeed lies open. We shall go that way. He may control all else, but Minos is not master of the air."

When he had spoken, Daedalus turned his mind toward unknown skills and changed nature, for he placed feathers in a row, beginning with the smallest, with a shorter one just below each longer one, so that you could almost believe the feathers had grown on such a slope.

Then he fastened the feathers at the middle with thread and at the end with wax. When they had been arranged thus, he bent them in a slight curve to imitate real birds' wings.

The boy Icarus was standing close by, and, with smiling face— not knowing he was handling things that would be dangerous for him—he now caught at the feathers that a random breeze had moved, now softened the golden wax with his thumb. So, by his play, he hindered the wonderful work of his father.

After the finishing touch had been placed on the undertaking, the craftsman himself balanced his own body on twin wings and hung in the moving air. Also, he instructed his son and said, "I warn you to go by a middle course lest, if you go too low, the water might weigh down the feathers or, if you fly too high, the heat of the sun might scorch them. Fly between the two. With me as your leader, take your course."

At the same time he gave the instructions for flying and adjusted the unfamiliar wings to his shoulders. Between the work and the warnings, the aged cheeks grew moist and the hands of the father trembled. To his son he gave kisses that were destined never again to be repeated. Then, lifted up by the feathers, he flew ahead and feared for his companion, like a bird that leads forth its tender offspring into the air from the high nest. And he urged him to follow and taught him the fateful art, as he himself moved his own wings and looked back at his son.

Some fisherman catching fish with trembling rod, or some shepherd leaning on his staff, or a plowman resting upon his plow handle saw them and was astonished; and, because they could make their way through the air, he thought they were gods.

Soon the island of Samos, sacred to Juno, was on their left, both Delos and Paros had been left behind, Lebinthos was on their right, and Calymne, rich in honey, had been passed, when suddenly the boy began to rejoice in the bold flight. He deserted his leader and, carried away by an eagerness for the sky, set his course higher.

The nearness of the destructive sun softened the fragrant wax—the fastening of the feathers—and the wax melted. He shook his bare arms and, because he lacked wings, could not make use of the air. And his lips, crying out his father's name, were swallowed up in the dark blue water that gets its name, Icarian Sea, from him.

But the unfortunate father, although no longer a father, called, "Icarus, Icarus, where are you? In what region shall I seek you?" As he kept calling, "Icarus," he caught sight of the feathers in the waves, and he cursed his craftsmanship. He buried the boy in a tomb, and the land of his burial was called Icaria, from his name.

From *Metamorphoses* VIII, 183–235

Oedipus and Sphinx

Oedipus was descended from Cadmus, the founder of Cadmea, the citadel of the future city of Thebes. He was destined to lead a life of tragedy from the cradle to the grave. It was the belief in ancient times that his name was derived from the Greek word oidipous, *meaning "swollen-footed," and was evidence of his suffering.*

In most accounts the Sphinx—part lion and part woman—was said to be the offspring of the monsters Echidna and Typhon.

As told in Greek prose by Diodorus Siculus

LAIUS, KING of Thebes, married Jocasta, sister of Creon, and, because he was childless for a long time, he consulted the god Apollo about the bearing of children. Pythia, the priestess of Apollo, answered him that it would not be to his advantage to have children, for, if a son were born to him, the son would be the murderer of his father and would fill his whole house with great misfortune.

Because Laius forgot the oracle's answer, however, and had a son, he pierced the ankles of the newborn child, bound them together with iron, and left him to die. It was for this reason that the name Oedipus was later given to the boy. The servants, however, who were to take the baby and leave him to die of exposure, were unwilling to do so and instead gave him as a gift to the wife of Polybus [Merope], for she was not able to bear any children.

After the boy had reached manhood, Laius decided that he would consult the oracle of Apollo about the infant child he had left to die. Oedipus, also, who had learned from someone that he was a foster child, set out to consult the priestess Pythia about the truth concerning his parents. When they came to Phocis and happened to encounter each other, Laius scornfully told Oedipus to step off the road to let him pass. Oedipus then killed Laius in anger, unaware that Laius was his father.

They tell the myth that, at this same time, a Sphinx, a beast of double shape, had come to Thebes and was setting forth a riddle to see if anyone could solve it, and many people were being killed because of the difficulty of finding the answer. Even though a large reward was offered to the one who could solve it —namely, that he would marry Jocasta and become king of Thebes—no one was able to find the answer to what was put forth to him, except Oedipus, the only one who could solve the riddle.

This was what was set forth by the Sphinx: "What is it that is of itself two-footed, three-footed, and four-footed?"

Although the others could not see through it, Oedipus replied that the answer was "man," for as an infant man begins to move as a four-footed being, when he is grown he is two-footed, and as an old man he is three-footed, leaning on a staff because of his weakness.

From *Bibliotheca historica* IV, 64, 1–4

Oedipus the King

Greek tragedy was presented in connection with religious festivals, especially the festival of Dionysus held at Athens each spring. It was in the fifth century B.C. *that Aeschylus, Sophocles, and Euripides brought the art of this form of dramatic production to the height of its perfection. Sophocles'* Oedipus Tyrannus, *one of those making up the Theban trilogy, is one of the finest tragedies of all time.*

A basic tenet of Greek tragedy was the belief that man had the power of free choice in regard to his own destiny, but was subject to the laws set by an eternal force greater than man and outside his understanding. When he had solved the riddle of the Sphinx, Oedipus was carried headlong into becoming the king of Thebes and marrying his mother, Jocasta. In spite of all his efforts to save himself and those close to him and because of his determination to bring the truth to light, Oedipus succumbed to the will of the gods and assumed the responsibility for his actions.

In the stories of the deaths of Oedipus, Antigone, and Eteocles and Polynices, the tragic sequence of events was later brought to a close. These accounts are given in Sophocles' Oedipus at Colonus *and* Antigone, *Aeschylus'* Seven Against Thebes, *and Euripides'* Phoenissae.

As told in Greek verse by Sophocles

CHARACTERS

OEDIPUS, king of Thebes
A PRIEST OF ZEUS
CREON, Jocasta's brother
CHORUS OF ELDERS OF THEBES
TIRESIAS, a blind prophet

JOCASTA, wife of Oedipus
FIRST MESSENGER, shepherd from Corinth
A SHEPHERD OF THEBES
SECOND MESSENGER, from the palace

Scene: Thebes, in front of the palace of Oedipus. Children, youths, and old men, led by a Priest of Zeus, are gathered at the altar in supplication as Oedipus enters.

OEDIPUS: O my children, the youngest generation of the ancient line of Cadmus, why are you seated here at the altar before me, bearing olive branches wreathed with wool? The city is filled with the scent of incense, filled with the sounds of hymns and mourning. I do not consider it right, my children, that I should learn of this from others, and so I have come here myself, I, Oedipus, whom all men call renowned.

Come now, O venerable one, tell me—since your age makes it proper for you to speak for all who are gathered here—what has brought you? Is it that you are afraid or have some request? Indeed, I would be glad to give you all the help you want, for I would, in truth, be most unfeeling if I did not feel compassion for suppliants such as these.

PRIEST: O Oedipus, lord and ruler of my land, you see how old and young alike are assembled at your altars—some still fledglings just beginning to try their wings, some burdened with the weight of years, priests, as I am the priest of Zeus, and some in the flower of their youth. The rest of our citizens, carrying garlands, are seated in supplication in the market place before the two altars of Pallas and at the oracle where Ismenus prophesies by fire. For our city, as you see yourself, is being tossed like a ship at sea and cannot raise her head above the surging waves of blood. A blight has fallen upon the budding fruit of our land, a blight upon the herds of grazing cattle, a blight upon the barren labor of our women. And a flaming demon, the fiery plague, has descended upon us, ravaging our city and consuming the house of Cadmus, while the dark kingdom of Hades is made rich with groaning and weeping.

It is not because we consider you one of the gods that I and these children have come to sit as suppliants at your hearth. But it is because we believe you to be the leader of men, both in the fortunes of life and in supplication to the gods, since you came to the city of Cadmus and freed us from the tribute that we paid to the hardhearted songstress. You were not aided by us in this nor given instruction, but it is believed and thought that you were helped by a god to restore the true course of our lives.

Now, O Oedipus, our mighty king, we, your suppliants, all beg you to find some help for us, whether it comes from an utterance of a god or from the skill of man. For I notice that the counsel of experienced men is most likely to prove to be the best.

O greatest of mortals, lift up our state again, rescue us again, and be on your guard, for now this land calls you its savior because of your earlier act of good will. Let no one remember your reign as the time when we were raised up only to be cast down again. Come, save our city and make it secure. Your happy omen brought us good fortune, and now show yourself equal to the task again. If you are to rule over this land, as now you do, it is better to rule over a land of men than over a wasted desert. For neither a walled city nor a ship is of any use if it is bereft of men and no one dwells within.

OEDIPUS: O my pathetic children, known, known all too well to me are the anxieties that have led you to come here, for I know full well what you all are suffering. Yet, as much as you are suffering, there is not one of you who feels pain as great as mine. Your distress falls on each one of you for himself alone and not for any other person, but my heart grieves at the same time for the city and myself and all of you.

You do not arouse me as one deep in sleep, for I am indeed one who has shed many tears, taken many paths in anxious, wandering worry. The one and only sign of hope I have found I have followed with action. I have sent the son of Menoeceus —Creon, my wife's brother—to Pythian Apollo at Delphi to inquire of the oracle by what deed or word I may rescue our city. And now, when I count up the number of days he has been gone, I am concerned about what has happened to him, for he has been away longer than one would expect. But when he returns, I would be a wicked man indeed if I did not carry out all that the god reveals.

PRIEST: You have spoken in good time, for even as you speak I see signs that Creon is coming toward us.

OEDIPUS: O lord Apollo, if only he may come bringing news as bright with hope as the joy in his eyes.

PRIEST: I would believe, in truth, the news is good, for otherwise his head would not be crowned as it is with laurel thick with berries.

OEDIPUS: We shall soon know, since he is near enough to hear us. (*Creon enters.*) Prince, my kinsman, son of Menoeceus, what word have you brought us from the god?

CREON: Good news, for I say that even insufferable burdens, if they happen according to the will of the gods, turn out well in the end.

OEDIPUS: What was the oracle? So far your words offer me neither hope nor fear.

CREON: If you wish to hear the oracle in front of all these people, I am ready to tell you. Or would you rather go inside?

OEDIPUS: Speak out in front of all, for the sorrow that I bear is more for these people than for my own life.

CREON: I shall then indeed relate all I heard the god say. Our lord Phoebus clearly bids us to drive away the poison that infects our land and to stop nourishing an incurable ulcer.

OEDIPUS: By what sort of purification? What is the character of this misfortune?

CREON: By banishment or by paying a ransom of blood for blood, for it is this bloodstain that is tossing our city about in storm.

OEDIPUS: Who is it then? Who is the man whose ill fortune is thus revealed?

CREON: Laius was, O king, the master of this land before you guided this ship of state.

OEDIPUS: I know that well, from what I've heard—for I never saw the man.

CREON: He met a violent death, and now the god clearly bids us take vengeance on his murderers, whoever they may be.

OEDIPUS: Where in all the world are they? Where in all the world can the dim traces of a crime of old be found?

CREON: "In this land," the god said. "What is searched for will be found, what is passed over will escape."

OEDIPUS: Was Laius in the palace or in the fields or in another land when he met this violent end?

CREON: He set out, so he said, on a journey away from home, but he never returned after he once started forth.

OEDIPUS: But was there no news, no companion on his journey who saw what happened; no one who could give information that could be pursued?

CREON: They all died, all but one who fled in terror and could report with certainty only one thing he saw.

OEDIPUS: What was that? For even one known fact might lead to many others if we could get even a small sign to give us hope.

CREON: He said that highwaymen attacked them—not just one brigand but a large band of robbers.

OEDIPUS: But how could a robber have been so bold—unless he was bribed with money from here?

CREON: So it was thought, but in the troubles that followed Laius' death no one came forward to avenge his murder.

OEDIPUS: What difficulty prevented a thorough search when a king had been struck down in such a manner?

CREON: The Sphinx, that creature of riddles, led us to set aside all thoughts of the dark past and to devote ourselves to what lay at hand.

OEDIPUS: Then I myself shall go back and begin at the beginning to bring the dark past to light once more. For Phoebus has shown worthy concern, and you, too, have shown just care for the dead. And now I also, as is right, will lend my support to avenging this crime against this land and the god as well. Not on behalf of some distant friend but for my own sake will I scatter this cloud that hangs over us. For whoever murdered that king might well want to lay a vengeful hand on me also. By taking up Laius' cause, therefore, I shall be serving my own as well.

Come now quickly, children. Get up from these altar steps

and take your olive branches with you. Let someone summon the people of Cadmus to assemble here. I shall leave no stone unturned, for we shall succeed with the help of the god or be destroyed if we fail.

(*Oedipus and Creon depart.*)

PRIEST: O my children, let us arise, for we came here seeking the answer to our prayers, which this man now promises to give us. And may Phoebus, who sent us his oracular response, also support us as our savior and deliver us from this affliction.

(*The Priest and the suppliants depart. A chorus of Theban citizens enters and sings.*)

CHORUS:

Strophe 1

O sweet-sounding child of Zeus, tell me, what word do you bring with you now as you come from the shrine of Pytho, rich with gold, to splendid Thebes? My heart is gripped by fear and quivers with fright. Oh, hear our cry, Apollo, physician of Delos, because I am afraid there is some debt for which I must pay, a debt unknown to me now or one to be revealed with the passage of time. Enlighten me, O child born of golden Hope, O immortal prophet.

Antistrophe 1

First, I call on you, daughter of Zeus, immortal Athena, for help; then on the protector of our country, your sister Artemis, who sits on her glorious throne above our market place spread out before her; and I call also on Apollo who shoots afar. Oh, reveal yourselves to me and be my threefold defense against doom, for if ever suffering fell upon our city in days past, you were quick to drive away the flaming evil. Come then, be with us now!

Strophe 2

Alas! Woe is me, for I bear trials without number. All my people are in distress, yet it is not within my power to forge a weapon of thought to defend them. Neither does the glorious earth bring forth her fruits, nor do our women, in the pangs of their labor, give birth to children. One life after another can be seen speeding more swiftly than a bird of fleet wing, more swiftly than an unquenchable fire, toward the horizon of the western god.

Antistrophe 2

Thus our city perishes under deaths without number, while her offspring lie on the ground with no one to mourn or bury them, spreading the germs of death. Wives and gray-haired mothers, too, cry out with shrieks of sorrow, lamenting on the altar steps in one place and another, bemoaning their utter despair. The solemn chant rings clear, and the mournful cry blends and rises above the paean: O golden daughter of Zeus, send us your merciful aid.

Strophe 3

Grant to me that the mighty Ares—who now, even without the brazen armor of shields, sets me ablaze amid the loud battle cries of his attack—turn and flee in headlong retreat from our fatherland, carried on a favoring wind to the great sea waters of Amphitrite or to the billowing waves of Thrace, so hostile to ships' anchors. For if night leaves us any respite from attack, day returns to bring renewed onslaught. O Zeus, who wields the fire-bearing lightning with his power, O father Zeus, consume him with your fiery bolt.

Antistrophe 3

Lycean king, I pray that from the taut string of your bow, strung with twisted gold, your arrows also fly forth to sing of your support for us against our enemy, and that the radiant torches of Artemis, with which she runs swiftly through the mountains of Lycia, light the way to our aid. And I call also upon you whose hair is bound with gold, the one for whom our land is named, Theban Bacchus, wine-colored Bacchus, with your band of maenads hailing you with the Bacchic cry, to come with the blazing flame of your brilliant light, our help against the god who is held without honor among the gods.

(*Oedipus enters just before the final notes of their song.*)

OEDIPUS: You are praying for help. Your prayers will be answered. If you will but listen to my words and take them to heart and apply them to your affliction, you may find help and relief from your distress. I speak to you as one who is a stranger to this episode, a stranger to this crime, since I myself could not trace it far alone if I did not have some sign from you. But now—for only after the event was I numbered a citizen among you citizens—I speak out in public before all the people of Thebes and make this proclamation:

If any one of you knows the man who killed Laius, the son of Labdacus, I command him to reveal everything to me. And if he is afraid to do so, he should know that he can remove the danger of accusation from himself by speaking out, for he will face a penalty no more severe than banishment from this land, without bodily harm. And furthermore, if anyone knows of a foreigner from another land to be the murderer, let him not be silent, for I shall repay him with a reward as well as my gratitude.

If on the other hand you remain silent, if anyone out of fear on behalf of a friend or himself makes light of my words, then hear what I must declare. I denounce this murderer, whoever he may be, and let no man in this land in which I hold the sovereign power and royal throne associate with him or speak a word to him, or allow him to take part in prayer or sacrifice to the gods or in rites of purification. Drive him away from your homes, all of you, in the knowledge that he is the contamination that the oracle of Pythian Apollo revealed to me but recently.

I am in this manner, therefore, the ally in the cause of both the god and the murdered man. Moreover, it is my fervent prayer that the murderer, whether he lies hidden in solitary guilt or had partners in his crime, may pass the rest of his wretched life surrounded by evil equal to his evil. And I vow that, if he should come to share my hearth with me with my secret knowledge, I shall pray I suffer the same curse I have just now called down upon all others.

And I lay a charge upon you to bring all this to pass for my sake and for the sake of the god and of our land, so wasted and stricken by the anger of heaven. For, even if action had not been pressed upon us by the god, it is wrong for you to leave the murder of this great man, your very own king, unpunished. You should pursue it to the bitter end.

And since now I hold the royal power that once he held, and have his bed and wife as well—and since, if he had not been unfortunate in his hope for children, we would have been kin through common offspring of the same wife, but, as it happened, an evil fate fell upon his head—I shall, therefore, take it upon myself to avenge his death as though he were my own father. I shall make every effort to search out and apprehend the one whose hands murdered the son of Labdacus, son of Polydorus, who was the son of Cadmus of old, of Agenor's ancient line.

As for those who disobey, I pray that the gods send them neither the fruits of the earth nor the offspring of the womb, but that they be wasted and destroyed by the plague they now suffer or by a fate even worse. But for all the rest of you, all the citizens of Thebes who are pleased with my plans, may Justice, our help and support, and all the gods smile on you and be with you forever.

CHORUS: As now you bind me under oath, under oath, O king, I will speak. I am not the murderer, nor can I point out the murderer. It was for Phoebus, he who posed this question, to say, if he would, who committed this crime.

OEDIPUS: You argue soundly, but no man alive has the power to force the gods to act against their will.

CHORUS: Then perhaps I might say what seems to me the next best thing.

OEDIPUS: Indeed, and if there is a third best, do not fail to speak of that, too.

CHORUS: There is a man we know, our lord Tiresias, a prophet very like our lord Phoebus, and if anyone seeks light on this problem from him, O king, he will find it clearly.

OEDIPUS: I have not overlooked even this in my efforts. For, on the advice of Creon, I have twice sent a guide to conduct him here, and for some time now I have been wondering why he has not yet arrived.

CHORUS: In truth, I recall rumors in the past, gossip of old.

OEDIPUS: What were they? Indeed, I want to look into every possibility.

CHORUS: It was said that Laius perished at the hands of some travelers on the road.

OEDIPUS: I have heard that, too, but it is not known who it is that saw it happen.

CHORUS: Yet, if the murderer has any knowledge of fear, he will not hesitate to flee when he hears the strength of your curse.

OEDIPUS: Words bring no fear to a man who feels no terror in his crime.

CHORUS: But here is one to find the culprit. For now, at last, they are bringing the godlike seer in whom the truth lives more deeply rooted than in any other man.

(*Tiresias enters, led by a boy.*)

OEDIPUS: O Tiresias, you who observe all things—those that may be taught and those that must be kept secret, both matters of heaven and matters of earth—you understand, even though your eyes cannot see the light of day, what a plague has fallen upon our city. We look to you now, O noble prophet, as our protector and only savior. For Phoebus, if you have not already heard the news from the messengers, has sent us an answer to our inquiry, saying that the deliverance from this plague would come only if we learned who were the murderers of Laius and put them to death or sent them in exile from the land.

Do not, therefore, begrudge us any signs you may find in the flight and cries of birds or any other means of divination you may have, but save yourself and your city, save me, save all that is being polluted by death. We are in your hands. To relieve the suffering of his fellow man by the full use of his greatest powers is man's noblest purpose.

TIRESIAS: Alas, alas! What a dreadful thing it is to be wise when wisdom is of no profit! Indeed, I had forgotten this lesson I knew so well, for otherwise I would not have come here.

OEDIPUS: What is wrong? What makes you come with such a feeling of depression?

TIRESIAS: Allow me to go home, for you will bear your burden more easily, and I mine, if you let me go.

OEDIPUS: You do not speak justly or with loyalty to this city that nurtured you if you withhold your word of prophecy.

TIRESIAS: In truth, I note that your words are not offered at an opportune time, and I, therefore, do not offer mine, for I fear the same fate would befall me.

OEDIPUS: By the gods I beg you not to turn from us if you have the knowledge of wisdom, for we have all prostrated ourselves before you in supplication.

TIRESIAS: In truth, for you are all without wisdom. But I will never speak out the evils that I know nor reveal these same evils that are yours as well.

OEDIPUS: What are you saying? Do you know but will not speak, and so will betray us and bring our city to destruction?

TIRESIAS: I will not bring grief upon myself or upon you. Why do you persist in asking me in vain for what you will never learn from me?

OEDIPUS: Will you never, O lowest of the low—for you would bring even solid rock to anger—will you never speak up? Will you never soften, never bend?

TIRESIAS: You reproach me for my temper, yet you do not see that which dwells within you, and you blame me.

OEDIPUS: Who indeed would not be angered by hearing what you say and how you are now holding our state in disrespect?

TIRESIAS: These things will all come to pass though I keep them shrouded in secrecy.

OEDIPUS: Since, then, they will indeed come about, it is your place to tell me.

TIRESIAS: I will say nothing more. Rage against me if you wish, and set free the savage anger of your heart.

OEDIPUS: In truth, I will not silence the anger that I feel but will speak out. I do believe you are the one who contrived this murder and even carried it out, except for using your own hands for the slaying. And if blindness were not your lot, I would also say that you, and you alone, had carried out the entire deed.

TIRESIAS: Would you indeed? I charge you, then, to stand by the proclamation you made with your own tongue and from this day forth to speak neither to these men here nor to me. You are the one; you are the guilty wretch who has brought pollution to this land.

OEDIPUS: How is it that you utter these reckless insults? And do you think you will escape your just rewards?

TIRESIAS: I have already escaped, for the strength of truth sustains me.

OEDIPUS: Where did you learn this? Certainly you did not learn it from your skill in prophecy.

TIRESIAS: From you, for you forced me to speak against my will.

OEDIPUS: Speak what? Speak again so I may comprehend it better.

TIRESIAS: Did you not follow my meaning before? Or are you provoking me to speak?

OEDIPUS: I did not understand what you said, so say it again.

TIRESIAS: I say you are the murderer of the man for whose murderer you are searching.

OEDIPUS: In truth, you will regret that you have twice spoken such malicious words.

TIRESIAS: What then? Should I speak even more, so you may be even more angry?

OEDIPUS: Say what you wish. You will be wasting your breath.

TIRESIAS: I say that you are living in shameful sin with the one closest to you and do not see the evil.

OEDIPUS: Do you think you can always go on talking thus and delight in it?

TIRESIAS: Yes, if there is indeed strength in truth.

OEDIPUS: There is for other men but not for you. It has no strength in your case, since you are blind in ear and mind and eye.

TIRESIAS: But the misery is yours in that you cast reproaches that all who are here present soon will cast at you.

OEDIPUS: One long, continuous night has nourished you, so that you can never bring harm to me or to any other man who sees the sun's light.

TIRESIAS: No, for your fate is not to fall by my hand. Apollo is quite capable of carrying out what is his concern.

OEDIPUS: Is it Creon's trick? Was it all planned by Creon, or by you?

TIRESIAS: Creon is not the one who causes you misery. It is you who makes yourself miserable.

OEDIPUS: O wealth and royal power and skill excelling skill in the fierce rivalry of life, how great is the jealousy that keeps watch over you if, because of this crown that the city has put upon my head—a gift all unsought by me—Creon, my faithful friend, Creon, my friend for so long, has turned on me without my knowledge, eager to drive me out; if he has contrived with this crafty magician, this scheming trickster who is well-versed only in the ways of gaining profit for himself but completely blind in his proper art of prophecy.

Tell me; come, tell me, when have you ever shown yourself to be a prophet? Why did you not, when the watchful Sphinx was here proposing her riddle, offer any solution to free these people from their bondage? Still the riddle could not be solved by the casual passer-by but required skill in prophecy, and you did not show that you had the power to interpret either the signs of birds or the wisdom of the gods. But I came—I, Oedipus, all untrained. And I brought her to an end when I arrived at the right answer by my own wits, not by the portents of birds. And yet I am the one you are attempting to overthrow, thinking you will take your place beside the throne of Creon.

It seems to me that you and the one who contrived this plan will have cause to regret that you plotted to cleanse the land of your scapegoat. Indeed, if it were not apparent that you are an old man, you would learn to your sorrow how exceedingly presumptuous you are.

CHORUS: To us it seems that both his words and yours, O Oedipus, were spoken in anger. We have no need for bitter speech but rather to consider how we can best follow out the oracular response of the god.

TIRESIAS: King though you may be, I have the equal right to make reply, for in this I, too, am a king. Indeed, I do not pass my life as your servant, for Loxias is my sovereign. I, therefore, will never register myself under Creon's patronage. This is my answer, since you deride me even for my blindness. You have eyes, but you do not see the evil that surrounds you, nor where you are living, nor who shares that house with you. Do you in fact know your lineage? No, you do not know, and in your ignorance you have become the enemy of all your kinsfolk, both those in the world of the dead and those on the earth above. And the double whip of your mother's and father's curse will drive you stumbling from this land one day, for though your eyes now see the clear light, they will then look on but the darkness.

What place will not be a harbor for your cries of despair? What rocky spot on all of Cithaeron will not soon echo with the sound of your wailing when you perceive the kind of wedding song under which you sailed into the port of your home, a port that was no haven, at the end of a voyage so smooth? And an overwhelming mass of other evils you do not even imagine will lower you to what you are and make you equal to your children.

Heap abuse on Creon's words and all I say, for there is no man among mortals who will ever be torn apart more terribly than you.

OEDIPUS: In truth, do I have to endure the insufferable words of this man? A plague upon you! Go! Go quickly! Don't ever come back again to darken my doors.

TIRESIAS: Indeed, I would never have come in the first place if you had not summoned me.

OEDIPUS: I had no way of knowing that you would speak such foolishness, or you would have waited a long time before I summoned you to my house.

TIRESIAS: So be it; I am, as you call me, a fool. But beside the parents who bore you, I am wise.

OEDIPUS: What? My parents? Wait! Who, indeed, were my parents?

TIRESIAS: This very day will reveal your birth and your death.

OEDIPUS: How you do like to speak in riddles and obscure speech!

TIRESIAS: But can there be anyone better at solving riddles than you?

OEDIPUS: Mock me for the skill in which you find me to be clever.

TIRESIAS: Even so, it was this very talent that brought about your ruin.

OEDIPUS: But if this same ruin preserved the safety of the city, that is compensation enough for me.

TIRESIAS: In that case, I shall leave you now. Come, boy, take me home.

OEDIPUS: Indeed, let him take you, for while you are here you are nothing but an annoyance, an affliction. When you have gone, you certainly cannot disturb me any more.

TIRESIAS: I will go, but first I am going to tell you what I came to say. I am not afraid to face you, for nothing you can do will hurt me. So I will tell you.

That man—the one you have been seeking all this time, threatening and denouncing him as the murderer of Laius— that man is right here. He was called a stranger who settled in our city. But soon he will be shown to be a native of Thebes, born in this city, yet he will not rejoice at this good fortune. No, blind and no longer endowed with sight, a beggar and no longer rich, he will set off for a strange land, feeling his way with his staff. And he will be disclosed to be both brother and father of the children who share his house, both son and husband of the woman who gave him birth, and successor to his father and his murderer as well.

Go inside and think this over, and if you discover I have spoken falsely, you will have the right then to say I have not the skill and mind for prophecy.

(*Tiresias departs, led by the boy. Oedipus goes into the palace.*)

CHORUS:

Strophe 1

Who is the man of whom the prophetic voice, issuing from the Delphic rock, has spoken—the one who has brought to pass horrendous deeds, unspeakable deeds, with his blood-stained hands?

Now the time is here for him to use feet fleeter than wind-swift horses in his flight, for the son of Zeus, armed with the fire of lightning, is about to pounce upon him. Even Apollo, and the fearful Fates, too, pursue him with a fixed course.

Antistrophe 1

Indeed, a commanding voice has just come, shining forth from snow-crowned Parnassus, summoning us to search out this unidentified man in every possible hiding place. For he roams wildly about in the deep woods, through the caves and rocks, like an injured bull, miserable in his wretched wandering, always seeking to flee from the words of the oracle at the very center of the earth—but always the phantom of fate flies about him, hovering above him.

Strophe 2

Terrible, terrible indeed are the words of the wise seer, and they fill me with dread. I cannot accept them, nor can I refute them. I do not know what to say. I am tossed between hope and fear and have no sight to see the present or the future. In truth, I never knew about any strife, either in the past or in our own time, between the House of Labdacus and the son of Polybus that could be used as evidence in attacking the popular reputation of Oedipus, or even in my attempt to avenge the unsolved death of one of the family of Labdacus.

Antistrophe 2

In truth, Zeus and Apollo both are wise indeed and know the ways of mortals. But among men it cannot, in fact, be proved that a mortal prophet can know more than I, a mortal too. Yet, it happens that a man can surpass another man in wisdom. Even so, I could never pass judgment until I saw the proof made clear. For once the winged maiden, the famous Sphinx, known to all, confronted him, and he was found to be wise and a true friend of our city. In my mind, therefore, he will never be guilty of the charge of crime.

(*Creon enters.*)

CREON: My fellow citizens, I have learned that Oedipus the king has accused me of a serious offense, and I have come here to protest my indignation. Indeed, if he feels, in all these misfortunes we are suffering, that he has been brought to any harm because of word or deed of mine, and if I must bear the burden of this shadow, I have no desire to live out the natural span of my life. For the stigma of this rumor does not affect me lightly, but most grievously if I am called a traitor to the city, a traitor to you, and to my friends.

CHORUS: But this accusation was, we doubt not, born of anger, spoken without thought and not from any reasoned judgment.

CREON: Then was it said that the prophet was prevailed upon by my urging to make false accusations?

CHORUS: These charges were made, but I know not with what motives.

CREON: But was this accusation brought against me with steady eyes and a calm mind?

CHORUS: I do not know, for I do not see what my master does. But see, here he is himself, coming from the palace.

(*Oedipus enters.*)

OEDIPUS: Is it you? Can it be that you have come back? Can you have the daring and the face to come near this house of mine—you, the recognized murderer of its master and the manifest robber of my sovereignty?

Come, by the gods I ask you, tell me, was it some cowardice or foolishness you detected in me that made you form this plot? Did you think I would not discover this deceit of yours creeping upon me by stealth or defend myself against it when I laid it bare? Don't you see you are the foolhardy one, pursuing, without supporters or friends, the royal power, a prize won only with followers and wealth?

CREON: Will you not listen? Hear what I have to say in answer to your words and then make the judgment yourself on what you have heard.

OEDIPUS: You are clever of speech, but I am at a loss to understand you, for I have discovered you are a dangerous enemy.

CREON: Then first let me explain this very charge.

OEDIPUS: Do not explain this charge to me; do not deny you are my enemy.

CREON: If you consider stubbornness without reason a quality worth having, your thinking is not straight.

OEDIPUS: If you think you can wrong a kinsman and not be made to pay the penalty, you are not of sound mind.

CREON: I agree that what you say is sound, but tell me—what is this injury you claim you suffered? Tell me.

OEDIPUS: Did you or did you not advise me to send for that revered prophet?

CREON: I did, and I still stand by that advice.

OEDIPUS: Tell me, how long has it been since Laius—

CREON: What are you trying to say? I do not understand you.

OEDIPUS: —disappeared from sight, met a violent end?

CREON: A long time ago, many years ago.

OEDIPUS: Was this same prophet practicing his art at that time?

CREON: Indeed, with the same skill and the same high esteem as he holds even now.

OEDIPUS: Did he ever mention me in any way at that time?

CREON: Not that I know of—never when I was there to hear it.

OEDIPUS: But was there no search made for the murderer?

CREON: An investigation was held, of course, but we learned nothing.

OEDIPUS: Why did this prophet not speak out at that time?

CREON: I do not know, and when I have no way of knowing I usually keep silent.

OEDIPUS: But one thing you do know and can surely make clear.

CREON: What is that? If I know about it, I shall not deny it.

OEDIPUS: That, if he had not talked with you, he would never have linked my name with the death of Laius.

CREON: If that is what he says, you yourself know best. But now I want to ask you a question myself.

OEDIPUS: Ask me whatever you wish, for I will never be proved a murderer.

CREON: Then tell me, did you marry my sister?

OEDIPUS: There is no denying such a question.

CREON: And do you rule over this land, sharing equal power with her?

OEDIPUS: Indeed, I grant her everything she desires.

CREON: And do I not share with both of you a third of the power?

OEDIPUS: It is just that point that reveals you as a false friend.

CREON: That is not true if you will look at it in the same light I do. First of all, consider this—does it seem to you that anyone would choose to rule in a time of trouble rather than a period of peaceful calm if he were to have his choice and the same power? In truth, I do not yearn by nature to be king but prefer to be king in deed alone, as does any man who knows how to reason soundly. For now I have all the advantages because of you, but without the fear. But if I were king, I would have to do many things against my will.

And how, to be sure, could the royal crown hold more pleasure for me than the enjoyment of power and rule without any of the pain and suffering? Not yet am I so misled that I would crave for glory other than that which holds profit. Now all men wish me well; now everyone greets me kindly; now all those who feel the need to see you seek a word with me, for in this approach lies all their hope of meeting with success. Why, therefore, should I give up all this and grasp at something else? No, a mind that is wise will not play me false. Indeed, I am not a follower of that sort of practice, and if another man undertook treasonable action, I could never bear to join him.

To prove what I say, go to Delphi and ask if I brought back a true report to you. Then, if you find out I have made any plot with the prophet, take me and put me to death, not by your judgment alone but by my own as well as yours. But I beg you not to set me apart and judge me in secret. For it is not right to pronounce bad men good at random, or good men bad. In truth, I consider it to be the same thing for a man to cast off a real friend as it is for him to throw away his own life, his most precious possession. In time, however, you will learn the whole truth. For time alone will prove an honest man, but an evil man is brought to light in a single day.

CHORUS: He has spoken well for a man who is being careful not to fall, O king. For those who are swift in thought are not sure of thought.

OEDIPUS: Whenever anyone takes swift steps to plot against me, I must be swift to make plans on my part. If I wait for him quietly, then it means he will win success while I will find only failure.

CREON: What then do you want? Do you want to cast me from the land?

OEDIPUS: Not at all. I would rather have you dead than banished. Thus your example will show what it is to be envious.

CREON: Does this mean you will not yield or believe me?

OEDIPUS: No, I am determined, for you are not to be trusted.

CREON: Indeed, I see clearly you are not very wise.

OEDIPUS: I am, at least, as far as I am concerned.

CREON: But you should be equally concerned for my interests also.

OEDIPUS: But you are an evil man.

CREON: But if you have no sense at all?

OEDIPUS: Still I must rule.

CREON: Not if you are ruling badly.

OEDIPUS: O my city, O Thebes!

CREON: Thebes is my city, too; not yours alone.

CHORUS: Stop, my lords! I see Jocasta coming from the palace and just in time, for with her help you can bring your quarrel to a just end.

(*Jocasta enters.*)

JOCASTA: Why, O foolish men, why are you waging this ill-advised battle of words? Are you not ashamed of exposing your private feelings when our land is sick with plague? Go inside now—and you, Creon, go home—and stop making so much over a little argument.

CREON: My sister, Oedipus, your lord, intends to punish me with one of two dreadful choices: to go in exile from my native land or to meet with death.

OEDIPUS: That is true, for I have caught him, my lady, carrying out evil against my very life with his wicked craft.

CREON: May I have no good fortune but die accursed instead if I have done any of the things you accuse me of doing.

JOCASTA: Oh, by the gods I beg you, Oedipus, believe him—primarily because of his oath sworn by the gods, but also because of me and all who are near you.

CHORUS:

Strophe 1

Trust, believe, be wise, O king, we pray you.

OEDIPUS: What then do you want me to grant you?

CHORUS: Respect the man who was not without feeling before and who now has sworn to his honesty by oath.

OEDIPUS: Do you know for what you are asking?

CHORUS: Yes, we know.

OEDIPUS: Then say what you mean.

CHORUS: Never make accusations against a friend who is under oath or let him be dishonored by rumor.

OEDIPUS: Know well, then, that when you seek this you seek in fact my destruction or my exile from this land.

CHORUS:

Strophe 2

No! By the foremost god of all the gods, by the Sun, no! Abandoned by the gods, abandoned by my friends, may I die by the worst of deaths if I ever had such a thought! But my spirit is distressed at the wasting of this ill-fated land and, more so, at the evils between you two heaped upon the evils already present.

OEDIPUS: Then, let him go, even though it means that I must surely die or be driven from this land in disgrace. It is your pleading, not his, that moves me to pity. But this man, wherever he may be, will always be hateful to me.

CREON: You are plainly as resentful in your yielding as you were violent in the extremes of your anger. But dispositions such as yours are justly most painful to those who bear them.

OEDIPUS: Now will you leave me alone and go away?

CREON: I shall go, now fated to be condemned by you but acquitted before all these others.

(Exit Creon.)

CHORUS:

Antistrophe 1

Lady, why do you wait to take him into the palace?

JOCASTA: I must know first what caused the quarrel.

CHORUS: Senseless suspicion born of rumors and wrongs that bring injury.

JOCASTA: Then were both of them to blame?

CHORUS: Yes, both.

JOCASTA: And what was said?

CHORUS: Enough, I have had enough. Our land is greatly troubled and now it is best to bring this strife to a halt.

OEDIPUS: Do you see how far you have gone, you with your well-meaning words, toward undermining and dulling my zeal?

CHORUS:

Antistrophe 2

O king—I have said it not only once—think how foolish we would be, how utterly senseless we would show ourselves to be, if we separated ourselves from you who piloted our beloved land on a safe course when she was foundering under adversity and who now can guide us safely once again.

JOCASTA: By the gods, tell me, too, my lord, what trouble has brought about this unbending anger.

OEDIPUS: I will tell you, for I respect you, my lady, above these others. It is Creon; Creon has been forming plots against me.

JOCASTA: Go on—try to tell me clearly—what brought on this quarrel?

OEDIPUS: He names me as the murderer of Laius.

JOCASTA: Does he really know, or did he take the word of someone else?

OEDIPUS: Indeed, he enlisted a prophet to do me evil, for he keeps his own mouth free of guilt.

JOCASTA: Then ease your mind about the matters of which you speak and listen to me, for you will learn that no one born of mortal shares in the prophet's skill. I will quickly give you proof of that.

An oracle's response was once brought to Laius—I will not say it was from Apollo himself but from one of his ministers—saying that the fate would fall upon him to die at the hands of the son who would be born to him and me. But what happened, so the report said, was that he was murdered by foreign highwaymen one day at a place where three roads come together.

For when the boy was no more than three days old, Laius had his ankles pierced and bound fast. Then the child was left, put there by the hands of others, on a pathless mountainside. And thus Apollo did not bring it about that the son should become his father's murderer or that Laius, according to the terrible deed he feared, should be slain by his son. Thus did the prophetic words of the oracle foresee the future. But do not pay any heed to them now, for whatever the god thinks fit to reveal, the god himself will easily make known.

OEDIPUS: As I listened to your words just now, my lady, uneasiness seized my spirit, turbulence struck my heart.

JOCASTA: What anxious thought disturbs you? Why do you speak thus?

OEDIPUS: I thought I heard you say that Laius was slain where three roads come together.

JOCASTA: So it was said, and that story is still repeated.

OEDIPUS: And where is the place where the tragedy occurred?

JOCASTA: Phocis is the name of the land. Roads branching from Delphi and from Daulia meet there.

OEDIPUS: And how long has it been since all this happened?

JOCASTA: Shortly before you were made king of this land, the news was reported to the city.

OEDIPUS: O Zeus, what has your will done to me?

JOCASTA: What is it, Oedipus, that weighs on your heart?

OEDIPUS: Do not ask me yet. Tell me, what was Laius' build? Was he still in the prime of life?

JOCASTA: He was tall, his hair just sprinkled with white, and not very different from you in appearance.

OEDIPUS: Oh, wretch that I am! It seems I have just called down a terrible curse upon my own head and knew not that I did so.

JOCASTA: What are you saying? I am filled with dread when I look at you, my king.

OEDIPUS: And I have dread fears that the prophet is not truly blind. But I will know better if you will tell me one thing more.

JOCASTA: Though I am very much afraid, I will answer whatever you ask of me.

OEDIPUS: Was he traveling with only a few companions or with many armed attendants, like a king?

JOCASTA: There were five men altogether, and one was a herald. Also one carriage, carrying Laius.

OEDIPUS: Alas! Everything is clear now. And who was it who reported all this to you, my lady?

JOCASTA: A servant, the only survivor to come back.

OEDIPUS: Is he by chance still in the household?

JOCASTA: He is not. As soon as he came back and found you were king in the place of the dead Laius, he put his hand on mine and beseeched me earnestly to send him to the pastures in the countryside, where he could live far away from the sight of Thebes. And so I let him go, for he deserved, though he was a slave, to receive even greater thanks than that.

OEDIPUS: Then can he not come back to us without delay?

JOCASTA: He can indeed. But why do you want to send for him?

OEDIPUS: I am afraid, O my lady, I have said more than I should have, and, therefore, I wish to see him.

JOCASTA: Then he will certainly come. But do not I, too, deserve to hear what is so burdensome to you, my lord?

OEDIPUS: Indeed, you will not be deprived of the truth now that my fears have reached this point. For who has a better right than you to hear the story of my trials and lot in life?

My father was Polybus of Corinth, my mother was Merope, a Dorian, and I was considered the most respected man of the city before a chance incident involved me—an incident to bring astonishment but not actually one to bring the great concern it did to me. At a dinner, a certain man who had had too much wine shouted at me in his drunken state that I was not the true son of my father. And though I was annoyed by this, I held back my anger for the time being. But on the next day I went to my mother and father and asked them, and they were grieved to learn that anyone would say something like that to me. And I was cheered by their answer, but still I kept wondering, for the rumor spread far.

Without the knowledge of my mother and father, I went to Delphi. And Apollo sent me away deprived of the assurance I had sought in supplication. Instead, his response revealed miseries, terror, misfortunes to come, prophesying that I would be mated with my mother, produce offspring that men could not bear to look upon, and be the murderer of the father who begot me.

And I, when I heard this, fled from the land of Corinth—for the rest of time I meant to cast my sights upon that city only through the stars—aiming for any place where I would never look upon the fulfillment of this horrendous fate. As I traveled I came to the place where you say the king was slain. There—I shall tell you, my lady, the truth—as I drew near to the place where the three roads meet, a herald and a man in a horse-drawn carriage, just as you described, came toward me. The man who was leading, and the old man, too, tried to push me off the road by force. Then I struck out in anger against the one who had pushed me aside—the driver—and the old man, when he saw this, waited until I was passing by his carriage and struck me squarely on the head with a two-pronged goad. I paid him back in full measure. In an instant, at one blow from the walking stick in my hand, he was rolled headlong from his carriage and fell flat. And I killed every one of them.

But if there was any relationship between this stranger and Laius, then what man is more wretched than I? What mortal is more hateful to the gods?—a man, in truth, whom no stranger, no citizen in our city, is permitted to take into his house or even speak to, whom all must drive away from their homes. And this very curse was called down upon me by none other than myself. Indeed, I am defiling the bed of the murdered man with these same bloodstained hands. Am I not in fact an evil man? Indeed, am I not wholly wicked?

For this I must flee into exile and suffer banishment from the sight of those who are close to me, never setting foot again on my native soil, or I am doomed to be joined in wedlock to my mother and to slay my father, even Polybus, who begot and reared me. If anyone should say some evil power set over man had pronounced this judgment against me, he would speak the truth. Let me not, O holy and awesome gods, let me not see that day. I would rather disappear from the sight of man before I lived to see myself marked with the stain of such disgrace!

CHORUS: Indeed, O king, the words you speak are full of grief. But until you have learned the story of the man you have summoned, keep your hope.

OEDIPUS: In truth, what little hope I have left must wait for the coming of the shepherd.

JOCASTA: And when he comes, what are you so anxious to learn from him?

OEDIPUS: I shall tell you. If he relates the same story you have, I have escaped disaster.

JOCASTA: And what words of such importance did you hear me speak?

OEDIPUS: You said the servant told that Laius was slain by robbers. If, therefore, he still says, as he did before, there were several robbers, then I was not the slayer, for one man cannot be said to be the same as many. But if he says a lone man committed the deed single-handed, then there is no remaining doubt that the scales are tipped against me.

JOCASTA: But you may be assured the story he first told was the same, and he cannot change it now, for the whole city, and not just I alone, heard it. And even if his wording should be slightly changed from his earlier account, he can never, O my king, he can never make it clear that the murder of Laius was truly in keeping with the oracle, for Loxias declared it was fated that he meet death through a son of mine. But that poor child never killed anyone; he himself died long before. As for prophecies, I would never again turn my eyes to the left or the right because of them.

OEDIPUS: Your reasoning is sound. Nevertheless, I want you to send someone to bring the shepherd here. Do not neglect to do this.

JOCASTA: I will send for him at once. But let us go inside now. I certainly will not do anything except what is pleasing to you.

(*Oepidus and Jocasta enter the palace.*)

CHORUS:

Strophe 1

May it still be my destiny to live a life that brings respect for purity of word and deed, ever following those sublime laws set forth on high, brought into being by the clear, bright sky of heaven, knowing no father but Olympus alone, born of no mortal man, never lulled to sleep by oblivion. For great is the god within them, and he does not grow aged.

Antistrophe 1

The insolence of pride breeds the tyrant, and pride, once it has feasted on vain and empty riches, wealth that is neither meet nor right for it, and has scaled the uppermost heights, is hurled down into the depths of ruin, where no foothold may be won. And I pray that our god may ever protect the man who labors on behalf of our city. I look ever to our god, our protector forever.

Strophe 2

If there is indeed any man who parades himself haughtily in word or deed, without fear of law and order, without respect for the images of the gods, and if he does not achieve his profit justly but carries out sinful deeds and strives to lay a profane hand on what is sacred, may a dread doom overtake him for his ill-starred arrogance. What man, in fact, can ever, in such circumstances, hope to shield himself against the avenging arrows of the gods? In truth, if wicked acts such as these are held in honor, why have I any reason to dance?

Antistrophe 2

No more shall I travel to the sacred temple at earth's center, to Abae's shrine, or to Olympia if the true word of the gods is not made manifest to all men in their troubles. O king, if you are rightly called king, O Zeus, king over all, may it not go unnoticed by you and your everlasting might. For the oracles surrounding Laius, spoken long ago, fade into forgetfulness and now are laid aside. Nowhere is Apollo made bright with honors, for the worship of the gods is faltering.

(*Jocasta enters.*)

JOCASTA: Elders of the state, the idea has come to me to go as a suppliant to the shrines of the gods, bearing wreaths and incense in my hands. For Oedipus is greatly disturbed at heart over all kinds of fears, and he does not, like a sensible man, measure his judgment of the present by the past but is at the mercy of any man if he speaks words of fear. Because now all my attempts at counsel are in vain, to you, O Lycian Apollo—for you are the one closest to us—I turn in supplication, bearing this offering, with the prayer that you may relieve us of this stain and cleanse us. For now we are all afraid as we look upon his fear, just as sailors who see their helmsman in panic.

(*A messenger enters.*)

MESSENGER: Could you tell me, O strangers, where the palace of King Oedipus is or, even better, where the king himself is?

CHORUS: This is his palace, and he is inside, O stranger. This lady is his queen and the mother of his children.

MESSENGER: Then may she always be blessed with happiness and this house blessed also, for she is his perfect, blessed wife.

JOCASTA: Blessings on you also, O stranger, for so your kind words deserve. But tell me what you have come to ask or what you want to point out to us.

MESSENGER: I have come with good news for your house and your husband, lady.

JOCASTA: What is your news? By whom were you sent?

MESSENGER: I come from Corinth. The message I shall deliver shortly will bring you joy, I am certain—or perhaps grief.

JOCASTA: What is it? What is this double meaning?

MESSENGER: The people want to make him king of the land of Corinth, as it was proclaimed there.

JOCASTA: But how is that? Is not the old man Polybus still reigning?

MESSENGER: In truth, he is not, for he is dead and buried.

JOCASTA: What are you saying? Is Polybus dead, old man?

MESSENGER: If I am not telling the truth, I deserve to die myself.

JOCASTA: Hurry, girl. Go quickly and tell this news to your master. O oracles of the gods, where are you now? This is the man from whom Oedipus fled for so long in fear lest he slay him, and now he is dead by some stroke of providence and not by the hand of Oedipus.

(*Oedipus enters.*)

OEDIPUS: Jocasta, my beloved wife, why have you summoned me from the palace?

JOCASTA: Listen to this man and, as you hear what he has to say, consider to what the awesome oracles of the gods have come.

OEDIPUS: And this man—who is he and what has he to say to me?

JOCASTA: He is from Corinth and comes with the news that your father, Polybus, is no longer living but has died.

OEDIPUS: What do you say, stranger? Tell me in your own words.

MESSENGER: If I must first report my message plainly, I assure you he is in fact dead.

OEDIPUS: Was it treachery or the result of illness?

MESSENGER: A slight tip of the scale sends the aged to their rest.

OEDIPUS: Then he died, poor soul, of natural causes, it seems.

MESSENGER: He did, and after a long, full life.

OEDIPUS: Alas, alas! Why should anyone, my lady, regard the Pythian oracle or the birds of omen screeching on high, by whose signs I was destined to slay my own father? He is dead and lies beneath the earth, while I am here before you and have not touched my hand to sword—unless it was that he pined away with longing for me. For in that case, his death was caused by me, and all the oracles now have been laid to rest in Hades with Polybus—worthless, gone.

JOCASTA: Did I not predict this long ago?

OEDIPUS: You did, but I was led astray by fear.

JOCASTA: And now let these fears weigh upon your heart no more.

OEDIPUS: Yet must I still not stand in fear of my mother's marriage couch?

JOCASTA: Why should any man be afraid when the power of chance prevails and there is no clear warning? It is best to live without plan, in whatever way one can. Have no fears about marriage with your mother, for it has happened that many men in their dreams have been wed to their mothers. But he who considers these dreams as next to nothing lives his life most happily.

OEDIPUS: All that you say would be fine if my mother were not still living. But now, since she is living, I am forced to live in fear, even though you reassure me.

JOCASTA: Even so, your father's death has made our outlook brighter.

OEDIPUS: Brighter, I agree, but I fear the woman who lives.

MESSENGER: And who is the woman you fear so?

OEDIPUS: Merope, old man, the wife of Polybus.

MESSENGER: But what is there about her that makes you afraid?

OEDIPUS: A dreadful prophecy sent by the gods, stranger.

MESSENGER: Is it one that can be told, or is it not right for another to know it?

OEDIPUS: Yes, you may hear it. Loxias once prophesied that I was destined to be joined in wedlock to my own mother and to shed the blood of my father with my own hands. It was for this reason that I settled long ago in a land far from my native Corinth. I have been happy in my choice, but still it is very sweet to look into the eyes of one's parents.

MESSENGER: Was it, in truth, this fear that made you an exile from your home?

OEDIPUS: This, old man, and the will to avoid being my father's murderer.

MESSENGER: Then why have I not removed this fear from you, O king, since I came on a mission of kindness?

OEDIPUS: And indeed it is right you should receive a just reward from me.

MESSENGER: In truth, that was the real purpose of my coming— that your return home would bring some good result.

OEDIPUS: But I will never go near my parents again.

MESSENGER: Oh my son! It is quite plain you do not know what you are doing.

OEDIPUS: What are you saying, old man! For the sake of the gods, explain to me.

MESSENGER: If this is why you are afraid to go home.

OEDIPUS: Indeed, I fear lest Phoebus' prophecy come true for me.

MESSENGER: You mean lest a stain fall upon you from your parents?

OEDIPUS: That very thing, old man—that is my unceasing fear.

MESSENGER: Then do you not know, in truth, that your fears have no foundation?

OEDIPUS: Why not, if I am the son of my parents?

MESSENGER: Because Polybus never was related to you by blood.

OEDIPUS: What are you saying? Polybus was my father, was he not?

MESSENGER: No more than I am, but as much.

OEDIPUS: And how could my father be on the same level with a man who is nothing to me?

MESSENGER: But he did not father you any more than I.

OEDIPUS: But then, why did he call me his son?

MESSENGER: He took you, I must tell you, long ago from my hands as a gift.

OEDIPUS: And yet, though I was the child of another, did he love me very much?

MESSENGER: He did, for the fact that he was childless till then won his love.

OEDIPUS: And what about you—did you buy this child you gave him or find me by chance?

MESSENGER: I found you in the wooded glens of Cithaeron.

OEDIPUS: How did you happen to be wandering in those hills?

MESSENGER: I was watching over flocks grazing in the mountains there.

OEDIPUS: Then were you just a shepherd traveling from place to place for hire?

MESSENGER: And I was also your savior, my son, in that very hour of your need.

OEDIPUS: And what pain had I when you took me in your arms?

MESSENGER: Your ankles could bear witness to you of that.

OEDIPUS: Oh, alas, why do you bring up that old distress?

MESSENGER: I removed the pin that bound your pierced ankles together.

OEDIPUS: Indeed, it was a dreadful disgrace I bore from my earliest memory.

MESSENGER: It was from this misfortune you were given the name you bear to this day.

OEDIPUS: Oh, for the love of the gods, was it the hand of my mother or my father? Tell me.

MESSENGER: I do not know. The man who gave you to me would know more than I.

OEDIPUS: What then? Did you get me from another and not find me yourself?

MESSENGER: No, I did not find you, but another shepherd gave you to me.

OEDIPUS: Who was he? Could you recognize him or point him out?

MESSENGER: I believe he was called by the name of one of Laius' household.

OEDIPUS: Do you mean the king who ruled this land long ago?

MESSENGER: Yes, he was one of that king's shepherds.

OEDIPUS: Then is he still alive? Can I see him?

MESSENGER: The people of this country would know best about that.

OEDIPUS: Is there any one of you standing here who knows the shepherd of whom he is speaking? Who has ever seen him either in the meadows or here in the city? Speak up! Now is the time to bring everything into the open.

CHORUS: I think he means no other than the shepherd whom you sought to see before. But our lady Jocasta could tell you best about that.

OEDIPUS: My lady, do you know the man for whom we sent a while ago? Is he the one this man means?

JOCASTA: Who is the one he means? Do not even think about it. Pay no attention to his idly spoken words.

OEDIPUS: But it should not happen that I fail to uncover the secret of my birth when I have such good signs.

JOCASTA: For the sake of the gods, if you value your own life at all, end your search. My misery is enough.

OEDIPUS: Take comfort! For you will not—even if I am proved to be the son of a mother in bondage, a slave through three generations—you will not be dishonored.

JOCASTA: But trust me even so, I beg you. Do not go on with this.

OEDIPUS: No, I cannot be dissuaded from learning the whole truth.

JOCASTA: But it is for your own sake that I advise you for the best.

OEDIPUS: That advice for the best has distressed me long enough.

JOCASTA: Oh, ill-omened man, may you never learn who you are!

OEDIPUS: Will someone go and bring the shepherd to me? And leave this woman to rejoice in her proud birth.

JOCASTA: No, no, you are doomed! There is no other name I can call you, never any other word.

(Jocasta rushes away.)

CHORUS: Why, Oedipus, did the queen hurry away in such wild distress? I am afraid now that from this silence there will burst forth a sudden storm.

OEDIPUS: Then let the storm break if it will! Even so, I am determined to learn my origin, no matter how lowly it may be. It may well be that the queen—for she has proud thoughts, as any woman has—is ashamed of my humble birth. But I, who consider myself to be a favored son of Fortune, she who bestows blessings, I shall not suffer shame. For I was born of this mother, and the moons, born of the same source, have looked upon me in my depth and in my height. With such a birth, I can never be other than true to what I am. Why, therefore, should I be afraid to search out the truth about my origin?

CHORUS:

Strophe

If indeed I am a prophet and blessed with wisdom, you will not, O Cithaeron—no, by Olympus—you will not, by the time of tomorrow's full moon, lack the knowledge that Oedipus honors you as one born in the same land, and both nurse and mother to him. And we shall celebrate your praises with choral dances as one who brings pleasure to our royal family. All hail, O Phoebus! May this be pleasing to you!

Antistrophe

Who was the mother who bore you, my child; who of all the immortals bore you in union with Pan, the god who roams the mountains? Or was it a wife of Loxias—for all the high pastures are dear to him—who gave you birth? Or perhaps it was Cyllene's lord and master or the Bacchic god, who dwells on the mountain peaks, who took you, a new babe, from one of the nymphs of Helicon, with whom he dearly loves to sport.

OEDIPUS: If it is right for me to judge, though never have I seen him before, I think, elders, I see the shepherd we have sought for so long. For he appears, by his advanced years, to be of the same age as this other aged shepherd, and, moreover, I recognize the men who are bringing him as servants of my own. But perhaps you would be in a better position than I to know whether you have seen this shepherd before.

CHORUS: Indeed, we recognize him, for we know him well. He was one of Laius' household, a shepherd as faithful as any man. (*The Shepherd enters.*)

OEDIPUS: I ask you first, stranger from Corinth—is this the man you mean?

MESSENGER: This is the man you see.

OEDIPUS: Come, old man, come here. Look at me and answer my questions. Were you ever one of Laius' household?

SHEPHERD: Yes, I was—not bought but born and raised there.

OEDIPUS: What was your task? How did you live?

SHEPHERD: For most of my life I tended sheep.

OEDIPUS: And in what districts were the pastures you used most often?

SHEPHERD: On Cithaeron or the hills close by.

OEDIPUS: Then you know this man? You have seen him before?

SHEPHERD: Seen him doing what? What man are you talking about?

OEDIPUS: This man here. Have you ever come into contact with him before?

SHEPHERD: Not so that I can say I recognize him quickly.

MESSENGER: And no wonder, master. But I shall recall what he has forgotten. I am sure he must remember the time when we watched our flocks together in the pastures of Cithaeron—he herded two flocks, I had one. For three whole seasons I was his companion from spring to the rising of Arcturus.* Then when winter came, I used to drive my flock to my own sheepfold, while he drove his to Laius' fold. Did it happen as I tell it or not?

SHEPHERD: You tell the truth, although it was a long time ago.

MESSENGER: Then tell me, do you remember that you gave me an infant boy at that time for me to raise as my own son?

SHEPHERD: What is it? Why do you ask?

MESSENGER: That man, my friend, was that child.

SHEPHERD: A plague take you! Can't you be silent?

OEDIPUS: Oh, do not be rough with him, old man, for your words deserve reproof more than his.

* A bright star rising in the morning in September, signaling the time for the cattle to come down from the high pastures and for the vintage.

SHEPHERD: What is it, O best of masters, I have done wrong?

OEDIPUS: Refusing to answer when he asked about the boy.

SHEPHERD: But he does not know what he is saying. He is making trouble over nothing.

OEDIPUS: If it does not please you to talk, you will be brought to speak to your sorrow.

SHEPHERD: Please, I beg you by the gods, do not harm an old man.

OEDIPUS: Quickly, someone hold his hands behind his back.

SHEPHERD: Oh, I am unlucky! What do you want? What more do you want to know?

OEDIPUS: Did you give this man the child about whom he is asking?

SHEPHERD: Yes, I did, and I wish I had died on that day.

OEDIPUS: And you indeed will meet your death if you do not tell the truth.

SHEPHERD: I will be much more likely to perish if I tell the truth.

OEDIPUS: This man, it seems to me, is looking for ways to delay.

SHEPHERD: No, I am not! I said before that I gave the child to him.

OEDIPUS: Where did you get the child? Did you get him from your own house or from another man's house?

SHEPHERD: The child was not mine. I got him from another man.

OEDIPUS: From someone in this city? From what house?

SHEPHERD: For the love of the gods, do not, master, do not ask anything more.

OEDIPUS: It will be the end of you if I have to ask again.

SHEPHERD: Then—it was a child from Laius' house.

OEDIPUS: Was he born a slave? Or was he one of Laius' own relations?

SHEPHERD: I am lost! I am on the bitter edge of saying it.

OEDIPUS: And I of hearing it, but still it must be heard.

SHEPHERD: It was said that the child was his own, but the lady inside, your queen, could tell you best about that.

OEDIPUS: How could she? Did she give him to you?

SHEPHERD: She did, my king.

OEDIPUS: For what purpose?

SHEPHERD: That I would do away with him.

OEDIPUS: His own mother, wretched woman?

SHEPHERD: She was afraid of dire prophecies.

OEDIPUS: What sort of prophecies?

SHEPHERD: The oracle said he would slay his own father.

OEDIPUS: Then why did you give him to this old man?

SHEPHERD: I pitied the child, master, and I thought he would take him away to the land from which he himself had come. But the child was saved for the height of shame. For if you are the person this man said you are, you may be certain you were born to be ill-omened.

OEDIPUS: This is the end for me! It has all come true, all is clear. O light of my world, may I look upon you now for the last time—I, cursed by my birth, cursed by my marriage, cursed by the killing I have done, revealed for what I am.

(*Oedipus rushes into the palace.*)

CHORUS:

Strophe 1

Oh, alas, you generations of mortals, what a mere nothing do I reckon your lives to be! For who is there, what man is there who achieves for himself any more happiness than a mere phantom, a fleeting vision that quickly fades away? Your example warns me. Your destiny, O Oedipus, is a lesson to me that no one born a mortal can be called blessed.

Antistrophe 1

This is the man who shot his arrow higher than all others and won the highest prize of success and wealth. O Zeus, this is the man who struck from her perch the maiden with the curving claws, the maiden who sang in riddles, and stood forth as a tower of strength against death in our land. From that day forth you were hailed as our king and held in the highest honor, the lord and ruler of mighty Thebes.

Strophe 2

And now what man can be called more wretched? Who bears sharper pangs of distress, or lives with deeper suffering, all his life's fortunes turned backward? Alas, famed Oedipus, did the same haven give you such shelter, both son and father, that your place of birth and your marriage chamber became one, for son and father alike? How, oh, how could the land your father tilled have endured you, wretched as you are, for so long a time?

Antistrophe 2

Time the all-seeing has found you out in spite of your efforts and has brought to judgment the fatal marriage of long ago between the begetter and the begotten. Alas, O child of Laius, if only, oh, if only I had never seen you! For I mourn for you as though a funeral dirge were pouring from my lips. If I were to speak the truth, I drew my breath anew from you, and now my eyes will close in sleep.

(*The Second Messenger enters.*)

SECOND MESSENGER: O elders, who are held in greatest reverence in our land, what deeds you will hear of, what sights you will look upon, what sorrows of mourning you will endure if, as loyal Thebans, you still respect the House of Labdacus. For I fear that not even the waters of Ister or Phasis could cleanse this house of its stains, so many are the evils it conceals and soon will bring to light—sins committed deliberately, not without purpose. Of all the world's suffering, the self-inflicted must be the saddest grief to bear.

CHORUS: But, in truth, the sorrow we have seen before was to us most grievous. What further burden could you add to our pain?

SECOND MESSENGER: It takes but a moment to tell and a moment to hear—our revered queen Jocasta is dead.

CHORUS: Oh, poor lady! How did it happen?

SECOND MESSENGER: She took her own life. You will be spared the real pain of the tragedy, for you did not see it. But you will learn from me, as well as my memory allows, the final conflict of the disconsolate lady's soul.

As soon as she was inside the palace doors, frenzied, she ran straight to the marriage couch, tearing at her hair with both hands, and slammed the doors behind her. She cried out to Laius, long dead, remembering the son she bore to him so long ago, the son who was his father's murderer, and his mother left to bear cursed offspring by her son. Then she wept for the marriage couch, where she, poor woman, had given birth not once but twice—giving birth to husband by husband and to children by her child.

What happened next and how she died I do not know, for Oedipus rushed in screaming, and our eyes did not see the end of her anguish, for they were staring at Oedipus pacing back and forth. Wildly he roamed, demanding a sword, calling on us to find the wife who was not a wife, the mother who bore a double brood, himself and his own children.

Then, as he raged, some evil spirit revealed the truth—for none of us, no mortal there spoke a word. With a wild scream, as if someone led the way, he threw himself against the double doors, forcing the twisting bolts from their sockets, and plunged into the room. We saw the woman hanging there, swinging from a rope. His eyes beheld the sight, and with a terrible cry he let down the cord. The luckless woman lay on the floor, and then the horrendous deed came. He ripped the gold brooches from her gown, raised them aloft, and plunged them straight into his eyes, proclaiming, "Nevermore will you see the wicked crimes I endured and brought about, but for the rest of time you will look in darkness upon the sights that should never have been seen, never knowing the sight of those I have longed to see."

And as he mourned this way, he raised his hands to smite his eyes not once but many times. And with each blow his bleeding eyeballs stained his cheeks, not oozing slowly with drops of blood, but gushing forth in one dark, bloody shower like hail.

Such evils have burst forth from the sins of two, not to fall on one alone but to join man and wife alike in a common disaster. Their happiness of former times was true happiness. But now today wailing, ruin, death, shame—every evil that can be named—are theirs, they all are theirs.

CHORUS: Then has the poor man still no relief from his pain?

SECOND MESSENGER: He cries out for someone to unbolt the doors and point out to all the people of Thebes his father's murderer, his mother's—I cannot speak that wicked word—even as he is about to cast himself forth from this land and remain no longer in the house cursed by the curse he laid himself. Yet now he has no strength and needs a hand to guide him, for his agony is more than man can bear. But you will see for yourselves. Look, the doors of the palace are opening, and soon you will look upon a sight so terrible that even those who turn in horror must feel pity.

(*Oedipus enters slowly.*)

CHORUS: Oh, dreadful sight for men to see! Oh, most dreadful of all the sights my eyes have yet seen! What madness, O stricken man, has come over you? Who is the demon who stalked you through your ill-fated life to pounce upon you now with a demon's leap? Alas, alas, wretched man! I cannot bear to look upon you, yet there is so much I want to ask you, so much I want to know, so much I want to examine. The cold chill of horror grips me.

OEDIPUS: Alas, alas, I am lost! Where is my misery carrying me? How is my voice borne from me in flight? Oh, dread destiny, where is your limit?

CHORUS: The end is in suffering not to be told, not to be seen.

OEDIPUS:

Strophe 1

Oh, a dread cloud of darkness has come over me, an unspeakable mist wraps me in dense and overwhelming blackness. Ah, woe is me, again I say woe is me! How I am stabbed by the points of these goads! How I am stung by the poisonous memory of these sins!

CHORUS: Yet it is no wonder in such extremes of misery that you should bear double sorrow with double sins.

OEDIPUS:

Antistrophe 1

Ah, my friend, you are still my constant attendant, my steady companion, for you still abide patiently with me, caring for the blind man. Alas! Alas! You are not unobserved by me, but I know well you are near; though I am blind, your voice is clear to me.

CHORUS: O you of fearful deeds, how could you blot out your sight this way? What demon drove you so far?

OEDIPUS:

Strophe 2

Apollo. It was Apollo, my friends, who brought these evils, my wicked suffering. But the hand that struck my eyes was no other but mine, my own miserable hand. Why, why would I have sight when nothing sweet was left to see?

CHORUS: It was even as you say.

OEDIPUS: What then was left for me to see, what for me to love, or what greeting for me to hear with pleasure, my friends? Lead me from this land with all haste. Lead away, O friends, this utterly destroyed being, this totally accursed man—yes, this mortal most hated by the gods.

CHORUS: Wretched as you are in both mind and fortune, I wish indeed that I had never known you.

OEDIPUS:

Antistrophe 2

May he be doomed, whoever freed my feet from their bonds there on the mountain slopes and kept me from slipping into death, for I give him no thanks. Could I have died then, there would be no sorrow now for my friends, no anguish now for myself.

CHORUS: And I also would wish it had been thus.

OEDIPUS: Then never would I have come to be the murderer of my father or to be named by men as the bridegroom of the mother who bore me. But now I am abandoned by the gods, a son of wickedness, successor to the bed of the father of my wretched being. If ever there was any misfortune greater than all others, it has fallen to the lot of Oedipus.

CHORUS: I do not know how I can say you reasoned well, for it would be better to be dead than living in blindness.

OEDIPUS: What was done was best done thus. Don't try to tell me, don't give me more advice. For I do not know with what kind of eyes I could have faced my father when I came to Hades, or my hapless mother, since my sins against those two are sins too great for death by hanging. But can you say the sight of my children, born as they were, was a delight for me to look upon? No, certainly not, never for my eyes. Nor this city and its towers, nor the sacred images of the gods. I, once the most distinguished of the Thebans, now the most miserable, have severed my cords to all that. I have ordained myself a wicked sinner for all to shun, unholy before the gods—I, a son of Laius.

How, in truth, was I, who revealed myself to be so stained by disgrace, how was I going to face these people and look them in the eye? Indeed no, for if I had seen a way to block off the spring of hearing, I would not have hesitated to cut off this miserable body of mine so neither sight nor sound could touch it. To live beyond the reach of thought or care for evil is sweet.

Alas, O Cithaeron, why did you give me shelter? Why did you not, as soon as you received me, reach out at once to kill me so that I would never have had to reveal to man the source of my birth? Oh, Polybus. Oh, Corinth. Oh, my fatherland, land that was called the home of my forebears, how fair then was the tender skin that cloaked the evils growing within! For now I stand revealed, a sinful man born of sinful lineage.

Oh, you three roads and secluded glen, you grove of oaks and narrow pass with triple paths, you drank of my very blood, the blood of my father, poured from my own hands. Do you remember, too, the deeds I undertook then and those I brought to pass after I came to this city? Oh, marriage rites, oh, wedding feasts, you gave birth to me, and when you had given me life, you again brought forth children of the same seed, producing fathers, brothers, children—all of kindred blood—brides, wives, and mothers—the most shameful disgrace that can happen to men. But it is not right to mention what should not even be thought about.

Quickly, for the love of the gods, hide me somewhere far from here, or slay me, or hurl me into the sea that you may never see me again. Come, condescend to touch the remnants of a man. Come, don't be afraid—it is I who must bear the burden of sins no other mortal can.

(*Creon enters.*)

CHORUS: Now, here comes Creon, and you can ask his help for what you want to do and plan, for he now is left alone, the sole protector of our land.

OEDIPUS: Woe is me! What words are there for me to say to him? How can I give him reason now to trust me when he has always known me to be against him in the past?

CREON: I have not come to mock you, Oedipus, nor to reproach you for evils past. (*To the attendants.*) But you, if you no longer have respect for the children of men, show reverence at least for our lord Helios, whose light nourishes all things, and be ashamed to expose guilt such as this in a nakedness that neither the earth nor the rain from heaven nor the daylight can endure with patience. Come now, take him into the house at once, for it is best that a man's misery should be seen and heard by his family alone.

OEDIPUS: By the gods' love, because your coming/ you the noblest of men/ brings me a flash of hope/ I the most wicked of men/ do me one favor. It is for you and not myself that I ask it.

CREON: And what request would you make of me?

OEDIPUS: Cast me from this land; send me in all haste to a place where no human voice will ever reach me.

CREON: I would have done so long before this if I had not thought it best to consult the oracle first.

OEDIPUS: But the will of the god has been made plain—to destroy me, the parricide, the one who has sinned against the gods.

CREON: That is what he declared, but it is better to ask again what we must do in our present need.

OEDIPUS: Then would you make inquiry for a man as wretched as I?

CREON: Indeed, for now you would trust the word of the god.

OEDIPUS: And I lay on you this charge. I humbly entreat you to give burial to the woman inside the house as you see fit, for you will carry out proper rites for one of your own. As for me, never let the city of my fathers be forced to have me living there while I am alive. Rather, let me live on the mountain slopes, even on Cithaeron, the mountain made mine when my mother and father placed me there in their lifetime in my destined tomb, so that now I may meet the death they appointed for me. And yet I know full well that neither sickness nor any other chance will carry me off, for I would never have been rescued from that early death had I not been saved for some dreadful doom.

But let my fate carry me where it will. My children—my sons, Creon, take no anxious care for them, for they are men and will not lack the necessities of life, wherever they may be. But my daughters, my two stricken girls, who never went to the table alone, who never partook of a meal without their father, who always shared my table with me, who always shared everything I had—oh, take care of them, please. If only I could touch them with my hands and mourn my sorrows. If only, O prince, if only, O noble prince! If only I could touch them, I would think they were with me just as when I could see.

(*His daughters, Antigone and Ismene, are brought in.*)

Am I imagining? It cannot be—do I hear my dear ones weeping? Has Creon taken pity and sent my dearest girls to me? Is it so?

CREON: It is true. I did this for you, for I knew the joy they would bring, the joy you had in former times.

OEDIPUS: May you be blessed, and for this kind act may good fortune smile on you more happily than she did on me. My children, where are you? Where? Come to me, come to your brother's hands, my hands, hands that blinded your father's bright eyes—hands of the man who, neither seeing nor realizing, was shown to be your father by the very one who gave birth to him.

And I weep for you both, though I have not the power to look upon you, when I think of the bitter days for the rest of your lives and how you are fated to live under the cruel scorn of all men. For what gathering of your fellow citizens can there be to which you will go, what festival that you will attend, from which you will not return home in tears instead of with merry hearts? And when you have come to the time when you are ready for marriage, who will be the man, who will there be, my daughters, who will risk taking on the stigma of such disgrace as must ever cling to your children as to mine? For what sins have not been committed? Your father killed his father, conceived children by the same mother who bore him, and became the father of you both by the very source of his own being. Such are the reproaches that will be cast upon you. Who, therefore, will marry you? There is no one, my poor children, no one, and you must surely pine away in wasted, unwedded maidenhood.

O son of Menoeceus, since you are the only father they have now—for we, the parents who gave them birth, we are both destroyed—do not let them wander poor and unmarried far from their own kin, and do not let them come to know bitter miseries such as mine. Have pity on them, for you see how young they are to be left alone, desolate but for your compassion. Give me your pledge, noble Creon, by touching my hand. My children, I would have given you both much advice if you were ready to understand. Now I can but pray you will find the best in life, and may the course of your lives turn out better than that of your father.

CREON: You have had tears enough. Come into the house now.

OEDIPUS: I must obey, though it breaks my heart.

CREON: There is a proper time for all that is right.

OEDIPUS: Do you know with what provision I will go?

CREON: Tell me and then I shall know.

OEDIPUS: Send me to live in exile from this land.

CREON: Do not ask me for what the gods must give.

OEDIPUS: But I am hated by the gods.

CREON: Then, in truth, it will soon come to pass.

OEDIPUS: You will really do it?

CREON: I am not in the habit of making idle promises.

OEDIPUS: In that case, take me away—I am ready.

CREON: Come now, let your children go.

OEDIPUS: Oh, no! Don't take my children away!

CREON: You cannot try to control everything, for even the control you did have did not follow you all your life.

CHORUS: O citizens of our native Thebes, behold: here is Oedipus, who solved the renowned riddle and became ruler of our city and was regarded with envy by every citizen because of his good fortune. Think of the flood of terrible disaster that has swept over him. Thus, since we all are mortal, consider even a man's final day on earth and do not pronounce him happy until he has crossed the finish line of life without the pain of suffering.

Oedipus Tyrannus

The Building
of the Walls of Troy

The early seeds of the Trojan War were sown with the building of the walls of Troy. Zeus sent Apollo and Poseidon to work for Laomedon, the king of Troy, for a year and to do his bidding for a set wage. Laomedon set for them the task of building the city walls. It was believed that the walls could not be breached if they were built by the gods. Because Aeacus helped in the building of the walls, the walls of Troy were vulnerable in the Trojan War.

As told in Greek verse by Pindar

WHEN APOLLO, the son of Leto, and Poseidon who rules widely were going to build walls around the city of Troy, they called upon Aeacus to help them in the work. It had been destined that, during the destruction of battle, the walls of Troy would breathe forth billows of smoke.

When the walls were just newly built, three gleaming serpents sprang upon the fortifications. But two fell back and died in amazement, whereas the third swiftly went over the wall with a loud noise. Apollo, turning over this adverse portent in his mind, said, "The citadel of Troy is overpowered, Aeacus, at the place where your hands have worked. A sign sent from loud-thundering Zeus the son of Cronus tells me this.

"This will not happen without your sons, however, for the capture of Troy will begin with the first generation of your descendants and will continue until the fourth generation." Thus, in truth, the god Apollo spoke plainly and then set out toward Xanthus. And Poseidon, the wielder of the trident, drove off in his swift chariot toward Isthmus on the sea, taking Aeacus with him in his chariot of gold.

From *Olympian Odes* VIII, 31–51

The Infant Heracles

Heracles, probably the most famous of the Greek heroes, was born to Alcmene, the wife of Amphitryon, after Zeus had assumed her husband's form. Heracles was thus the son of one of the gods while his twin brother, Iphicles, was the son of a mortal father. Hera's jealous anger was aroused against Heracles because of his paternity.

Perseus and Andromeda were grandparents of both Alcmene and Amphitryon. The story of the birth of Heracles may have been the result of the attempt by the people of Thebes to claim the hero for their city.

Heracles became a hero of nations other than Greece, especially those in the East. He later became very popular among the Romans—who called him Hercules—and served as the model for many other heroes. Although not a god, he was sometimes the recipient of worship.

As told in Greek verse by Pindar

I RECALL the story of old telling how, when Heracles, the son of Zeus, and his twin brother were born into the light of day, he did not escape the notice of Hera. The queen of the gods, with anger in her heart, sent two serpents. They indeed, entering at the doorway, went into the great inner chamber of the house, eager to wrap themselves around the infants in their cradle.

But Heracles sat right up and tried his skill at battle for the first time, grasping the two serpents in his strong bare hands and strangling them. Even their mother, Alcmene herself, jumped to her feet quickly and tried to ward off the attack of the savage creatures.

At once the Cadmean chiefs rushed in with their bronze weapons, and their father, Amphitryon, with a bared sword in his hand, came in, struck with sharp pains of distress. He stood there astonished, with mixed fear and delight, for he realized the unusual courage and strength of his son.

Then Amphitryon summoned a neighbor who was the eminent prophet of mighty Zeus, the true prophet Tiresias. And Tiresias prophesied to him and to all who were gathered there the fortunes the boy would meet, telling how many savage monsters he would kill on land and how many on the sea. And he told that Heracles himself, in truth, when he was at rest after all his great labors, would have as his just and special prize everlasting peace in the homes of the blessed; and that he would receive Hebe as his wife and celebrate the marriage with a feast, praising his majestic home before Zeus the son of Cronus.

From Nemean Odes I, 33–72

The Labors of Heracles

Both Eurystheus and Heracles were descendants of Perseus—a native of Argos—and Zeus had declared that the first boy to be born on a certain day would rule over the Argives. Hera, jealous of the fact that Heracles had been born of Zeus' union with Alcmene, therefore caused the birth of Heracles to be delayed and that of Eurystheus to be hastened. Hera then agreed that, after Heracles had performed certain labors for Eurystheus, he was to become immortal.

Closely associated in the minds of the Greeks, Mycenae and Tiryns were only nine miles apart. Both had large palaces built on citadels standing high above the Argive plain and surrounded by cyclopean walls. Excavations begun at Mycenae by Schliemann in the nineteenth century are still being carried on there and at Tiryns. The extensive remains continue to shed light on the Mycenaean civilization.

As told in Greek prose by Apollodorus

It FELL to the lot of Heracles that he was driven to madness because of the jealousy of Hera, and he threw his own children and Iphicles' two children into the fire. As a result, he punished himself by exile and went to Delphi to ask of the god where he ought to live. Pythia, the priestess of Apollo, then called him Heracles for the first time* and told him to go to Tiryns and live in servitude to Eurystheus for twelve years and to carry out the ten labors he would set for him. She said, also, that when he had performed these labors he would become immortal.

---

* In his youth Heracles was called Alcides, a name meaning "son" or "descendant of Alcaeus." Alcaeus was the father of Amphitryon.

When he had heard the oracle, Heracles went to Tiryns and carried out the tasks as Eurystheus ordered him to do. First Eurystheus commanded him to bring back the hide of the Nemean Lion, an animal that could not be wounded and was an offspring of Typhon. When Heracles arrived at Nemea and found the lion, he first shot at him with his bow, but when he realized the creature was invulnerable, he chased after him with his club raised on high.

When the lion fled into a cave with two entrances, Heracles blocked up one of the mouths and went in after the lion through the other. Then, throwing his arms around the animal's neck, he strangled the lion to death and then carried it off on his shoulders. Heracles offered a sacrifice of thanksgiving to Zeus and took the lion to Mycenae. Eurystheus was so filled with terror at Heracles' manly strength that he forbade him to come into the city in the future and ordered him to show the prizes of his labors from outside the walls.

For his second labor Eurystheus ordered Heracles to kill the Hydra of Lerna, which lived in the swamp of Lerna and went out into the countryside killing cattle and laying waste to the land. The Hydra had an enormous body and nine heads, one of which was immortal. Heracles went to Lerna in a chariot driven by Iolaus and found the Hydra on the brow of a hill next to the springs of Amymone, where it had its den. Shooting at it with flaming arrows, Heracles drove the creature out, and then, when it came close, he grabbed it and held it tight. But the Hydra wrapped itself around his foot, and he was not able to get free by striking off its heads with his club, for as soon as one head was cut off two grew in its place.

In addition, a huge crab came to the aid of the Hydra and kept biting his foot. He, therefore, killed the crab and called to Iolaus to help him. Iolaus set fire to a part of the woods nearby and, by burning the stumps of the heads with firebrands, kept them from growing out again. Then Heracles cut off the immortal head, and, when he had buried it in the ground, he put a heavy rock over it. Then he split open the body of the Hydra and dipped his arrows in its poison.

Eurystheus, however, said that this labor should not be counted as one of the ten, for he had not overcome the Hydra alone, but with Iolaus' help.

For his third labor Eurystheus ordered him to bring the Cerynean Hind back to Mycenae alive. The deer had horns of gold and was sacred to Artemis. Heracles, therefore, because he did not want to kill it or hurt it, pursued it for a whole year. Then, when the deer, exhausted from being hunted, fled for safety up onto a mountain called Artemisius and from there to the river Ladon, Heracles, shooting it with an arrow as it was on the point of crossing the river, put it over his shoulders and started off through Arcadia. But Artemis, accompanied by Apollo, chanced upon him and wanted to take the deer from him, and she accused him of slaying her sacred animal. Heracles, however, pleading innocence on the grounds of necessity and placing the blame on Eurystheus, soothed the anger of the goddess and took the deer to Mycenae alive.

As the fourth labor, Eurystheus ordered him to capture alive the Erymanthian Boar, which was destroying the countryside around a mountain called Erymanthus, where he lived. Along the way Heracles was entertained by the centaur Pholus, the son of Silenus and a nymph. When Heracles asked for wine, he told him he was afraid to open the wine jar, because it belonged to all the centaurs. Urging him not to fear, Heracles opened it himself, and in a short time, when they smelled the aroma, the centaurs, armed with stones and pine trees, came to the cave of Pholus. Heracles, pelting them with firebrands, turned back the first who ventured to come inside and then shot at the rest with arrows, chasing them as far as Malea.

From there they fled for safety to Chiron, who, when he had been driven from Mount Pelion by the Lapithae, had settled in Malea. As they gathered around him in fear, an arrow shot by Heracles lodged itself in Chiron's knee. Heracles ran over to him in distress and pulled out the arrow and put the ointment Chiron gave him on the wound. But when Chiron's wound could not be healed he went off into a cave, ready to die. This was impossible, however, since he was immortal. But Prometheus offered himself to Zeus to become immortal in his place, and thus Chiron died.

The other centaurs fled in all directions, and some went to

Mount Malea, and Nessus fled to the river Evenus. Poseidon gave refuge to the rest at Eleusis and hid them on a mountain. Pholus, however, pulled an arrow from one of the bodies, amazed that a little thing could kill such big creatures. But the arrow slipped out of his hand onto his foot and killed him at once. When Heracles went back and found Pholus dead, he buried him and then went on with his hunt for the boar. He drove the animal out of his lair and chased it into the deep snow, where he caught it in a net, and carried it off to Mycenae.

The fifth labor Eurystheus set for him was to clean out the stables of Augeas in one day. Augeas was the king of Elis, and he had many herds of cattle. Heracles went to him and, not telling him the instructions of Eurystheus, said he would clean the stables in a single day, if he would give him a tenth of his cattle. Augeas agreed, thinking it could not be done.

Heracles, after he had called Augeas' son Phyleus as a witness to the agreement, tore away part of the foundations of the stable and diverted the Alpheus and Peneus Rivers into the stables, letting them run out through an opening he had made on the other side. But when Augeas learned that this task had been carried out under orders from Eurystheus, he refused to repay Heracles with the cattle. Phyleus bore witness for Heracles against his father, declaring he had promised to pay him a reward.

In anger Augeas ordered both Phyleus and Heracles to leave Elis. Phyleus, therefore, went to Dulichium to live, and Heracles proceeded to Olenus, where King Dexamenus was being forced to promise his daughter in marriage to the centaur Eurytion. When Dexamenus called on him to come to the rescue, Heracles slew Eurytion.

Eurystheus, however, would not accept this labor as one of the ten, saying that it had been carried out for hire.

As his sixth labor he ordered Heracles to drive off the Stymphalian birds. There was at Stymphalus, a city in Arcadia, a lake called the Stymphalian Marsh, nestled in deep woods, to which huge birds had flocked in fear of being the prey of wolves.

When Heracles was at a loss as to how he could drive the birds away from the woods, Athena gave him some bronze rattles she had been given by Hephaestus. By shaking these against a mountain beside the marsh he frightened the birds away, for they could not stand the noise and flew up in fear, and in this way Heracles was able to shoot them with his arrows.

The seventh labor Eurystheus ordered Heracles to perform was to bring back the Cretan Bull. Acusilaus* says this was the bull that carried Europa to Crete for Zeus, but some people say this was the bull that Poseidon sent out of the sea when Minos vowed he would sacrifice to Poseidon whatever appeared from the sea. They say, also, that when he saw how beautiful this bull was, Minos set it out to pasture with his herds of cattle and sacrificed another bull to Poseidon, and that, because the god was angered by this, he made the bull fierce.

When Heracles went to Crete to get the bull and asked for help in capturing it, Minos told him to seize the bull by himself. He did catch the bull, and he took it to Eurystheus and showed it to him and then set it free. The bull wandered off to Sparta and through all of Arcadia; then, crossing the Isthmus, it came to Marathon in Attica, where it harassed the countryside.

As the eighth labor Eurystheus ordered Heracles to bring the mares of Diomedes of Thrace to Mycenae. Diomedes, the son of Ares and Cyrene, was the king of the Bistones, a tribe of Thrace, and the owner of man-eating mares.

Heracles set sail, therefore, with a company of followers, and, when he had overpowered those who took care of the horses and stables, he herded the mares toward the sea. But when the Bistones came to rescue the mares with weapons, he entrusted them to the care of Abderus, who was a son of Hermes and a trusted follower of Heracles. But the mares dragged Abderus to his death, and Heracles, therefore, fought with the Bistones, killing Diomedes and putting the others to flight.

Heracles founded the city Abdera† close to the grave of Abderus and took the mares to Eurystheus and gave them to him. Eurystheus, however, turned them loose, and they made their way to Mount Olympus, where they were killed by wild animals.

---

* A Greek writer of about the sixth century B.C. who wrote chronicles and also a prose version of Hesiod's *Theogony*.

† Abdera, colonized by the Greeks in the seventh century B.C., was the home of Protagoras and Democritus.

The ninth labor Eurystheus ordered Heracles to perform was to get the warrior's girdle of Hippolyte. She was the queen of the Amazons, who lived near the Thermodon River. They were a race powerful in war, for they followed manly pursuits. Hippolyte had a girdle given to her by Ares as a symbol that she excelled all the other Amazons. Heracles was sent to bring back this girdle, because Eurystheus' daughter Admete wanted to have it. He gathered together, therefore, those who wanted to accompany him and set sail with one ship.

After he reached Mysia, he was entertained by Lycus, the king. When Lycus fought against Mygdon, the king of the Bebryces, Heracles helped him and killed a great number of the enemy, among them King Mygdon. And he seized a large amount of land from the Bebryces and gave it to Lycus, who gave it the name Heraclea.

After he had reached the port of Themiscyra, Hippolyte came to him and asked him why he had come. Then she promised that she would give him her girdle, but Hera, taking on the likeness of one of the Amazons, mingled with the women, saying that the strangers who had come were seizing the queen. The Amazons, therefore, armed themselves and raced down to the ship on horseback. When Heracles, however, saw they were armed, he thought it was a trap, and so he killed Hippolyte and took her girdle. Then, when he had fought off the other Amazons, he set sail and put in at Troy.

It happened that at that time Troy was suffering a misfortune because of the anger of Apollo and Poseidon. For Apollo and Poseidon, wanting to test Laomedon's insolence, took on the likeness of mortal men and agreed to build the walls of Troy for pay. When they had built the walls, however, he would not pay them. As a result, Apollo sent a plague and Poseidon sent a sea monster, which was washed up by a flood tide and carried away the people who lived in the plain.

When the oracle, however, said Laomedon would be delivered from his punishment if he offered his daughter Hesione as a sacrifice to the monster, he chained her to a rock beside the sea. When Heracles saw Hesione exposed to danger, he offered to rescue her, if Laomedon would give him the horses that Zeus had given to Tros in recompense for his taking of Ganymede, the son of Tros. After Laomedon said he would give him the horses, Heracles killed the sea monster and rescued Hesione. Laomedon did not, however, give him the horses as he had promised, and so Heracles set sail, threatening to make war upon Troy.* Then, when he reached Mycenae with the girdle, he gave it to Eurystheus.

For his tenth labor he was ordered to bring the cattle of Geryon back from Erythea, an island near the ocean. Geryon had the body of three men grown together and joined at the waist, and he had red cattle, watched over by his herdsman Eurytion and by Orthrus, a two-headed dog. As he went across Europe, therefore, to get the cattle of Geryon, he killed many wild beasts. Then he went to Libya and on to Tartessus, where, as symbols of his journey, he set up two pillars opposite each other at the extreme limits of Europe and Libya.

Then, because he was hot from the sun on his journey, he shot an arrow at the god Helios, who, in wonder at his daring, gave him a golden goblet in which he crossed the sea. And when he came to Erythea he went to Mount Abas. The dog, however, found him and went for him, but he struck him down with his club, and he also killed the herdsman Eurytion when he came to the rescue of the dog. When Geryon heard what had happened, he caught up to Heracles at the river Anthemus while he was herding the cattle before him, and Geryon was killed by an arrow as he tried to fight him off. Then Heracles loaded the cattle into the goblet, and, when he had crossed over to Tartessus in it, he gave the goblet back to Helios.

At Rhegium one of the bulls broke loose and, dashing into the sea, swam across to Sicily and came to the kingdom of Eryx, the son of Poseidon, who put the bull in with his own herd. Heracles, therefore, placed the cattle in the care of Hephaestus and went in search of the bull. When he found the bull in the herd of Eryx, who refused to give it up unless Heracles overcame him in a wrestling match, Heracles defeated him three times. He then

---

* Heracles later carried out his threat and attacked Troy. He sacked the city and killed Laomedon and all his sons with the exception of Priam.

killed him in the next match and took the bull and herded it with the other cattle to the Ionian Sea.

When Heracles reached the coast of the sea, however, Hera sent a gadfly upon the cattle, and they broke away and ran into the foothills of the mountains of Thrace. He went after them and drove those he rounded up to the Hellespont, but those he did not catch ran wild from that time on. Heracles took the cattle he had recovered to Eurystheus, who offered them as a sacrifice to Hera.

After Heracles had spent eight years and one month in the performance of these labors, since he did not count that of the cattle of Augeas or of the Hydra as acceptable labors, Eurystheus ordered him, as his eleventh labor, to bring the Golden Apples of the Hesperides back to him.

The Golden Apples were not in Libya as some say, but near Atlas in the land of the Hyperboreans, and Earth had presented them to Zeus when he was wed to Hera. They were guarded by an immortal dragon, the offspring of Typhon and Echidna, which had a hundred heads and many different voices. The Hesperides— Aegle, Erytheia, Hespere, and Arethusa—also guarded the Golden Apples.

As he was traveling through Illyria and arrived at the river Eridanus, he came upon the nymphs, the daughters of Zeus and Themis*, who showed him where Nereus was. Heracles then seized Nereus while he was asleep, and, when Nereus transformed himself into all sorts of shapes, Heracles bound him up and would not let him go until Nereus told him where the apples and the Hesperides were to be found.

As soon as he got the information, Heracles started out across Libya, where the ruler was Poseidon's son Antaeus, who was in the habit of doing away with strangers by compelling them to wrestle. When Heracles was forced to wrestle with him, he picked Antaeus up and killed him by holding him in the air and breaking his body—for when Antaeus was touching the earth he had the power to grow in strength, and for this reason some people said he was Earth's son.

---

* Themis is generally said to be the mother of the Hours and the Fates by Zeus.

When Heracles had traveled across Libya to the sea beyond, he crossed over to the continent opposite, and on the Caucasus he brought down with his arrow the eagle, the offspring of Echidna and Typhon, that was eating out Prometheus' liver. Then he set Prometheus free and turned Chiron over to Zeus to die—even though he was not mortal—in place of Prometheus.

When Heracles reached the land of the Hyperboreans and came to the place where Atlas was, because Prometheus had instructed him not to go after the apples himself but to hold up the heavens for Atlas and send him for the apples, Heracles followed this course and took up Atlas' burden. When Atlas got possession of three of the apples of the Hesperides, he went back to Heracles. Because he did not want to hold up the sky, Atlas said he would take the apples to Eurystheus himself, and he instructed Heracles to keep on supporting the heavens himself. Heracles then assured him he would, but, by using a trick, he transferred the vault of the heavens to Atlas again. For, as Prometheus had proposed he should do, he urged Atlas to take up the sky so that he could put a pad across his shoulders. When Atlas heard this, he put the apples on the ground and relieved Heracles of the vault of the heavens.

And so, when he had gathered up the apples, Heracles started on his way. Some people, however, say Heracles did not receive the apples from Atlas, but that he killed the serpent that guarded the apples and picked them himself. When he returned to him, Heracles gave the apples to Eurystheus. Eurystheus, however, presented them to Heracles, but Athena took them from him and carried them back again, for it was against divine law for them to be set down anywhere.

The twelfth labor Eurystheus set for him was to bring Cerberus from Hades. Cerberus had three dog-heads, a dragon's tail, and on his back he had the heads of all kinds of snakes.

When Heracles reached Taenarum in Laconia, where the entrance that leads down to Hades is located, he made the descent through it. And when the spirits of the dead saw him, they all fled from him except for Meleager and Medusa, the Gorgon. Then he drew his sword on the Gorgon, as though she were living, but he was informed by Hermes that she was only an empty shade.

Then when he drew near the gates of Hades he found Theseus and also Pirithous, the one who had sought Persephone in marriage and was for this reason bound there. When they saw Heracles, they reached out to him with their hands as though they expected to be raised up from the dead by his strength. And Heracles did, in truth, take Theseus' hand and raised him from the dead, but when he wanted to raise Pirithous he gave up, because the land shook with an earthquake.

When Heracles asked Pluto for Cerberus, Pluto told him to take him, if he could overpower him without the help of his weapons. Heracles found Cerberus at the gates of Acheron, and he threw his arms around his neck and did not loosen his strangle hold until the dog was subdued, even though he was bitten by the dragon in the dog's tail. Then he took the dog off with him and ascended to earth again at Troezen. And when Heracles had shown him to Eurystheus, he took Cerberus back again to Hades.

From *Bibliotheca* II, iv, 12–v, 12

Heracles

Even as early as the time of Homer and Hesiod, Heracles was considered to have the status of a hero worthy of dwelling among the Olympians. His mortal wives were Megara, daughter of Creon, and Deianira, but after achieving immortality and going to live on Mount Olympus, home of the gods, Heracles was wed to Hebe. This marriage with Hebe, referred to as early as the Odyssey, *indicates that some reconciliation took place between Hera, Hebe's mother, and the greatest of the Greek heroes.*

The following accounts predate that of Apollodorus by about 600 years. They illustrate the manner in which the more popular myths were developed and embellished as time passed.

As told in Greek verse in the *Homeric Hymns*

TO HERACLES THE LION-HEARTED

I SHALL sing of Heracles, the son of Zeus, indeed the strongest of the men on earth. Alcmene gave birth to him in Thebes, the city of beautiful dances, after the cloud-wrapped son of Cronus had lain with her. He was once sent roaming over endless stretches of both land and sea by King Eurystheus, accomplishing many reckless deeds by himself and undergoing many bold adventures. Now, however, he dwells in happiness in the glorious abode of snow-covered Olympus and has as his wife beautiful Hebe. Hail, king, the son of Zeus. Give me prosperity and happiness.

Homeric Hymns XV

As told in Greek verse by Hesiod

CHRYSAOR AND Callirrhoë, the daughter of glorious Ocean, were the parents of three-headed Geryon. Mighty Heracles killed him in a struggle over Geryon's heavy-footed cattle in seagirt Erythea on that very day when he had stolen Geryon's broad-browed oxen. On that same day Heracles had driven them off to holy Tiryns and had crossed over the narrow path of Ocean and had slain Geryon's dog Orthrus and his herdsman Eurytion in the misty expanses on the other side of glorious Ocean.

She* gave birth also to the dauntless goddess Echidna, who is half nymph, with snapping eyes and beautiful cheeks, and also half serpent, monstrous and fearful. It is said that Typhon, fearful and unbridled and wicked, was united in love to this maiden with the snapping eyes. First of all she gave birth to Orthrus, Geryon's dog. Next she bore a second monster, invincible and unmention-able—Cerberus who eats raw meat, the hound of Hades with voice of brass, fifty-headed, shameless and powerful. Then she gave birth to a third monster, the sorrowful Hydra of Lerna, whom the goddess Hera caused to thrive, since she was exceed-ingly angry with the mighty Heracles. But Heracles, the son of Zeus, with the help of warlike Iolaus, killed the Hydra with his pitiless bronze sword, according to the will of the goddess Athena.

Echidna, because she had yielded to Orthrus in love, also bore the dread Sphinx, the destroyer of the people of Thebes, and the lion of Nemea, which Hera, the proud wife of Zeus, nourished and trained to stalk the countryside of Nemea, a constant threat to mortals. He plagued the numbers of the men who had their homes there, but the might of powerful Heracles subdued him.

From *Theogony*, 287–332

* The use of the pronoun here would seem to indicate that Echidna's mother was Callirrhoë, but she is generally considered to be the daughter of Phorcys and Ceto.

Theseus

Theseus, the great-grandson of Pelops and the son of King Aegeus of Athens, became the national hero of Athens and Attica. The myths connected with him parallel in many ways the legends surrounding his friend Heracles. According to some, Euripides among them, Poseidon was the father of Theseus. As in the case of Heracles, both a mortal and an immortal father were ascribed to him, thereby increasing his heroic stature.

The temple erected on a rise of land just to the west of the Agora of Athens has been popularly known as the Theseum because it was thought to have been dedicated to the hero. Modern archaeological research has shown, however, that this temple was dedicated to Hephaestus, or to Hephaestus and Athena.

The Panathenaea mentioned in this account was a great festival celebrated in honor of the goddess Athena. Various games and contests were held, and the festival culminated in the procession to the summit of the Acropolis to present a new robe to Athena. It was this procession that formed the subject of the Parthenon frieze.

As told in Greek prose by Apollodorus

WHEN PANDION was in Megara his sons, Aegeus, Pallas, Nisus, and Lycus were born. After the death of Pandion, his sons led an army against Athens, banished the sons of Metion, and divided the rule among the four of them. But Aegeus held all the power. He first married Meta, daughter of Hoples, and his second wife was Chalciope, daughter of Rhexenor. Because no child was born to him and he feared his brothers, he went to Pythia to consult the oracle about begetting children.

The god answered him, saying,

"The extended mouth of the wineskin, O greatest of men,
Loosen not before you arrive at the summit of Athens."

Although he did not understand the response of the oracle, he
started back toward Athens. And as he was traveling through
Troezen he was a guest at the house of Pittheus, the son of
Pelops, who, understanding the oracle when he heard it, made
him drunk with wine, causing him to lie with his daughter Aethra.
But on the same night Poseidon also lay with her.

Aegeus then instructed Aethra that, if she gave birth to a boy,
she should raise the child but not tell anyone whose he was. Then
he left underneath a certain rock his sword and sandals, saying
that whenever the boy was able to roll the rock away and get
these tokens she was to send him off with them.

Then Aegeus continued on to Athens and carried out the games
of the Panathenaean festival, in which Androgeus, the son of
Minos, defeated all his competitors. Aegeus sent him against the
bull of Marathon,* and he was killed by the bull. Some say, however, that, while Androgeus was traveling to Thebes to enter the
games in honor of Laius, he was ambushed by jealous contestants
and slain.

Soon after that, since he was master of the sea, Minos sent his
fleet to attack Athens. When the war dragged on and he was not
able to capture Athens, Minos prayed to Zeus to bring vengeance
on the Athenians.

Then, when famine and plague had fallen upon their city, the
Athenians, following the advice of an ancient oracle, first sacrificed the daughters of Hyacinthus on the grave of Geraestus the
Cyclops. But when this was of no help, they asked the oracle how
they could be rid of these evils. The god told them to give Minos
whatever satisfaction he chose to ask of them. They sent envoys
to Minos, therefore, asking him to state what satisfaction he
wanted. Minos then commanded them to send seven boys and the
same number of girls, without weapons, every year as food for
the Minotaur, which was confined in a labyrinth. Anyone who

* The bull of Marathon was the one given to King Minos by Poseidon
and later captured by Heracles. After it was freed the bull wandered in the
area of Marathon.

entered was powerless to find the way out, for many intricate twists and turns closed off the secret exit.

Aethra had borne to Aegeus a son, Theseus, who, when he had grown up, lifted up the rock and took the sandals and the sword and set out on foot for Athens.

On the way Theseus made the road safe from villainous highwaymen, for first, at Epidaurus, he overcame Periphetes, the son of Hephaestus and Anticleia, who, because of the club that he carried, was called the club-bearer. Periphetes, since his legs were weak, carried a club of iron, and used it to kill passers-by. After he took the club away from him, Theseus continued to carry it himself.

Second, Theseus killed Sinis, the son of Polypemon and Sylea, daughter of Corinthus. Sinis was called the pine-bender, for he haunted the Isthmus of Corinth and forced travelers to hold onto pine trees he had bent down. They, however, were not strong enough to do this and so were pulled up to their death by the trees. Theseus killed Sinis in this same way.

From *Bibliotheca* III, 15, 5–16, 2

Third, at Crommyon Theseus killed the sow named Phaea, the same name as that of the old woman who kept it. Some say the sow was the offspring of Echidna and Typhon.

Fourth, he slew Sciron the Corinthian, the son of Pelops, or, according to some, of Poseidon. Sciron, in the district around Megara, held sway over the rocks called Scironian after his name and forced passers-by to wash his feet and then kicked them into the sea, where they were swallowed up by an enormous turtle. But Theseus seized him by his feet and cast him into the sea.

Fifth, in Eleusis he slew Cercyon, the son of Branchus and the nymph Argiope. Cercyon compelled all passers-by to wrestle with him and killed them in the struggle. Theseus, however, lifted him into the air and dashed him against the earth.

Sixth, he slew Damastes, whom some people call Polypemon. Beside the road Damastes had his dwelling place, where he made up two beds, one small and the other large, and extended hospitality to the passers-by. But he laid the short men on the large bed and beat them with a hammer to the size of the bed; and the tall men he put upon the small bed and sawed off whatever parts of the body hung over it.

Thus, when he had made the road safe, Theseus came to Athens. Medea, however, who was then married to Aegeus, plotted against him and convinced Aegeus that he should be on his guard against Theseus as a traitor. And so Aegeus, who was unaware that Theseus was his own son, was in fear of him and sent him against the bull of Marathon. But when he had slain the bull, Aegeus brought him a poison that Medea had given him that same day. Just as Theseus was on the point of being made to take the drink, he gave his father the sword. Aegeus recognized it and dashed the cup out of his hands. When Theseus was thus made known to his father and learned about the plot, he drove Medea from the kingdom.

And Theseus was chosen to be one of the third group offered to the Minotaur—or, as some people say, he volunteered to go. Because the ship had a black sail, Aegeus instructed his son that, if he came back alive, he should hoist white sails on the mast. When Theseus reached Crete, the daughter of Minos, Ariadne, who was in love with him, promised to help him if he would make her his wife and take her away to Athens. When Theseus had sworn himself to these terms on oath, she begged Daedalus to reveal the way out of the labyrinth. Following his advice, she gave Theseus a thread when he went in, and Theseus tied this to the door, trailing it after him as he entered. And when he came upon the Minotaur in the farthest corner of the labyrinth, he killed him with his bare hands and then, by winding up the thread, found his way out again. And during the night he reached Naxos with Ariadne and the young people.*

There Dionysus fell in love with Ariadne, carried her off to Lemnos, and became the father by her of Thoas, Staphylus, Oenopion, and Peparethus.

---

* The manuscripts of Apollodorus are fragmentary here. According to Theocritus and other earlier versions of the events that followed, Theseus forgot Ariadne and left her on Naxos. Plutarch and others give several different reasons for her abandonment, among them the appearance of Dionysus to Theseus in a dream advising Theseus to leave Ariadne and sail for home.

Theseus, however, in his distress over Ariadne, forgot as he was sailing back to port to hoist the white sails on his ship. Aegeus, therefore, when he caught sight of the ship from the acropolis and saw the black sail, thought Theseus had been killed, and so he jumped to his death.

Theseus then succeeded to the kingship of Athens and slew the sons of Pallas, who were fifty in number. And in like manner he put to death all others who tried to oppose him, and thus he alone held all the power.

From Epitome I, 1–11

The Marriage of Peleus
and Thetis

Catullus presented the myth of the marriage of Peleus and Thetis in the form of an epyllion, or brief epic. The main theme is idyllic in type, concentrating on the joyous occasion of the wedding. In sharp contrast to this is the digression, or second theme, a characteristic of the epyllion, centered on Ariadne's unhappiness. The marriage song, sung by the Fates, forms another division in the poem. Unity is given to the whole by another contrast, the high moral tone of man during the age of heroes, the time to which Peleus and Thetis belonged, set against the low moral fiber of later ages, including Catullus' own time.

According to Pindar, Jupiter had himself been in love with Thetis, but it had been prophesied that she would bear him a son greater than his father. On the advice of the prophetess Themis, who revealed this oracle to the gods, Jupiter therefore urged his grandson Peleus to wed Thetis. In most accounts Prometheus, who was punished for stealing fire, was rescued by Heracles. In Aeschylus' Prometheus Bound, *however, he was the one who knew the secret about Thetis and used that knowledge to bargain for his freedom.*

As told in Latin verse by Catullus

PINES THAT once grew to their full size on Pelion's summit moved, so it is told, through the clear-flowing billows of Neptune's realm to the waters of the Phasis and the kingdom of Aeëtes. Then chosen heroes, the flower of Argive youth, eagerly seeking to carry off the golden fleece from Colchis, dared to sail their swift ship across the depths of the sea, skimming over the dark blue surface with sweeping oars.

Athena, the goddess who preserves the citadels of lofty cities, built this vessel with her own hands to fly before the light breeze, joining a fabric of pine in union with the curved keel. This craft was the first to school untutored Amphitrite in charting a course. The moment their ship's prow broke a furrow through the choppy deep and the waves, twisted beneath their oars, grew white with spray, wild countenances raised themselves up from the foaming eddy—the faces of the sea nymphs, daughters of Nereus, full of wonder at this monster of the sea. Then, and then only, mortals looked upon the nymphs of the sea with their naked bodies exposed to view, standing out breast-high above the waters. Then Thetis, it is said, set Peleus on fire with love, then Thetis scorned not marriage to a mortal, then Jupiter himself, the father of all, blessed the union of Peleus and Thetis.

O heroes born in the happiest period of time, hail, race of the gods, O noble mothers' sons, again hail! I shall urge you on time and again with my song, and you, enriched beyond all others with a marriage of happy omen, you the mainstay of Thessaly, O Peleus, to whom Jupiter himself, even the father of the gods, yielded his beloved. Was it you whom Thetis, the most beautiful of the Nereids, held spellbound? Was it to you that Tethys granted permission to wed her granddaughter, and Oceanus, too, who embraces the whole circle of the world with his waters?

When first dawned the light of the appointed day they had so eagerly awaited, all Thessaly gathered in a throng at the palace. The royal abode is brimming over with the joyful company, bearing gifts in their hands, proclaiming joy by their countenances. Scyros is deserted, Tempe is left behind, and so too were Thessaly's homes and walled cities. No one tills the fields, the necks of the oxen grow soft, neither is the humble vineyard cleared with the curving sickle, nor does the bull turn over the sod with the sloping plowshare, nor does the pruning hook diminish the shade of the tree's leafy branches, and squalid rust falls upon the deserted plows.

But the palace of Peleus, as far as the rich abode extends, glistens with shining gold and silver. Ivory gleams on the thrones, goblets shine bright on the tables, the whole dwelling rejoices with the splendor of royal treasure. Indeed, the wedding couch of the bride divine stands in the inner hall, made of polished tusks from India and covered with a spread tinted rosy purple from the dye of the shellfish.

This coverlet, embroidered with the figures of men of old, set forth with wondrous skill the courageous deeds of the heroes. There, gazing out from the wave-resounding shores of Dia, Ariadne watched Theseus as he sailed swiftly out of sight, and she held fierce anger within her heart. Nor, indeed, could she believe that she really saw what she beheld. Small wonder, since only then, just aroused from her deceptive sleep, did she realize she was deserted, alone and miserable on the shore, while her thoughtless lover beat the sea with his oars in his flight, leaving behind him empty promises tossed lightly on the breezes.

At the water's edge, Minos' daughter followed Theseus into the distance with tear-filled eyes, standing like a stony statue of a bacchante, gazing out at him—alas, gazing—and she was buffeted back and forth under the great waves of her anguish. No hold had she on the delicate scarf over her golden hair, no more was her bosom hidden by the fine covering of her cloak, no longer was the fullness of her breasts restrained by slender bands, but the garments which had all slipped away from her body and scattered here and there at her feet were lapped by the salt waves. With no care then for her veil, no thought for her garments floating in the water, with her whole heart, Theseus, with her whole soul, with her whole mind she was focused in her utter despair on you.

Then, as Ariadne prayed in her anguish for vengeance against this heartless deed, the king of the gods heard her plea and granted her request with the invincible majesty of his nod—a nod that caused the earth and the ruffled seas to tremble as the firmament shook the twinkling stars. And Theseus in fact, his mind drenched in a dark cloud, dismissed from his forgetful heart all the instructions he had kept in the fastness of his thoughts before and did not raise the happy signal to show his anxious father he was safely coming into the port of Athens at last.

It is said that when Aegeus entrusted his son to the winds as he set sail from Athena's walls he embraced him and instructed him thus: "My son, my only son, far dearer to me than life, my son, only recently restored to me in the declining years of my old age, whom I am forced now to send off to an unknown fate, I shall not allow you to sail with the signs of good fortune. No, I shall hang dyed sails from your swaying mast, canvas deeply stained with Spanish ochre so that the sails may match the dull gloom of my grief, the dark flame in my heart.

"But if the goddess Athena, who promised to be the protector of our people and our city, grants that your hand be sprinkled with the bull's blood, then as soon as your eyes are within sight of our hills let the yardarms give up their garb of mourning, every inch of it, and let the twisted ropes raise pure white sails so that when first I see them my joyful, happy heart may know that a glad day has brought you back to me in safety."

These instructions, held firmly in mind before, forsook Theseus even as clouds, driven by a blast of wind, depart from the lofty summit of a snowy peak. Then Aegeus, watching from his place atop the citadel* and peering expectantly with straining, tear-filled eyes to catch sight of the ship, as soon as he saw the hue of the sails full-spread, hurled himself headlong from the summit of the rocks, believing that he had lost Theseus to a grim fate.

It was thus that Theseus in his pride entered his home, a home made a house of mourning by his father's death, and found in his turn just such anguish as he had brought to Minos' daughter by his thoughtlessness.

Ariadne was revolving a tangle of cares in her wounded heart as she stared pitifully at her lover's ship disappearing from view. But there in another part of the coverlet joyous Bacchus came in all haste to Dia, and a band of reveling satyrs and sileni from the east attended him. He came seeking you, Ariadne, he came out of love, a burning love for you.

Thus royally adorned with embroidered figures such as these, the coverlet enveloped the marriage couch in its embrace. Then when the young people of Thessaly had fulfilled their eager desire to examine the details of the cloth, they gave place to the im-

---

* The best vantage point from which to watch for the returning ship would have been the Promontory of Sunion. In some versions Aegeus jumped into the sea—an impossibility from Athens—thereby giving his name to the Aegean.

mortal gods. And so, departing from the splendid courtyard, the mortal guests started out on foot, scattering, each to his own home.

After their departure, first of all Chiron came from Pelion's summit bearing sylvan gifts—a wealth of blossoms that the fields bring to flower, that Thessaly brings forth on her mountainsides, that the gentle breeze of Favonius nourishes by the river banks, all these he brought in profusion, woven into streaming garlands, and the house, charmed by their sweet scent, smiled.

Peneus, too, leaving lush green Tempe—Tempe, a vale edged about with wooded slopes—leaving the bands of Dorian nymphs to dance alone, was among the first to come, nor did he come empty-handed. He was bearing lofty beech trees, roots and all, and bay trees with tall, straight stems, waving plane trees, supple poplar and slender cypress. All these he set about in masses that the approaches, decked with the soft foliage, might be gay with green.

Behind the river god came Prometheus—he of clever mind— carrying the fading traces of the old punishment he endured when, his limbs bound with chains to a rock, he hung on a steep cliff.

Then the father of the gods came with his revered wife and their offspring, leaving only you, Apollo, with your twin sister alone in the heavens.

As soon as the immortals were comfortably seated in the ivory-white palace the tables were served with a bountiful wedding feast. Then, their bodies shaking with the tremor of age, the Fates began to chant their words of prophecy. Their hands were busy at the everlasting task that was rightfully theirs. The left hand held the distaff with its mass of soft wool, the right hand, gently drawing the fibers down, shaped them into thread between upturned fingers, then rolled the taut thread onto the spindle, starting it with thumb pressing hard and palm turned down, and set the spindle, steadied by its balancing disk, twirling. While the hands were working thus the mouth kept smoothing the fibers, and the woolly fuzz that stood up roughly on the light thread stuck to their parched lips. Baskets of wicker at their feet guarded the fluffy fleece of the shining wool.

Then with clearly sounding voices, drawing the wool from the distaff, the Fates poured forth their prophecies in divinely inspired song—song that no later age shall find false, singing:

O glory growing ever greater by great deeds,
glorious defender of Thessaly, most glorious son,
hear what the sisters reveal to you on this joyous day,
hear their prophecy truly told.
But turn, O spindles, turn, spin the threads of destiny.
     Hesperus will come, bringing you all a bridegroom longs for,
your bride will come under an auspicious star,
flooding your captured soul with your heart's love,
yielding to you in soft, languid sleep,
cushioning your manly neck in her gentle arms.
Turn, O spindles, turn, spin the threads of destiny.
     No house ever sheltered love so true,
no love ever joined lovers so firmly,
as the deep love, the harmony between Peleus and Thetis.
Turn, O spindles, turn, spin the threads of destiny.
     There will be born to you a son, fearless Achilles,
known to the enemy only by his brave breast, never his back,
so often the victor in the swift-footed race,
outstripping the fiery steps of the fleet stag.
Turn, O spindles, turn, spin the threads of destiny.
     Not a hero will match him in war
when Phrygian fields flow with Trojan blood
and Agamemnon, third in descent from Pelops,
besieges and destroys the walls of Troy in a long war.
Turn, O spindles, turn, spin the threads of destiny.
     Mothers, even at their sons' funerals,
even as they tear their disheveled white hair
and bruise their withered breasts with aged palms,
will tell of his mighty courage, tell of his famous deeds.
Turn, O spindles, turn, spin the threads of destiny.
     For just as the reaper, cutting a swath in the thick grain before
          him,
harvests his golden crop under a warm sun
so Achilles will cut down the Trojan host with his sharp sword's
          edge.
Turn, O spindles, turn, spin the threads of destiny.
     Scamander's waters will witness his high courage,

Scamander that loses itself in the Hellespont's swift tides,
choking its waves with the piled bodies of the slain
and warming its deep current with mingled blood.
Turn, O spindles, turn, spin the threads of destiny.
   So come now, join together in your heart's desire.
Let the husband take his goddess bride in happy wedlock,
let the wife take her long expectant bridegroom in joyful marriage.
Turn, O spindles, turn, spin the threads of destiny.

Chanting such notes of happiness to Peleus, the Fates sang prophetic strains divinely inspired. For that was in the time when the gods, before religious piety fell into neglect, used to visit the guiltless homes of the heroes in bodily form and revealed themselves in mortal gatherings. Often the father of the gods, returning when the festal days of his annual rites came round and seated in his gleaming shrine, would watch as a hundred bulls fell to earth.

But after the earth was steeped in wicked crime and the greed of all men put justice to flight, brothers stained their hands in the blood of their brothers and a son ceased to mourn for the death of his parents. The wicked mixture of all things, just and unjust, in the madness of sin has turned the righteous hearts of the gods from us. And so it is that the gods shun the gatherings of men and do not suffer themselves to appear in the open light of day.

From Catullus 64, 1–408

Ixion

Although Ixion had murdered one of his own relatives, Zeus had purified him of the crime. Ixion's consequent actions, however, showed a lack of thankfulness and respect toward Zeus.

From the union of Ixion and Nephele—nephele is the Greek word for "cloud"—was born Centaurus, the father of the centaurs.

As told in Greek verse by Pindar

MEN SAY that Ixion, who rolls around and around on his winged wheel at the command of the gods, teaches us that we should repay our benefactor with continued gratitude and kindly appreciation.

Ixion learned this well, for, although he was granted a pleasant life among the gods, the gracious children of Cronus, he was not satisfied with his great blessings. But he longed madly for Hera, who was allotted in happy marriage to Zeus. But indeed his proud daring urged him on to arrogance, and soon this man suffered a fitting and just punishment.

It is right that one should always view the fitness of all he does according to his own limitations. Improper love has hurled the offender into deep suffering before, and now this came upon Ixion also.

Ixion had made love to what was only a cloud, embracing it in a false dream, completely unaware as he was—for the cloud appeared in the shape of Hera, the daughter of Cronus and queen of the gods. The hands of Zeus had placed the cloud before him as a deceit and a beautiful source of misery.

It was in this way that Ixion brought about his own punishment and was bound to the four spokes of a wheel. When he had been chained thus to the wheel and was unable to escape, Ixion served as a warning to all mankind.

From *Pythian Odes* II, 21–41

The Argonauts

Zeus had fashioned Nephele to deceive Ixion. She was later married to King Athamas of Boeotia and became the mother of Phrixus and Helle. When Phrixus' stepmother, Ino, daughter of Cadmus, wanted to sacrifice him to Jupiter (the Roman counterpart of Zeus) to end a drought, Phrixus and his sister fled to King Aeëtes of Colchis. For his flight Mercury, the messenger of the gods, sent him a ram with a golden fleece. Phrixus later sacrificed the ram to Jupiter at Colchis and gave the golden fleece to Aeëtes. On the way Helle had fallen from the ram into the sea at the strait (now the Dardanelles) that received its name, Hellespont, from hers.

The expedition of the Argonauts took place a generation before the Trojan War. The men who sailed in the Argo *were already famous throughout the Greek world as heroes and demigods. A number of them must have watched in later years as their sons sailed off to Troy.*

As told in Latin verse by Valerius Flaccus

My story is of the seas first sailed upon by the great heroes, the sons of gods, and of a ship, driven by fate. The ship had dared to follow the shores of the Black Sea and to rush in between the Clashing Rocks, holding a straight course, and to come to rest at the last on gleaming Olympus, home of the gods.

Phoebus Apollo, may you inspire me and happily assist me in this undertaking, so that my words may reach and spread through all the Roman cities.

From his earliest years King Pelias had ruled in Thessaly. He had long been held in awe by his people, and now he was old. His mind, however, was active with plans, because he feared Jason, his brother's son. He feared, also, the warnings of the gods, for the prophets foretold that Jason would bring destruction upon his uncle, the king.

Pelias, therefore, made haste to cast aside his fears and to consider by what means and opportunities he might bring about the death of Jason, son of his brother Aeson. But he saw that there were no wars in Greece and no monsters in any of the cities of Greece that might destroy Jason. The anger of the sea and the dangers of the vast ocean seemed the best way.

Then, looking at the young man with a calm expression and a countenance giving the impression of truth to his false words, Pelias spoke to Jason, saying, "Give me your agreement to this adventure, which will be finer than any deeds of the past, and show me your eagerness for the expedition. The strength I once had has grown dull with the years, and my son is not yet ready for rule and the affairs of war or the sea. May you—since now you are strong in responsibility and vigorous in spirit—go to Colchis, my fine young man, and bring the golden fleece back to a shrine in Greece. And may you be worthy to meet and overcome all risks."

With such words Pelias urged on the young man and even ordered him to set forth. Quickly the king's secret tricks were laid bare, and Jason understood that the golden fleece alone was not the goal, but that he was indeed being driven away from his rightful kingdom and onto the boundless sea by jealous hatred. How would he be able to carry out these orders? By what means, moreover, could he seek Colchis, where the golden fleece lay guarded? Alas, what should he do?

Should he rely on the help of Juno, queen of the gods, and on Pallas Athena, resounding with armor, and enter upon the voyage as he was commanded, trusting that he could win fame by overcoming the dangers of the sea and accomplishing his task? Stretching his hands toward the stars, he prayed reverently, "Juno, all-powerful gueen, grant that I may reach the Black Sea and Colchis, and may you, Pallas Athena, keep me safe. Then I shall offer up the golden fleece in your temples."

The goddesses heard Jason's prayer and sought their different ways, slipping swiftly through the air. Pallas Athena flew quickly down to the city where her valued Argus, builder of ships, lived.

She instructed him to build a ship and to fell great oaks with his ax, and she went with him into the shady woods of Pelion to carry this out.

Meanwhile, Juno went to all the cities of Greece, telling the people that Jason, the son of Aeson, was setting out before untried winds and that his proud ship would soon stand ready and in need of those who could man the oars and bring the ship safely back again to Greece. She told them they would be raised to the heavens because of the fame of their adventure.

A great band of heroes who had already faced wars and tasted fame, and many who, in the flower of early manhood, were making their first attempts and had not yet been given an opportunity for glory, were eager for the voyage.

Straightway Hercules hastened forth willingly to the adventure. Rejoicing in the task, the boy Hylas carried on his shoulders the hero's bow and the arrows inflamed with poison. Indeed he wished to take it, but his hand was not yet equal to the weight or size of Hercules' club.

The goddess Juno turned her gaze toward the waters of the Aegean. There a large gathering of men worked busily. At the same time, she saw that a grove of trees had been felled on all sides and that the shores were resounding with the steady blows of the double-edged ax. Already Argus was cutting pines with the thin blade of a saw, and the sides of the ship were being fitted together. She saw, too, planks being softened over a slow fire until they bent to the proper shape. The oars had been fashioned, and Pallas Athena was seeking out a yardarm for the sail-carrying mast. When the ship stood finished, strong enough to plow through the pathless sea, and when fine wax had filled the hidden cracks, the builder Argus added varied ornamental paintings.

Although the men were amazed at the wondrous ship and the painted scenes, Jason, the son of Aeson, thought to himself, "Alas, we are unfortunate men, both sons and fathers! Are we, gentle souls, being sent against the storms in this vessel? Will the sea rage only against me, Aeson's son? Should I not carry off my young cousin Acastus, son of Pelias, so he may undergo the same adventures and the same dangers as I? In that case, Pelias would wish that the ship might have safe seas and would pray with our mothers for calm waves."

As Jason was planning this, an eagle, the armor-bearer of Jupiter, approached, flying through the sky on the left, and caught up a lamb, holding it fast in his strong claws. But in the distance shepherds, aroused from the pastures, followed the bird with a shout, and the barking of dogs pursued it. Swiftly the eagle kidnapper took to the air and escaped out over the vast Aegean.

Jason watched this good omen and happily made for the home of proud King Pelias. Before Jason reached the palace, Acastus, the king's son, ran out toward his cousin and embraced him.

Jason spoke first, saying, "I have not come, Acastus, to make unworthy complaints, but I have in mind to make you a comrade in our undertaking. I think no young man more worthy to seek the golden fleece. Think of the new lands and how much of the world we shall see! Perhaps now you consider the task too difficult. But when the lucky ship sails back again and I return to my beloved homeland, then indeed what shame you will have when you hear of our adventures! What envy you will feel when I tell about all the places we have seen!"

The king's son, not allowing Jason to say more, spoke: "Enough! I am prepared for whatever you call upon me to do. Indeed, I shall deceive my unsuspecting father, lest his too anxious care should hinder me. Then I shall quickly join you by the time you are ready and the ship is putting out from the shore's edge."

Jason heard the promises Acastus made and noted his courage with pleasure. Then he turned toward the shore with quick steps.

Meanwhile, at the word and command of their leader, the companions of Jason, a great throng, lifted the ship on their shoulders and ran down headlong, with straining knees, into the sea. There was no lack of shouting from the panting sailors or of sweet music from the lyre of Orpheus.

Then, rejoicing, the men erected altars. The greatest honor was given to Neptune, ruler of the waters, and to Zephyrus, the gentle west wind. Jason himself, pouring forth an offering from a goblet three times to Neptune, father of the sea, spoke thus: "O thou who dost shake the foaming kingdoms of the deep at thy will and dost encircle all lands with the sea, grant me thy favor. I know that I alone out of all the world am starting out on untried ways and am deserving of stormy weather. I am not, however, carried forth of my own free will. Pelias has given these harsh commands and has brought about this journey to Colchis in order to bring grief upon me and my people."

Thus Jason spoke and poured the wine upon the flame as an offering to the god of the sea. Jason, leader of the Argonauts, then addressed his men, saying, "Since, my comrades, the highest hope is placed in this great undertaking, may you also now bring to our adventure the spirit and courage of your fathers. It is not for me to blame the tyrant Pelias or his suspected plots. It is Jupiter who has ordered it. Jupiter himself has willed that men should join in fellowship throughout his world and should engage together in great tasks such as this. Come with me, men, and, although the adventure be dangerous, accomplish it successfully. It will be one that will be pleasing to remember and will inspire our grandsons. Now, comrades, may you spend this coming night in pleasure upon the shore with pleasant talk and pastimes."

And now Chiron the centaur came running down from a hilltop. He was holding the young Achilles, who called out to his father, Peleus, from afar. When the boy saw Peleus look toward his familiar voice and stretch out his arms for a wide embrace, he sprang forth and clung for a long time to his beloved father's neck.

The boy Achilles was fascinated by the heroes as he drank in their boasting words and turned his face close to Hercules' lion's skin. But Peleus hugged his son happily and kissed him. Then, looking toward the heavens, he prayed aloud: "O gods above, may you wish that I, Peleus, sail through calm seas and travel on favoring winds. So, also, may you keep this, my child, safe. And may you, Chiron, take care of all else for me."

Then an eagerness for the voyage came upon each man. With their spirits high, they were ready to cross over the sea. They held a vision of the golden fleece far away and of the *Argo*, their ship, returning soon, ornamented with garlands of gold.

The sun set and the waves of the sea carried away all the light of day from the joyful Argonauts. Lights, scattered along the curving shore, appeared.

And now the talking and laughter came to an end, and, laid upon their quiet beds, all were still. Their leader Jason, alone among the rows of sleepers, was unable to sleep. Aeson, his aged father, and his mother, Alcimede, likewise sleepless, watched their son and held to him with tearful eyes. Jason, speaking gentle words, cheered them and calmed their troubled hearts.

Soon, when their eyelids had closed, overcome by deep sleep, the oak of Jupiter, the gleaming guardian of the garlanded ship, seemed to urge the leader on with these words: "I shall go with you over the sea. Now is the time; come, delay no more! Even if the uncertain sky be covered with clouds while we sail over all the sea, even now cast aside your fears, trusting in the gods above and in me."

Jason, trembling—although the omen of the gods was a happy one—jumped up from his couch. At the same time, Aurora, the nourishing dawn, ruffling the sea with the light of a new day, brought forth all the Argonauts from their sleep. They hurried to and fro on the decks. Some set the yardarm of the lofty mast into position, others tried out the oars on the shining surface of the sea, and Argus lifted the anchor to the lofty prow.

The weeping of the mothers grew louder, and the brave hearts of the fathers grew heavy. Weeping, they clung to their sons in long embraces. And now it was time. With its sad signal the trumpet, sounding three times, loosened the embraces that were both wasting the breeze and delaying the ship. Each one of the men gave his name to his oar and to his rowing-bench. Here on the port side Telamon, the father of Ajax, took his place. Higher than he, Hercules sat on the starboard side. The other youths took their seats on each side.

The fame of the *Argo*, the ship of Thessaly, drew even you to the sea, Nestor—you who would wonder some years from now at the sea, white with sails and a thousand ships' captains sailing to the Trojan War. There, too, was the prophet Mopsus, whose white cloak flowing around his purple-red boots reached to his feet and whose helmet was bound with a spray of laurel at its peak. And Tydeus, too, sat at his oar in the row with Hercules.

You also, Philoctetes, rowed toward Colchis. Then you were

famous for your father's spear, but in the future you would see the island of Lemnos twice and shoot the arrows of Hercules. Nor was Peleus, trusting in his wife, the sea goddess Thetis, and in her parents, deities of the sea, missing from their number. His lance was glittering from the lofty prow, longer than all the other lances.

Erginus, the son of Neptune, also was carried over the waters free from care. He had a knowledge of the dangers of the sea, of the stars of the clear night, and of what wind Aeolus, their king, chose to set free from his caves.

Pollux carried boxing gloves of bull's hide adorned with lead that wounds. Castor, who knew how to break the mouths of horses to the bridle, was with him. They wore cloaks gleaming alike with brilliant purple, remarkable work that Leda, their mother, wove on twin looms.

Meleager, the clasp that held your mantle gathered together was loose. It showed your strong shoulders and an expanse of fine chest equal to the strength of Hercules.

Idas struck the blue water with a shorter oar and sat far off, the last in his rowing-bench. But his brother Lynceus was kept for great purposes. It was he who could break through the earth and seek out the silent Styx with his piercing vision. From the middle of the sea, Lynceus would point out the land to the pilot and would show him the stars to guide the ship. He alone would see through the clouds when Jupiter had hidden the sky in shadows.

Nor indeed did Orpheus exert himself on the rowing-benches or break the waters with an oar, but with a song he showed the oars their rhythm, lest they come together without order on the surface of the waves.

Argus, you had the care of your own ship. Pallas Athena gave you your skill. It was your lot to be on guard lest the vessel let in water in any place unobserved, and to stop up either with pitch or soft wax the cracks caused by the pounding of the waves.

Tiphys, ever watchful, fixed his gaze on the Great Bear. It was he who, by good fortune, found a use for the slow-moving stars, steering a course over the sea with the heavens as a guide.

Behold, Jason recognized Acastus, bristling with javelins and shimmering with the light of his shield as he ran down a shortcut on the mountain slope, and was joyful and happy in his own trickery.

Then Jason, jumping onto the ship in the midst of the shields and the men, cut the cables with his flashing sword. At once the vessel, driven ahead, moved out. The mothers stood on the shore and followed with their eyes the bright sails and the men's shields catching the light of the sun, until finally the sea appeared higher than the mast and the limitless space took the ship from their sight.

Then Jupiter, looking down from his starry citadel and seeing the noble undertakings of the Greeks and the great mass of work they were beginning, was glad. All the gods rejoiced with him. But the sun god Apollo was fearful of the dangers that lay ahead and poured forth these words from his heart: "Jupiter, father of us all, is this expedition thy wish? Does the *Argo*, the ship of the Greeks, now sail over the waves with you as the guide and with thy good wishes?"

Then Jupiter, the father of gods and men, answered, "All these events have been planned by me. They will proceed in due order and remain fixed in their course.

"For a long time the region that stretches from the boundless East to the waters of the Hellespont has flourished with a wealth of horses and men. No force has dared to rise up against the East or to struggle against her in war. Thus did I myself favor her fates and her cities. But the final day of Asia is hastening on. The Greeks now demand from me their opportunity for success. To this end the Argonauts are being sent forth over the sea.

"A way has been made through the waves and through the seas for thee, Bellona, goddess of war. May the mountains, woods, lakes, and all the narrow passages of the sea lie open. Let hope and fear be the judge of all men. I myself shall test each kingdom to decide which shall rule over all people for the longest time and where I shall place the reins of empire with most certainty."

Then Jupiter turned his eyes toward the deep blue Aegean Sea. He looked upon the strength of Hercules and the twin sons of Leda—Castor and Pollux—and spoke thus: "Strive toward the stars, men! I have set a hard and painful road to heaven for you."

Meanwhile Boreas, the fierce north wind, looking out from the mountain heights of Macedonia, saw the sails of the *Argo* well out to sea. He hastened to Aeolia, home of the clouds and winds and the ship-breaking storms. Aeolus, ruler of the winds, is an all-powerful king whose commands the wild band of winds obeys. Within the mountains of Aeolia, iron and double walls of stone hold in the stormy east winds. When Aeolus, their king, can no longer curb their roaring, by his own wish he breaks open the doors of their prison. By giving them freedom he pacifies their wild murmurings.

Boreas roused Aeolus from his lofty throne, bearing this news: "What a dreadful thing, Aeolus, I have seen from the heights of Macedonia! Greek heroes are sailing forth in a great new ship built with their axes and cross the sea rejoicing in their huge sails. I have not the power to stir up the waters from their depths of sand as I could before I was held by the bonds of the prison of the winds. Because the Greeks see that I, Boreas the north wind, am ruled by you, king of the winds, they have faith in their own courage and in the strength of the ship they have built. Grant that I may overwhelm and sink the mighty ship of the Greeks."

Thus spoke Boreas. And all the winds within the cave began to roar and clamor for the sea. Then Aeolus struck open the great door with a mighty thrust. The joyful winds burst forth from their prison—Zephyrus the west wind, and Notus the south wind, whose wings were the color of the night, along with the offspring of the rain clouds, and also Eurus the east wind, his hair wild with storm blasts, his head yellow with blowing sand.

The winds brought on a tempest, and, roaring on their course with single purpose, they drove the raging sea onto the shore. They did not stir up only the kingdom of Neptune, god of the sea; but even the sky was on fire with lightning and was filled with the great roar of thunder. Night covered up all things in a pitch-black sky. The oars were pulled from the rowers' hands. The ship's prow was turned broadside, and her side was pounded by resounding blows from the waves. A sudden whirlwind ripped the sails and left them flapping on the swaying mast. Then what terror seized the trembling Argonauts when the darkened heavens glowed and lightning flashes fell before the quaking ship, and when the sail went under on the port side and rose again wet from the yawning waves!

Then with a mournful murmur the Argonauts cried out, "Hardly have we set sail from the shore and the Aegean has risen up with such an uproar! Does an even more dangerous sea lie ahead for us in our misery?"

Thus they bemoaned their fate, mourning that they were to die a lingering death. Even the stout-hearted Hercules saw that his arrows and club of oak were useless against the storm. Suddenly the wood was loosened, and the ship took in the waters of the sea through its vast gaps. Now Eurus the east wind, twisting the vessel this way and that, lashes it; now Notus the south wind, whistling with Zephyrus the west wind, catches it up.

On all sides the sea raged, when suddenly Neptune, carrying his three-pronged spear, raised his sea-blue head from the deep. "Let Pallas Athena, my sister," he said, "softening my heart with weeping, rescue this ship from me."

So spoke the god of the sea, and he quieted the raging waters and the battered shores and drove away the winds. The daylight was revealed and shone forth. A rainbow stretched across the sky, and the clouds returned to the mountaintops. Then the ship stood out on placid waters.

Therefore, Jason, leader of the Argonauts, covered his shoulders with a sacred cloak and took up a cup. Then he poured an offering of wine into the sea and spoke this prayer: "O gods, who hold the rule over the waves and the loud storm and whose palace stretches far within the broad sky, may the will of the gods be more favorable to me now. Grant that I may bring these men back to land and embrace once again the threshold of my native home. Then a great number of sacrifices will nourish your deserving altars everywhere."

Thus Jason spoke. A shout arose, and the raised hands of all marked agreement with the words of their leader. And behold, they saw the gentle west winds gliding toward them. The great ship flew forward under full sail, cutting the sea and plowing up foam with its three-pronged prow. Tiphys had the helm, and his quiet helpers stood by for his commands.

From *Argonautica* I, 1–689

Jason and Medea

Jason and the Argonauts had a number of adventures en route to Colchis, but they finally reached their destination. Hera, Athena, and Aphrodite continued to favor and aid Jason as they had from the beginning.

A number of writers, including Apollonius Rhodius, Pindar, Sophocles, Euripides, and Ovid, told the story of the aftermath of the expedition of the Argonauts. On their return to Greece, Medea restored Jason's father, Aeson, to youth by her magic. Then, pretending to do the same for Pelias, she brought about his death. After Pelias' murder, Jason and Medea were forced to flee and took refuge in Corinth. In time, Jason deserted Medea in order to marry Creusa (also called Glauce), the daughter of King Creon of Corinth. Medea killed her rival with a poisoned robe, murdered her two sons by Jason, and fled to Athens, where she married King Aegeus, the father of Theseus.

As told in Greek verse by Apollonius Rhodius

DURING THE night, under the skillful guidance of Argus, the ship came to the wide river Phasis where it meets the sea at Colchis. At once they lowered their sails and used their oars to enter the great mouth of the river. On their left they saw the lofty Caucasus Mountains and the city of Aea, and on the other hand the plain and sacred grove of Ares where a serpent guarded the fleece, which was spread out over the leafy branches of an oak tree.

Then Jason, the son of Aeson, poured a libation of honey-sweet wine into the river from a gold goblet in offering to Earth and the gods of this land and to the spirits of its heroes who had died, and he entreated them to favor him with their kind aid and a welcoming harbor for their ship. Then they spent the rest of the night there, and before long the eagerly awaited dawn appeared.

Thus the men waited, hidden by the thick reeds, but Hera and Athena saw them and consulted with each other. At length Hera spoke out and explained her plan, suggesting, "Come, let us go to Aphrodite the Cypriote and let us approach her together, urging her to persuade her son Eros—if only he will—to send one of his arrows at the daughter of Aeëtes, the enchantress Medea, binding her with a love for Jason. I feel certain that, with her help and advice, he will carry the fleece off to Hellas." So she spoke, and her shrewd plan was pleasing to Athena.

Then they set forth and went to the great palace of Aphrodite, which her husband, the lame god Hephaestus, had built for her when he received her from Zeus as his bride. Hephaestus had gone to his forge and anvils, and Aphrodite was alone, seated on a beautiful chair facing the door. She smiled at them as she asked, "Good ladies, what purpose or desire brings you here after such a long time? For what reason have you come, you who are the greatest of goddesses?"

Then Hera answered her, saying, "Our hearts are filled with foreboding, for Aeson's son has brought his ship into the river Phasis, coming in search of the fleece. Indeed we are most fearful for all of them, since their task now looms before them."

Aphrodite was struck with awe as she beheld Hera entreating her in supplication, and she answered her kindly, saying, "Revered goddess, may there be no one more base than I, the goddess of Cyprus, if I make light of your wishes by either word or deed or whatever my weak hands may accomplish for you. And let there be no return given for this favor of mine."

Then Aphrodite started off through the valleys of Olympus in search of her son. And she found him in the luxuriant orchard of Zeus, not alone but with Ganymede, whom Zeus had once brought to live in the heavens among the immortals, because he had been captured by his beauty. Aphrodite went up to her son and, taking his chin in her hand, spoke to him thus: "Come now, if you are willing to carry out for me this task, which I shall explain to you, I shall give you Zeus' very lovely plaything, which his dear nurse Adrastea made for him—a golden ball. If you throw it into the air, like a star it will leave a blazing trail through the sky. I shall give you this ball if you strike Medea with your arrow, binding her to Jason in love. But let there be no delay, for then my gratitude will be less."

So she spoke, and at once Eros picked up his quiver, which was leaning against a tree, and put it over his shoulder. Then he took his curving bow in his hand and went off through the garden of Zeus' palace and out through the gates of lofty Olympus, where the way descending from the heavens begins.

The heroes were seated on the benches of their ship, far off at the river's edge, talking over their plans together. And Jason said, "My friends, I shall tell you what I should like to see done, and it is up to you to carry it out. You will all stay here quietly on the ship, while I go to the palace of Aeëtes, taking the sons of Phrixus and two other men with me. When I get there, I shall try to determine by talking to him whether he will give us the golden fleece willingly or not." So he spoke, and the young men quickly agreed with Jason's plan.

Then Jason called upon Phrixus' sons and Telamon and Augeas to accompany him, and when he had taken up Hermes' wand they left the ship and set out toward the hill rising from the plain. As they went on their way, Hera thoughtfully laid a dense mist over the city so they might reach the palace of Aeëtes without being seen by any of the people of Colchis. But when they reached the palace, Hera drove the mist away again.

Meanwhile, Eros made his way through the gray mist without being seen, and, standing in the doorway, he quickly strung his bow and drew a fresh arrow from his quiver. Then, still unseen, he ran across the threshold, glancing around sharply, and as he stood close to Jason, Aeson's son, he drew his bow wide and shot his arrow at Medea. And her heart was struck dumb with love.

When the servants had placed a banquet before them and the men had feasted on the welcome food and drink, Aeëtes addressed the sons of his daughter Chalciope, asking, "Sons of my daughter and Phrixus, come tell me who these men with you are and where you left your hollow ship."

Then Argus, because he was somewhat afraid for Jason's quest, answered politely, "Aeëtes, if you wish to know what they want,

I shall not conceal it from you. A certain king who had a keen desire to drive this man out of his native country and away from his possessions, because he was more powerful than any of the sons of Aeolus, sent him here on a hopeless voyage. Pallas Athena built his ship and Jason manned her with the bravest heroes of all Achaea and has come here to your city with the hope you will give him the fleece."

King Aeëtes was filled with anger as he listened to Argus, but Jason, the son of Aeson, calmed him by speaking to him gently: "Aeëtes, bear with us. Fate and the heartless command of a rash king brought me here. Grant us this favor we ask of you, and I shall fill all Hellas with your wondrous glory."

Then Aeëtes interrupted Jason, saying, "Stranger, you do not need to tell us all the details. I shall set a task for you as a test of your courage and strength. I have two bulls grazing on the plain of Ares that have feet of bronze and breathe forth fire. I yoke them and drive them over the rough soil of the field, ploughing as much as four acres, and I sow the furrows not with seeds of Demeter's corn but with the teeth of a fierce dragon, which spring up in the shape of armed men. Then I cut them down with my sword at once as they rise against me everywhere. I yoke the bulls in the morning and I finish harvesting by evening. And you, if you can carry through such a task, can carry off the fleece by the end of that same day to the palace of your king. But I will not give it to you before, and do not expect me to."

Jason answered the king, "Aeëtes, you hold me to your will indeed, since you are the judge. I shall undergo the trial, therefore, no matter how overpowering it is, even if it brings death to me."

Since Aeëtes had made the conditions clear, Jason rose to leave, and Augeas and Telamon went with him. As they went out of the hall, the son of Aeson stood out above the others because of his handsome appearance and grace, and the maiden Medea, holding her veil aside, watched him from the corner of her eye, and her heart burned with the first pangs of love.

Soon night drew the shadow of darkness over the earth. The sailors on the sea looked up from their ships at the Bear and the stars of Orion, and there were no longer any dogs barking in the city or any sounds at all, only silence hanging over the deepening night. But sweet sleep did not come to Medea, for in her longing for Jason many cares kept her awake.

Medea was afraid because of the great strength of the bulls, and her heart quivered within her breast, just as a sunbeam dances up and down on the wall of a house. One minute she thought she would give him a magic drug against the bulls, the next moment she thought she would not give him the charm but would herself die instead. Then she thought she would not die and would not give him the drug, but would just calmly endure her misery in silence. Then she sat down and thought over the various possibilities.

At length, swayed by the influence of Hera, Medea no longer hesitated, but she longed to have the dawn come quickly so she could give Jason the magic drug as she had planned and actually see his face before her. It was a welcome sight to her when the early light of day appeared and people began to move about the city. She put on a beautiful robe, fastened with fine brooches, and threw a silver-white veil over her lovely head.

She summoned her maids, twelve in number, and instructed them to yoke the mules to her carriage with speed, to take her to the splendid shrine of Hecate. While her handmaidens were preparing the carriage, Medea took a magic drug from its box. Then, leaving the well-paved streets of the city behind, she drove over the plain and came to the shrine.

Argus took Jason aside, away from his comrades, as soon as he learned from his brothers that Medea had set out at dawn for the sacred shrine of Hecate. Then he led him across the plain, and it was not long before Jason came in sight, just as Medea had been hoping he would. But Medea did not know what to say first, so anxious was she to say everything at once. Then she showed him the charm, and he accepted it from her gladly. She delighted in his need of her, and her heart grew warm within her, melting as dew melts upon roses warmed by the morning sun.

At length Medea began to speak to him, saying, "Listen carefully now to the way I plan to help you. In the early morning dampen this magic drug and anoint your body with it as you would with oil; and from it you will gain great courage and strength, so that you will seem the equal not only of any man but even of the immortal gods. You will not, however, feel like this for long, but only for a day.

"I shall tell you also of something else that will be helpful. As soon as you have yoked the mighty bulls and have plowed over the rough field, and when you have sown the dragon's teeth in the dark furrows and the giants begin to spring up on all sides, wait until you see them rising out of the earth in numbers. Then, without being seen, throw a boulder into their midst, and they will slaughter each other as they fight over it like hungry dogs. And so in this way, you can take the fleece and carry it off to Hellas, taking it far away from Aea, far from here. But remember, when you have returned to your home, the name of Medea, and I in turn will remember, even though you may be far away."

While she was speaking and as the tears came to her eyes, Eros overpowered Jason also, and he answered her in this way: "Indeed I am certain that never, either by night or by day, will I forget you if I escape from death and if I reach Achaea again safely and if Aeëtes does not set another task, even worse than this, in the way."

Thus they came to understand each other through gentle words, and then they parted. Jason went off in a happy frame of mind to rejoin his companions on the ship, while Medea returned to her handmaidens, who all ran toward her as she came.

In the meantime, Jason, following Medea's advice, moistened the magic drug with water and sprinkled it over his shield and his sturdy spear and sword. Next he sprinkled it on his own body, and a mighty strength, indescribable and fearless, came to him. By then the men were ready for the task, and they delayed no longer but took their places at the rowing benches and rowed on up to the plain of Ares.

As soon as the men had moored the ship, Jason jumped ashore, looking very much like Ares in some ways, and in other ways like Apollo of the golden sword. And then, from some hidden den in the earth below where they had their stalls, places filled with smoke and flame, the two bulls burst forth together, breathing fiery flames. The scorching heat surrounded Jason, striking him like a bolt of lightning, but Medea's charm kept him from harm.

Then Jason seized the tip of the horn of the bull on the right and threw it down, bringing it to its knees by a swift kick on its bronze foot. He threw the other bull to its knees in the same way, striking it with one blow as it charged at him. Aeëtes was amazed at Jason's strength. The sons of Tyndareus [Castor and Pollux], who were standing by, picked up the yoke from the ground and handed it to Jason, who fitted it tightly across the necks of the bulls.

Soon the bulls, spurred on with Jason's spear, began to move forward, and the rough earth was broken up behind them, split apart by the strength of the bulls and the rugged ploughman. Jason sowed the teeth as he ploughed, and the bulls toiled on, plodding with feet of bronze. But when a third of the day was left and the four acres had been ploughed, Jason set the bulls free from their yoke, and they ran off across the plain in fear.

Presently, earthborn men were springing up all over the field, but Jason remembered the instructions of crafty Medea. He picked up a huge round boulder and hurled it far from him and into their midst. Then he quickly crouched down behind his shield, out of sight and confident. The earthborn men, just like swift hounds, jumped all over each other, shouting and killing. They fell to the earth, their mother, struck down beneath their own spears, as pine trees or oaks are blown over by a windstorm. And then, as a fiery star shoots across the heavens, the son of Aeson fell upon the earthborn men, drawing his sword from its sheath, and mowed them down. Thus Jason cut down his crop of earthborn men, and the sun set and his task was finished.

Aeëtes, in truth, sat in his palace throughout the night, his heart burning with anger over the result of the test, nor was he at all certain that it had been carried out without help from his daughters. And Hera filled Medea's heart with the agony of fear, for she soon realized clearly that the help she had given Jason had not escaped the notice of her father—she also feared her handmaidens might reveal what they knew. And indeed she would have put an end to her life without delay by taking a poison drug, if the goddess Hera had not encouraged her, distracted as she was, to take flight with the sons of Phrixus.

Then, with tears running down her cheeks, she left the palace and ran barefoot along the narrow streets, holding her cloak over her forehead with one hand to hide her pretty face and lifting up the hem of her skirts with the other hand. She quickly passed beyond the walls of the city without being recognized by any of the guards.

Medea hurried on in her flight and was happily relieved when she reached the bank of the river and saw on the shore opposite the glow of the fire that Jason and his men kept burning all through the night in celebration of Jason's victory. Then she called out clearly in the darkness to Phrontis, the youngest of the sons of Phrixus, and he and his brothers, and Jason also, recognized her voice. Their companions were silent with amazement when they learned that it was really Medea. Medea called three times, and three times Phrontis called back in answer, while the men kept rowing swiftly toward her.

Before they had even cast the ropes ashore, Jason jumped to the bank quickly, and close behind him came Phrontis and Argus, two of Phrixus' sons. Medea threw her arms around their knees and begged, "Save me, friends, have pity on me. Save yourselves, too, from Aeëtes, and I shall give you the golden fleece by putting the dragon that guards it to sleep for you."

Raising her to her feet, Jason comforted her in his arms, saying, "My dear, let Zeus himself be my witness, and Hera his queen, that I shall take you to my own house as my wedded wife, when we have traveled safely back to the land of Hellas."

Then Jason took Medea's right hand in his, and she urged them to row in haste to the sacred grove nearby so that they might seize the fleece while it was still night and carry it off in spite of Aeëtes. Then, taking her aboard, they shoved off from the river bank at once. At the hour when hunters begin to drive sleep from their eyes, Jason and Medea set foot ashore at a grassy place, which they call the Ram's Bed.

Nearby and black from smoke was the base of the altar that Phrixus had erected to Zeus at the time when he sacrificed the golden fleece, as Hermes had told him to do. Jason and Medea went along a path to the sacred grove, making their way to the great oak tree on which the fleece was hanging, gleaming like a cloud that is tinged with red from the flaming splendor of the rising sun. But directly before them, stretching out his long neck and hissing fiercely as his sharp, sleepless eyes saw them approaching, was the dragon.

Just as endless billows of smoke whirl up from smoldering logs, so the monstrous creature rolled his boundless scale-covered coils along the ground. But as he undulated toward them, Medea stood before his eyes calling with her sweet voice on Sleep to come to her aid and bind the monster with his spell. Then, singing a chant, she sprinkled over his eyes a potent charm, and as the powerful scent of the drug spread all about he stretched out in sleep.

Medea called out to Jason, and he quickly seized the golden fleece from the oak. Then at last Jason urged her to start back to the ship, and she left the shady grove of Ares. Dawn was spreading over the earth when they joined the others again, and the young men looked in wonder at the great fleece shining as brilliantly as the lightning of Zeus. They all came forward, each one eager to touch it and take it in his hands, but Aeson's son kept them from it and laid a newly made mantle over it.

Then Jason led Medea to the stern and gave her a seat before he addressed his men, saying, "Do not delay any longer, my friends, the return to our homeland. For now the quest for which we undertook this grievous voyage and endured painful suffering is over. It has been successfully accomplished through the wise counsel of this maiden. I intend to take her back home with me to become my wedded wife."

The men shouted their eager approval, and, drawing his sword from its sheath, Jason cut the cables from the ship's stern. Then he went and stood near Medea, beside the helmsman Ancaeus, and the ship sped forward under the oars.

From *Argonautica* II, 1260–1285; III, 6–1407; and IV, 6–210

Atalanta

Atalanta was a contemporary of Meleager of Calydon, who, as a youth, had gone with Jason on the expedition of the Argonauts. Atalanta had taken part in the hunt for the Calydonian Boar and it was she who wounded the boar before it was killed by Meleager. She is comparable in a number of ways to the goddess Diana, especially in her love of the woods and the hunt.

In some accounts Atalanta is the daughter of Iasus of Arcadia and in others her father was Schoeneus of Boeotia. The latter was a son of King Athamas and thus a half brother of Phrixus and Helle.

As told in Latin verse by Ovid

WHEN VENUS' son Cupid was kissing his mother, he, without realizing it, pricked her breast with an arrow that protruded from his quiver. The injured goddess pushed her son away from her, but the wound had gone quite deep, although she herself did not notice this when she first saw it. Then, captivated by a handsome mortal, she no longer cared for Cythera or Paphos, but she preferred Adonis even to the heavens. She clung to him, she was his constant companion, and she—who was always in the habit of lounging in the shade and protecting her beauty by taking good care of it—now roamed over the mountain ridges and through the forests and over stony places full of brambles with her skirts pulled up above her knees in the manner of Diana.

She warned you also, Adonis, to fear wild animals, saying, "Be brave against timid creatures, but boldness against bold creatures is not safe." When he questioned her, she replied, "I shall tell you a tale and you will wonder at the strangeness of a crime of old." Thus she began her story.

"Perhaps you have heard the story of the girl who outran the swiftest of men in footraces. The story is not an empty legend, for she did in truth outrun them, and, in addition, one could not say whether she was more exceptional for her reputation as a runner or for her beauty. When she consulted the oracle of Apollo at Delphi concerning a husband, the oracle answered, 'You have no need, Atalanta, for a husband. Avoid marriage. But you will not escape, however, for you, although continuing to live, will be deprived of yourself.'

"Alarmed by the god's oracle, she lived unwed in the depths of a forest and drove away the numerous suitors who sought her hand by setting a condition for them. 'I cannot be won,' she said, 'unless I am first defeated in a race. Run a race against me. The reward of the swift will be marriage; death will be the price paid by the slow. Let these be the terms of the contest.' She was indeed harsh, but so great was the power of her beauty that a large and daring throng of suitors came to contend with her even under these conditions.

"Hippomenes sat watching the unevenly matched races and said, 'Why would anyone seek a wife under such disadvantages?' Thus he condemned the excessive eagerness of the other men. But as soon as he saw the beauty of the girl when she tossed aside her clothing, he lifted up his hands in amazement, saying, 'Forgive me, you whom I condemned just now. I did not know then how valuable was the prize you sought.'

"As he praised Atalanta he felt the early flames of love. He hoped that no one of the youths would outrun her, yet in his jealousy he feared someone might. 'But why do I leave the chances of this running contest untried?' he wondered. 'The gods themselves help those who are bold.' Even as Hippomenes was musing thus, the girl flew by on winged feet. He wondered at her beauty, heightened now by running, and watched her as she reached the goal and was crowned winner with the wreath of victory. The men she had defeated groaned as they paid the promised death penalty.

"Hippomenes, however, not deterred by their fate, stepped forward and, looking directly at Atalanta, said, 'Why do you seek an easy victory by overcoming the slow of foot? Race with me, and, if Fortune makes me the winner, you will not be disgraced by losing to such a one as I am. My father is Megareus of Onchestus, and his grandfather is Neptune. I, therefore, am the great-grandson of the king of the seas, nor is my manliness any less great than my lineage. Or if I am defeated, you will have gained a great and memorable reputation by surpassing Hippomenes.'

"While he was speaking, Atalanta watched him kindly, and she was not sure whether she wanted to lose or win. And so she mused thus, half to herself, half aloud, 'What unjust god wants to destroy this handsome youth and urges him to seek marriage at the risk of his life? I am not, in my opinion, worth that much. I am not moved by his handsome appearance—although I could be—but by the fact that he is still a boy. He himself does not move me, only his youth. What if he does love me and believes marriage to me worth such a price? While you can, stranger, go back home and abandon the idea of a marriage that is stained with blood. No girl would be unwilling to marry you. Is this man also to die and suffer death undeservedly as the price for his love? I wish that you would change your mind; or, since you are so foolhardy, I wish you were swifter! Ah, poor Hippomenes, I wish you had never seen me! You deserved to live.'

"So she spoke, and she was touched by the first signs of love, and, not realizing what was happening, she loved but was not aware she loved. Meanwhile, her father and the people were calling for the races to continue, and Hippomenes called on me for help as he prayed, 'I pray that Venus may aid me in my daring attempt and further the love she has instilled in me.' A friendly breeze wafted his entreaty to me, and I was moved, I confess. There is a meadow—the natives call it the field of Tamasus—in the land of Cyprus, which the people of ancient times dedicated to me. In the meadow is a tree shining with golden foliage, its branches rustling with yellow gold. By chance I was just coming from there, carrying three golden apples, and, without anyone seeing me, I gave these to Hippomenes and told him how to use them.

"When the trumpets gave the signal, they both streaked forth headlong from the starting place and skimmed over the sandy track on swift feet. The shouting and cheers of the spectators gave the young man encouragement. Oh, how often, when she could have passed him, she tarried and then, with a lingering look, unwillingly left him behind. His breathing was weary, his mouth dry, and the goal was still far away. Then at last he rolled one of the three golden apples toward her.

"The girl was surprised, and, in her eagerness for the shining apple, she turned from the course and picked up the rolling fruit of gold. Hippomenes passed her, and the onlookers applauded loudly. She made up the time she had lost by running fast, and again she left the youth behind her. Again, delayed by the tossing of a second apple, she caught up to and passed him. Finally the last part of the course remained. 'Now,' he said, 'be with me now, goddess, bestower of this gift,' as he quickly threw the shining golden apple well to the side of the field, so that she would take longer to return.

"The girl seemed to hesitate about going after it, but I compelled her to pick it up, and I added weight to the apple, hindering her equally by the heaviness of her burden and her delay. And to end my story with the race, he passed the girl, and as the victor, carried off his prize.

"Was I not worthy of thanks; was I not worthy, Adonis, of an offering of incense? But, forgetting me, he showed no gratitude, burned no incense. Then, suddenly stirred to anger and hurt by their forgetfulness, so that I would not be treated with indifference in the future I planned to make an example of them, and I spurred myself on against them both. They were passing a temple hidden in the deep woods, which renowned Echion had erected long ago to the mother of the gods in fulfillment of a vow, and the length of their journey forced them to rest. There, aroused by my divine will, an uncontrollable desire to lie with her overcame Hippomenes. Near the temple there was a dark and sheltered corner, like a cave and formed from the native porous stone—a place made sacred by ancient religious rites, where a priest had set many wooden statues of the gods of old. Hippomenes entered this place, and he desecrated the sanctuary by forbidden lust. The holy images averted their eyes, and the tower-crowned Mother [Cybele] hesitated on the point of plunging the sinful couple into the Stygian waters, since that punishment seemed light. Instead, therefore, tawny manes began to conceal the smoothness of their necks, their fingers and toes curved into claws, their arms became legs, their whole weight was centered in their chests. They brushed the sandy ground with tails; their expressions were fierce, and they uttered roars in place of words. They frequented the forests as their marriage chamber, and, lions now, terrifying to others, they were broken to the bit in submission to the bridle of Cybele. And so, my dear one, shun, I pray you, these animals and all the other wild beasts that do not turn in flight but show their breasts to battle, lest your manliness be the destruction of us both."

From *Metamorphoses* X, 525–707

Orpheus

Orpheus—by some accounts the son of a Thracian king, and by others the son of Apollo and the Muse Calliope—had accompanied Jason and the Argonauts to Colchis. He was married to Eurydice after his return from that expedition.

Many of the details of the myth of Orpheus are found in the accounts of Aeschylus and Euripides, and in numerous representations in art as far-reaching as architectural sculpture at Delphi and wall paintings in the Catacombs.

Orphism, a religious cult that developed around the worship of Orpheus, continued well into Christian times. The Orphic Mysteries were based on the doctrine of the need to purify the soul of guilt according to the religious rites said to have been initiated by Orpheus. Plato and other Greek philosophers set forth a discussion of a number of the concepts of Orphism, including punishment and purification, the transmigration of souls, and the afterlife.

As told in Latin verse by Ovid

HYMEN MADE his way to the shores of Thrace, for Orpheus had summoned him there—although it was to be in vain. He came indeed, but he brought neither festive words nor joyful faces nor a happy omen. The torch he held kept hissing with smoke that brought tears to the eyes, while no amount of waving could make it burn. The outcome was even worse than the omen. While the new bride, accompanied by a throng of naiads, was wandering through the grass, she fell dead from a snakebite in her heel.

Her husband, the Thracian bard, mourned her for a long time in the world of the living, and then, lest he leave even the world of the dead untried, he dared to descend to the world of Styx by the gateway of Taenarum in search of her. Passing through the shades and shadows of the dead, he came to Proserpina and her husband, the lord and master of the gloomy realm of the spirits. Then, plucking his lyre in accompaniment, he addressed them in song: "O rulers of the world below the earth, to which all of us who are mortals return at length, I have not journeyed here to see the dark regions of Tartarus. The reason for my journey is my wife, into whom a snake she had stepped on poured his venom, taking her life in the years of her youth.

"I tried to bear this grief—I do not deny I tried—but Love overcame me. This god is well-known in the upper world. I don't know whether he is known here too, but, if the story of the kidnapping of Proserpina is true, I assume that Cupid joined you in love also. I beg you, restore the life of Eurydice, the life cut short too soon. We all come to this kingdom in the end; this is our final home, and you hold the longest reign over the human race. She, too, when she has lived out the full number of her years, will be yours by right. I ask only to have her in the meantime. But if the fates deny this favor to me, I am resolved not to return to the upper world, and you may, instead, take pleasure in the death of both of us."

As the bloodless spirits listened to Orpheus' words, sung to the music of his lyre, they wept. Tantalus did not try to reach the waters receding from him, Ixion's wheel stood still, and you, Sisyphus, sat down upon your stone. Then for the first time, the report is, the cheeks of the Furies were wet with tears, so overcome were they by his song.

Neither the queen nor the king of the lower regions could bear to deny his request, and they summoned Eurydice. She was among the newly arrived shades of the dead, and she walked with a slow step because of her wounded foot. Thracian Orpheus was given back his wife, and he also accepted the condition that he not turn his head to look back at her until he had passed beyond the valley of Avernus, or the gift would be useless.

They started up along the path through the deep silence, climbing a dark hill, misty and thick with clouds. They were not far from the edge of the upper world when he, fearing she might not be there and eager to see her, turned his head in love. At once she slipped back away from him, and, stretching out her arms striving to reach him and hold him, she, unfortunate as she was, grasped nothing but the yielding air. And now, dying a second time, she spoke no word of complaint against her husband—for of what might she complain except that she was loved?—and uttered a final "Farewell," which he was scarcely able to hear, and sank back out of sight.

Orpheus was stunned by this second death of his wife. Though he prayed to cross into Hades a second time, the ferryman denied his vain wish, and for seven days he sat on the bank of the Styx without washing or tasting food. Grief and mental anguish and tears of sorrow were his nourishment. Then, lamenting the cruelty of the gods of Erebus, he went back to lofty Rhodope in Thrace.

Three times the sun had completed a year and had reached watery Pisces, while Orpheus kept himself apart from the love of all women. Many women felt a love for him and sought to win the love of the bard. And as many grieved when their love was repulsed, while he gave his thoughts to young boys in the springtime of life and the early flower of youth.

There was a hill, and atop the hill was a broad field green with grass but without shade. When the heaven-born bard sat down there and played his sweet-sounding lyre, shade trees came to that place. Among their number was the cone-shaped cypress—now a tree, but once a boy dear to that god who controls the strings of the lyre and the bow, Apollo.

The bard Orpheus was seated in the grove he had brought to the hilltop, amid a gathering of wild animals and birds. Then, when he tested the chords by striking them with his thumb and heard that the different notes were in harmony of tone, he began to sing this song: "With thoughts of Jupiter, O Muse Calliope, my mother, inspire my song. I have often sung before of the might of Jupiter, but now I must sing a lighter song."

While the Thracian bard charmed the trees and wild animals with his music, and while they gathered around him to listen, behold, the frenzied women of Thrace caught sight of Orpheus from the top of a hill, and one cried, "See, see, there is the one who scorns us!" Then she hurled a spear at Apollo's bard as he sang, but it was buried in foliage and left a mark without wounding him. Another's weapon was a stone, which was overpowered in mid-air by the melody of his song harmonizing with the lyre and fell before his feet like a suppliant begging forgiveness for its daring intent.

But the mad attack grew bolder, for all restraint was gone and wild fury reigned. Indeed, all of their weapons, spellbound by Orpheus' music, would have been harmless, but the loud clamor of the bacchantes drowned out the sound of his lyre. Then, at length, the rocks grew red with the blood of the bard they could no longer hear, as the women rushed at him, some throwing clods of earth, others branches stripped from trees, some hurling stones.

The sorrowful birds wept for you, Orpheus, the wild beasts mourned you, and the stones and the trees that had gathered so often to listen to your songs wept for you. And they say the rivers, too, swelled their banks from their own tears.

From *Metamorphoses* X, 1–152 and XI, 1–48

Midas

Bacchus was angered because Orpheus had been killed by Thracian bacchantes. Because of this he left Thrace to go to Asia Minor, where he was held in high esteem. Midas, who was king of Phrygia at that time, was said to have been taught the religious mysteries of Bacchus by Orpheus.

In most accounts Midas is the son of King Gordius of Phrygia, who tied the Gordian knot. Phrygia was the center for the worship of Cybele, a goddess of nature and fertility who was known as the Great Mother and was later identified with the Greek goddess Rhea. Cybele was said by some to have been the mother of Midas, an example of the frequent merging of the myths and cults of the Asiatic and Mediterranean peoples.

As told in Latin verse by Ovid

BACCHUS DESERTED the countryside of Thrace and sought out the vineyards of his well-liked Mount Tmolus and the Pactolus River, although at that time it was not golden nor was it envied for its precious sands.

His usual company of satyrs and priestesses thronged around Bacchus, but Silenus was missing. Some Phrygian countrypeople found him, staggering from the burden of his age and too much wine, and took him to King Midas. As soon as Midas recognized the friend and companion of Bacchus' sacred rites, in honor of his guest's arrival, he happily held a festival, lasting twice five days and nights. Then the king went gladly to the land of Lydia and returned Silenus to his young charge, Bacchus.

Rejoicing that he had recovered his foster father, the god gave Midas the pleasant—but destined to be harmful—reward of choosing a gift. Midas, about to make a bad choice, asked, "Grant that whatever I touch may be turned to gleaming gold." Bacchus agreed to the king's choice and granted his wish, although it was going to bring harm, and felt sad that he had not chosen better.

Midas, the Berecyntian hero, went away happy and rejoiced in what would prove a misfortune, and tested the worth of the gift by touching several objects. Then, scarcely trusting himself, he broke a branch, green with foliage, from a low oak tree; the branch became gold. He picked up a rock from the ground; the rock also turned yellow with gold. He then touched a clod of earth; the earthen lump became a nugget of gold at his powerful touch. He plucked ears of ripe corn; his harvest was golden. He held an apple picked from a tree; you would think the Hesperides had given it to him. If he reached toward a high door with his fingers, the door seemed to gleam. Even when he washed his hands in clear water, the golden water flowing off his hands might have deceived Danaë.* Scarcely could his heart contain his hopes, that all he touched would turn to gold.

Servants placed tables laden with meat and filled with bread before him as he rejoiced. Then indeed, if he touched the gifts of Ceres, the grain became rigid, or if he prepared to bite into the meat with eager teeth, a piece of gold pressed against his mouth as it drew near. He mixed wine with fresh water; you might have seen liquid gold running through his mouth.

Astonished at this new and evil turn, both rich and wretched, he wished to escape from his wealth, and he hated the gift he had prayed for only a short time earlier. No abundance relieved his hunger; dry thirst burned his throat, and, as he deserved, he was tortured by the now hated gold. Raising his hands and splendid arms toward the heavens, he begged, "Forgive me, Bacchus, Lenaean father, for I have sinned. But pity me, I pray, and rescue me from this splendid evil."

The divine will of the gods is merciful. Bacchus restored Midas to his former state, because he confessed he had sinned, and took from him the gift he had given him in fulfillment of the agreement. "And lest you might remain encircled by the gold you desired, go," said Bacchus, "go to the river near the great city

* Zeus, appearing to Danaë as a shower of gold, had made her the mother of Perseus.

Sardis and make your way upstream against its flowing waters along the Lydian ridge of Mount Pactolus until you come to the source of the river. And plunge your head in its foaming spring where it spouts forth at full force and wash off not only your body but wash away your guilt at the same time."

The king went to the river as he was commanded. His power of changing things to gold colored the river and passed from his mortal body into the waters of the stream. And even now its sands, which took on the seeds of that metal and were colored by the sodden lumps, are hard with the ancient gold.

From *Metamorphoses* XI, 85–145

Philemon and Baucis

The elderly couple Philemon and Baucis are unidentified except for their names and the fact that they lived in Phrygia. Their story was told by Lelex—whom Ovid calls "the hero of Troezen"—when Theseus and his companions were visiting the river god Achelous and after Pirithous had expressed doubt about the power of the gods.

As told in Latin verse by Ovid

LELEX, A man of mature wisdom and years, spoke thus: "The power of heaven is measureless and has no limit, and whatever the gods will is done. And so that you may have no doubts, in the Phrygian hills an oak stands beside a linden tree, and a low wall surrounds them. I myself have seen the place.

"Not far from this spot is a marsh, once a habitable land, but now waters frequented by birds and waterfowl. To this place came Jupiter in the guise of a mortal, and Mercury the staff-bearer, grandson of Atlas, had laid aside his sandals and had come with his father.

"A thousand homes they approached, seeking a place to rest; a thousand homes were bolted against them. One home, however, took them in at last—a small one indeed, thatched with straw and marsh reeds. But the devout old couple, Baucis and Philemon, of equal age, had been wed in that cottage in the time of their youth. In that cottage they had grown old together, and they had made their poverty seem light by facing it and bearing it with a spirit of contentment. It made no difference whether one asked for masters or servants there, for the two old people were the entire household—they were equally servants and masters together.

"Therefore, when the gods came to their humble home and, bending their heads, entered the lowly doorway, the aged man invited them to rest themselves on a bench that he pulled up for them and over which Baucis quickly threw a homespun covering. Then she stirred up the warm ashes on the hearth and rekindled yesterday's fire, nourishing it with leaves and dry bark, and blew it into flames with her feeble breath. Next she stripped the outer leaves from the cabbage that her husband had cut from the well-watered garden.

"Philemon, with a forked stick, lifted down a smoked side of bacon hanging on a smoke-blackened beam, cut off a small piece of the meat they had saved for so long, and set it to cook in boiling water. Meanwhile, they passed the time of waiting with talk.

"The old woman, with her skirts tucked up and her hands trembling with age, laid the table. But one of the three legs was too short, and she made it even with a piece of broken pottery. After this had corrected the slant, she wiped the leveled table with fresh mint. Then she placed green and black olives—the fruit of the chaste goddess Minerva—on the table, and autumnal cornel-cherries pickled in the brine of wine, also endives and radishes, a piece of cheese, and eggs lightly cooked in the low embers, all served in earthen dishes.

"There was only a short interval before the hearth sent forth its steaming food, and wine that was made but recently was brought out. Then, setting this aside, a way was made for the dessert. Here were nuts, here dried figs and dates, plums, and fragrant apples in wide baskets, and grapes gathered from the purple vines; a clear honeycomb stood in the center of the table. In addition to all this, kind faces and sincere and generous hospitality surrounded the table.

"Meanwhile, they saw the wine bowl was being refilled of its own accord as soon as it became empty, and the wine was supplied anew by itself. Astonished by this strange sight and lifting up their hands in prayer, both Baucis and Philemon, trembling alike, begged forgiveness for the scanty and simply prepared meal.

"The aged couple had one goose, the guardian of their tiny farm, and this they prepared to kill in honor of their divine guests. The goose, however, swift of wing, wore out the old people, slow with age, and escaped them for a long time, until at length he seemed to have fled to the gods themselves for refuge. The gods would not allow the bird to be killed. 'We are gods,' they said, 'and the wicked people living around you will pay the penalty they deserve; but it shall be granted to you to escape this disaster, if you will but leave your house and come with us as far as the slopes of that high mountain close by.'

"They both obeyed, and, supported by walking sticks, they struggled step by step up the long slope. When they were as far from the summit of the mountain as an arrow can reach in a single shot, they looked back and saw everything covered with water and only their own house remaining clear.

"While they wondered on these things, while they wept at the fate of their neighbors, that old cottage, small even for its two masters, was turned into a temple. Columns took the place of the wooden props, the thatch turned yellow, and a golden roof appeared, and also doors embellished with relief work and pavement of marble on the ground.

"Then Jupiter, the son of Saturn, spoke to them gently: 'Ask, O righteous old man, and you also, a wife worthy of this fine husband, for whatever you wish.'

"When he had spoken a few words with Baucis, Philemon revealed to the gods their common decision: 'We ask to be the priest and priestess and to watch over your temple. And, since we have passed our lives together in harmony, may the same final hour carry us both off and may I never see the tomb of my wife nor be buried by her.'

"Fulfillment followed their request. They were the guardians of the temple as long as their lives lasted. At the end, when, weakened by the years and their great age, they were standing by chance before the steps of the temple and were recalling all that had happened at this spot, Baucis saw that Philemon was putting forth leaves, and the old man Philemon saw that Baucis also was becoming leafy. And even as the treetops were growing over both their faces, as long as they still had the power of speech they exchanged words. And they cried out together, 'Farewell, O life's mate,' just as the branches hid their mouths and closed over them.

"The people of Bithynia [Phrygia] still point out the place where the trees stand side by side, growing from a double trunk."

From *Metamorphoses* VIII, 617–720

The Judgment of Paris

Paris, a son of King Priam of Troy and Hecuba, had been ex-
posed on Mount Ida at birth because his mother had dreamed she
would bear a firebrand that would set Troy aflame. Paris, who was
also called Alexander or Alexandros, was brought up by shepherds
and loved the nymph Oenone.

The golden apple does not appear as part of the myth before
Lucian and other later writers.

As told in Greek prose by Apollodorus

ERIS THREW an apple to be contended for by Hera and Athena
and Aphrodite as the prize for beauty. Then Zeus instructed
Hermes to lead them to Alexander on Mount Ida, so that he might
decide which one was the most beautiful.

The goddesses promised to give Alexander gifts. Hera, in truth,
promised that if she were judged the most beautiful of all she
would make him ruler over all men; Athena promised him victory in battle; Aphrodite promised him marriage to Helen. He
chose Aphrodite as the most beautiful and then sailed off to
Sparta, where he was entertained as a guest by Menelaus. On the
tenth day, however, when Menelaus went away to Crete to pay
his last respects to his grandfather Catreus, Alexander prevailed
upon Helen to leave with him. And so, leaving her nine-year-old
daughter Hermione behind, Helen took most of her possessions
with her and sailed away with him under cover of night.

Hera, however, sent a severe storm upon them, forcing them to
put into port at Sidon. Because he was afraid they might be followed, Alexander remained in Phoenicia and in Cyprus for quite
some time. Then, when he believed the danger of pursuit was
over, he went on to Troy with Helen. Some people, however, say

that Helen was carried off by Hermes, according to the instructions of Zeus, and taken to Egypt. They also say that there she was given to Proteus, the king of the Egyptians, to protect and that Alexander arrived at Troy with only a phantom of Helen shaped from clouds.

When Menelaus learned that Helen had been carried off, he went to Mycenae to urge Agamemnon to gather together an army to go against Troy and to raise troops throughout Greece. He himself, sending a herald to each one of the kings, reminded them of the oath they had taken to come to his aid in case anyone wronged him in regard to his marriage. And he advised each of them to watch out for the safety of his own wife, telling them that the insult was shared in common by all of Greece.

From *Epitome* III, 2–6; *Bibliotheca* III, x, 9

Hector and Achilles

The seer Calchas had prophesied that Troy could not be captured without Achilles. But in the tenth year of the war Achilles withdrew from the fighting in anger against Agamemnon, who had taken his captive maiden, Briseïs, from him. During the period when Achilles was not fighting in the war, Hector and the Trojans were victorious.

The story of the rivalry of Hector and Achilles forms a large part of the subject matter of the Iliad, *through which it runs like a thread.*

Although Achilles does not meet his death in the Iliad, *Hector predicted that he would be killed at the Scaean Gate by Paris and Apollo.*

As told in Greek verse by Homer

TELL ME now, Muses who have your homes on Olympus—for you are goddesses, and you have the power, and you know all things, whereas we hear only rumor and we do not know anything—who were the leaders and captains of the Danaans. Indeed I could not mention or name all the throng of men, not even if I had in fact ten tongues, and ten mouths, and an untiring voice, and a heart of bronze within me if the Olympian Muses, daughters of aegis-bearing Zeus, did not recall to my memory all those who came to Ilium.

Now, in truth, all those who lived in Pelasgian Argos and who inhabited Phthia and Hellas, the land of beautiful women, and who were called Myrmidons and Hellenes and Achaeans had as the captain of their fifty ships Achilles—swift-footed, godlike Achilles.

The leader of the Trojans was noble Hector of the flashing

helmet, the son of Priam, and he commanded by far the largest number and the finest of the Trojan troops pressing forward with their spears.

Hector of the flashing helmet, going on his way, quickly came to his own splendid house, but he did not find white-armed Andromache in the halls—for she had gone with her child and well dressed handmaiden to watch from the top of the wall, where she stood weeping and sobbing. Then Hector, when he did not find his fine wife at home, spoke to the maidservants, saying, "Come now, maidservants, tell me the truth. Where did white-armed Andromache go when she left the house? Did she go to the house of any of my sisters or my brothers' well-dressed wives or to Athena's temple, where the other fair-haired Trojan women are seeking to win over the revered goddess?"

Then one of the busy housemaids answered him, saying, "Hector, since you bid us indeed to speak the truth, she went to the great wall of Ilium, because she heard that the Trojans were suffering defeat and the Achaeans were winning a great victory. She, therefore, hurried off to the city wall in a frenzy, and the nurse went with her, carrying the child."

Thus she spoke, and Hector ran from the house back over the same route, along the well-built streets. When he came near the gate as he hurried through the great city—the Scaean Gate, from which he intended to go out onto the plain—then his highly gifted wife came running to meet him—Andromache, the daughter of great-hearted Eëtion, who was the ruler of the people of Cilicia, for it was indeed his daughter who was wed to bronze-armored Hector. With her came her handmaiden carrying the child in her arms—a tender child, just a baby, the beloved son of Hector, resembling a lovely star—whom Hector called Scamandrius but others called Astyanax.

Then, in truth, Hector smiled as he looked at his son without speaking, and Andromache clung close to him, weeping, and slipped her hand in his as she spoke to him, saying, "My good Hector, this spirit of yours will consume you. And you do not take pity on your infant son or on me, your poor wife, who will soon be your widow; for soon all the Achaeans will rush upon you and kill you. Indeed it would be better for me to die if you are lost to me, for there will no longer be any comfort for me when you have gone to meet your fate, only grief.

"I have no father, no queenly mother. For, in truth, mighty Achilles slew my father and destroyed the great city of the Cilicians. And my seven brothers all went to the house of Hades in a single day, all slain by mighty Achilles. As for my mother, he brought her here along with all the spoils he had taken, but he set her free again after he had received an enormous ransom. And then Artemis, who delights in arrows, struck her down in her father's halls. Hector, you are now father and mother to me, and brother also, even as you are my splendid husband. So come now, I beg you; take pity on us and stay here with us on the wall, lest you make your child an orphan and your wife a widow."

Then great Hector of the shining helmet answered her: "In truth, I also am anxious about all these things, my wife, but I would feel very deep shame before the Trojans and their long-robed wives if I should avoid battle and keep away from it like a coward. Nor does my heart permit this. For I know this well, deep in my mind and heart, that there will come a day when sacred Ilium will be destroyed, and also Priam and the soldiers of Priam armed with good ashen spears. But the sorrow of the Trojans that will follow in the wake of this does not distress me as much as does the thought of the grief you will feel when some one of the bronze-clad Achaeans will drag you off in tears, will take away your freedom. But let me die and let a mound of earth cover me before I hear the sound of your cries as they carry you off."

So spoke glorious Hector, and he stretched out his arms to take the boy, but the child shrank back into the bosom of his nurse crying, frightened by the appearance of his loving father and alarmed at the bronze helmet with its crest of horsehair. Then his loving father and queenly mother laughed aloud, and straightway glorious Hector took off his glistening helmet and set it on the ground. Then he kissed his dear son as he took him into his arms playfully, and he called on Zeus and the other gods in prayer:

"Zeus and all of the gods, grant that this child, my son, may one day become, even as I am, foremost among the Trojans, and as strong and brave, and that he may rule over Ilium with valor.

And one day may someone say, 'And indeed he is far better than his father,' and may his mother feel pride in her heart."

As he ended his prayer, he placed his child in his beloved wife's arms, and she held him close in her embrace, smiling through her tears. And her husband was moved to pity when he noticed this, and he caressed her cheek with his hand and spoke, saying, "Dear one, do not let your heart be too troubled over me, for there is not any man who will send me down into Hades before the time destined for me. But I believe that no man has ever escaped his fate, whether he might be a cowardly man or a brave man, once he has been born. So go back home and occupy yourself with your own work, your loom and your distaff, and bid your handmaidens to set about their work also, and let war be the care of men, of all men—and myself especially—who live in Ilium."

Thus, in truth, spoke glorious Hector. And then he picked up his helmet with its crest of horsehair, and his dear wife walked away in the direction of their home, turning often to look back while the tears streamed down her cheeks. And soon she reached the well-built palace of Hector, victor over men, and found her many handmaidens within, and she aroused tears of lamentation among them all. Thus indeed, even while he lived, they grieved for Hector in his own house, for they feared that he would not return home again from the war or escape violence at the hands of the Achaeans.

Then shortly, Paris overtook great Hector just as he was about to turn and leave the spot where he had been talking with his wife, and glorious Hector went out through the gate quickly, and his brother Paris went with him. They were both eager indeed in their hearts for war and battle. And just as a god gives a fair breeze to sailors who have been longing for it, even so, in truth, did they appear to the anxious Trojans.

Meanwhile, Patroclus, the brave son of Menoetius, was taking care of the wounded Eurypylus in the camp, but the rest of the Argives and Trojans were fighting on in full force. And indeed the Danaans' ditch and the broad wall that they had built to defend their ships could not withstand attack much longer. At that time the battle and the cries of war were raging about the ramparts, and the Argives, subdued by the lash of Zeus, were penned up next to their hollow ships and were held in check from fear of Hector, the mighty source of terror. And Hector himself, moreover, went into the battle as he always did, like a whirlwind.

Everywhere now the walls and fortifications were spattered with the blood of men from both armies, Trojans and Achaeans. But still they were not able to put the Achaeans to flight, for they held firm. Thus indeed was their fighting, and the war stretched in the balance until the time when Zeus granted victorious glory to Hector, son of Priam, who became the first to dash inside the wall of the Achaeans. Then he gave a piercing shout, calling to the Trojans, "Move fast, Trojan horsemen. Break through the wall of the Argives and hurl blazing firebrands upon their ships."

Thus he urged them on, and when they heard him they all made straight for the wall as one man. And Hector picked up a rock that happened to be lying in front of the gate and was wide at the bottom but sharp at the top. He carried the stone right up to the doors that protected the solid and close-fitting gates. They were high double doors, and two crossbars on the inside held them closed, and a single bolt fastened them together. Hector went up very close, and then, taking a firm stand, he struck them directly in the middle, standing with his legs well apart so that his throw might not lack power, and he broke apart both hinges.

And the stone went through to the other side before it fell, and the gates groaned, and the bars did not hold. The doors were sent flying in every direction under the force of the stone, and glorious Hector at once bounded in, his face looking like sudden nightfall. He glistened with fearful bronze and held a spear in each hand. Certainly no one who met with him could have held him back when he jumped in through the gates—no one except one of the gods. Then, whirling around toward the crowd of Trojans, he called to them to scale the wall, and they obeyed his command. At once some scaled the wall, while others poured in through the gate. The Danaans fled in panic among the hollow ships, and the din of battle rose without pause.

Hector indeed did not linger among the throng of Trojan fighting men, but just as a tawny eagle swoops down on a flock of birds feeding at a river's edge, just so he made straight for a dark-prowed ship. And Zeus pushed him on from behind with his mighty hand and urged his soldiers forward with him. Then a bitter battle raged beside the ships, and the black earth streamed with blood. And when Hector had taken a hold on the stern of a ship, he did not let go but grasped it firmly with his hand and shouted to the Trojans, "Bring fire, and raise the war cry all together. Now Zeus is granting us a day that will repay us for everything—today we take the ships."

While they fought thus around the well-equipped ships, Patroclus went to Achilles, the prince of his people, shedding hot tears and saying, "O Achilles, son of Peleus, by far the mightiest of the Achaeans, do not be angry with me, for great distress has overwhelmed the Achaeans. For indeed all those who were always the bravest are now lying beside the ships, struck down by arrows or wounded by spears. Odysseus, famous for his spear, has been wounded, and Agamemnon also. Permit me to put your armor upon my shoulders so that the Trojans may mistake me for you and stop the battle, and the warlike sons of the Achaeans may catch their breath, for they are weary. Certainly we could easily, if we were refreshed, drive the exhausted Trojans back to their city and away from our ships and huts."

Thus Patroclus spoke, beseeching Achilles. But he was a foolhardy man, for he was in reality begging for what would be his own evil death and fate.

Tell me now, O Muses who dwell on Olympus, how fire was first started among the ships of the Achaeans. Hector took his stand right in front of Ajax and struck his ashen spear hard with his own great sword and broke it off completely. Then Ajax knew deep in his noble heart—and shuddered at the thought—that this was the work of the gods and that Zeus who thunders on high had chosen victory for the Trojans. Then he fell back, away from the falling arrows, and the Trojans threw fire without ceasing onto the swift ship, and at once unquenchable flames engulfed her.

Thus did fire envelop the stern, and Achilles slapped his thighs and spoke to Patroclus: "Go now, good Patroclus, master rider. Indeed I see the flames of ravaging fire among the ships. Put on my armor quickly, and I shall assemble the men." So he commanded him, and Patroclus armed himself with the glistening bronze. But he did not take the spear of Achilles, the peerless son of Aeacus, a great heavy spear. This alone he left behind, for no other one of the Achaeans was able to wield this spear—no one, only Achilles himself. And Achilles then, going to all the huts, alerted all his Myrmidons to arm themselves, and they streamed forth like ravenous wolves.

Patroclus called forth the strength and spirit of every man, and they fell upon the Trojans in a mass. Patroclus was the first to hurl his shining spear directly into the midst of the place where most of the men were milling about together in a throng. He drove them away from the ships, and the Danaans poured in among the hollow ships as the incessant noise of battle rose up, and they rescued their ships from the ravaging fire.

Thus the Danaans rushed upon the Trojans, and their minds were filled with fear as they forgot their eager courage. Hector, in truth, now realized the victory in the battle was falling to the other side, but even so he kept on fighting and tried to save his loyal men. But from the ships there came the shouts of their flight, and they began to flee in confusion out over the ramparts again. And his swift-footed horses carried Hector off fully armed, and he left behind him the Trojan fighting men, who were held back in their efforts to escape by the deep trench.

Patroclus, shouting anxiously to the Danaans, followed in hot pursuit of the Trojans, who filled all the roads in the noisy flight of their broken ranks. And his swift horses easily cleared the trench as he drove them on, for his heart was eager to strike at Hector. But Hector's swift horses, too, carried him onward.

Patroclus, shouting at his horses, pursued the Trojans and made a great mistake by his foolhardiness. For if he had kept in mind the warnings of Achilles the son of Peleus, he would, in truth, have escaped the dread fate of black death. But always the will of Zeus is stronger than the purpose of men, and it was he who now put angry boldness in Patroclus' heart.

Hector had reined in his horses at the Scaean Gate, for he was in doubt whether he should drive them into the throng of the enemy again and fight, or should order his men to reassemble inside the city walls. While he was debating this, Phoebus Apollo came to him in the likeness of a valiant and strong man—in the form of Asius. Then Apollo the son of Zeus addressed Hector, saying, "Hector, why have you withdrawn from battle? This does not become you. Come now, drive on your sturdy steeds against Patroclus, and you may even yet overpower him, and Apollo may grant you the victory."

Then glorious Hector ordered bold Cebriones to lash his horses into the battle. But Apollo went and mingled with the throng and sent cowardly confusion into the Argives and gave glory to the Trojans and Hector. Hector did not seek the other Danaans or try to slay them but drove his sturdy steeds at Patroclus. And Patroclus jumped from his own chariot onto the ground, holding his spear in his left hand. With his other hand he picked up a shining jagged stone, took a firm stand, and hurled it, striking Hector's charioteer, Cebriones, an illegitimate son of glorious Priam, on the forehead while he was holding the reins of the horses. Cebriones fell from the mighty chariot like a diver, and his spirit left his body. Then Patroclus fell upon noble Cebriones with the force of a lion, and at once Hector jumped to the ground from his chariot on the other side. And thus they fought over Cebriones like two lions over a slain deer.

As long as Helios was crossing the middle of the sky, the missiles of both sides reached their mark, and men kept falling. But when he turned toward evening, then indeed the Achaeans proved to be the better men, even beyond their appointed lot, and they dragged noble Cebriones away from the range of the arrows and the shouts of the Trojans. And then Patroclus leaped upon the Trojans with evil in his mind. Three times he rushed at them, equal to Ares in swiftness, shouting a terrible cry, and three times he killed nine men. But when he fell upon them for the fourth time like a demon, then—for you, Patroclus—the end of life appeared; for Phoebus Apollo met you face to face in fierce combat —Phoebus, a dread god.

The god stood behind him and struck him on his broad back and shoulders with the flat of his hand, and Patroclus' eyes rolled in his head. And Phoebus Apollo knocked the helmet from his head, and it clanged as it rolled under the hoofs of the horses. Then a blindness swept over his mind, and his fine legs grew weak beneath him, and he stood in a daze. Then one of the Dar-

danians, Panthous' son Euphorbus, from close behind struck him
right in the back between the shoulders with his sharp spear.
And Patroclus, overpowered by the blow of the god and the
thrust of the spear, fell back into the crowd of his comrades,
trying to escape his doom. Then when Hector saw high-spirited
Patroclus retreating and wounded by the sharp bronze, he came
up close to him and struck him in the abdomen with his spear and
drove the bronze clear through. And Patroclus fell with a thud,
and the host of the Achaeans grew silent with grief.

Meanwhile, many a fine weapon fell at the trench and all
around it, dropped by the fleeing Danaans, and there was no rest
from battle. Thus they kept fighting like a blazing fire. And
Antilochus ran in haste to bring the news to Achilles, and he
found him in front of his high-beaked ships, brooding in his heart
over what had now come to pass. The son of King Nestor came
up to him, shedding hot tears, and told him the tragic news: "Alas,
son of wise Peleus, you must be prepared to hear sad tidings, sad
news I wish had never happened. Patroclus lies dead. They are
fighting around his body, and Hector of the flashing helmet has
taken his armor."

At this report a black cloud of grief engulfed Achilles. Then
he gave a terrible cry, and his queenly mother, seated in the
depths of the sea beside her ancient father, heard him. Then she
cried aloud, and all the other goddesses gathered round her, all
the daughters of Nereus who were in the deep sea. She left the
cave, and the other nymphs went with her. And when they came
to the deep-soiled land of Troy, they came up one after another
onto the beach where Achilles lay grieving amid the ships of the
Myrmidons drawn up there in close order. His queenly mother
came up beside him and took his head in her hands and spoke to
him in winged words: "My son, why do you weep? What grief
has entered your heart? Tell me and do not hide it."

Then, sighing deeply, Achilles the swift of foot answered her,
saying, "Mother, my dear friend is dead—Patroclus, whom I loved
best of all my comrades, even as much as my own life. I have lost
him, and Hector, who has slain him, has stripped my splendid
armor from him. My heart does not will me to live on and stay
here among men unless Hector first, struck down by my sword,

may perish and thus repay the price for the death of Patroclus, the son of Menoetius, and the plundering of his body. And now I will go forth and find the murderer of my dearest friend, the murderer Hector. Do not try to keep me from battle. However much you love me, you will not hold me back."

Then the goddess, silver-footed Thetis, answered him: "In truth, you are right, my son, to think it is no mistake to defend your comrades from sheer destruction. But your splendid armor is held by the Trojans, and Hector of the gleaming helmet is wearing it himself on his own shoulders. Do not go into battle until you see me come back here again, for I shall return in the morning at sunrise and bring you fine armor from the master Hephaestus."

Then the goddess, silver-footed Thetis, at once set off for Olympus to bring back splendid armor for her dear son. And she came directly to the house of Hephaestus—a house that was indestructible, sparkling as a star, outstanding among the dwellings of the immortals, made of bronze by the god with the lame foot himself. He was making tripods, but he put his bellows down, setting them away from the fire, and limped over to Thetis and sat down on a splendid chair. Then he took her hand and spoke, saying, "Why, Thetis of the flowing robes, have you come to my house? Tell me what you have in mind. My heart bids me do for you anything I can if I am able to do it and it can be done."

And Thetis answered him with tears running down her cheeks, "Hephaestus, I have come to beg you in supplication asking if you will kindly give my son, who faces an early death, a shield and helmet, fine greaves fitted with ankle clasps, and a breastplate. For the armor that he had before was lost when his faithful friend was slain by the Trojans, and now he is lying on the ground in grief."

Then the famous lame god answered her, saying, "Take courage and do not let these cares distress your heart. I shall make him splendid armor that will be a wonder to all men who behold it."

So saying, he left her and went back to his bellows and turned them toward the fire and ordered them to set to work. And he put indestructible bronze on the fire, and tin and precious gold and silver. Then he laid a great anvil on the anvil-block and took up a great hammer in one hand and tongs in the other hand. First he made a shield—a large and strong shield, skillfully adorned—and around it he put a triple rim, bright and gleaming, and from it he hung a silver strap. The shield was made of five layers, and on it he very skillfully fashioned many designs. When he had finished the great, sturdy shield, he next made Achilles a breastplate brighter than a blazing fire. He also made for him a great helmet and put a crest of gold on the top and fashioned greaves of pliant tin for him.

Then, when the famous lame god had finished making all the armor, he took it and laid it before Achilles' mother. And Thetis, like a falcon, flew down from snowy Olympus, carrying the sparkling armor from Hephaestus.

As Dawn with her saffron robe rose from Ocean's stream to bring the daylight to immortals and mortals alike, she came to the ships bearing the gifts of the god. The lovely goddess stood beside her son and took his hand in hers, saying, "My son, even though it grieves us, we must nevertheless leave Patroclus lying here, since he has indeed been slain by the will of the gods. Now take this splendid armor made for you by the skill of Hephaestus, armor more glorious than any man has ever worn before."

When Achilles saw the armor, even greater anger came over him, and he was pleased when he held the fine gifts of the god in his hands. Then he addressed his mother with winged words: "Mother, indeed these arms the god has fashioned for me are like the work of the immortals and not such as any mortal man could make. Now, in truth, I shall arm myself for battle with these." Then, in anger against the Trojans, he put on the gifts of the god, the arms that Hephaestus had made for him with such care, and the armor seemed to give him wings.

Achilles moved quickly through the ranks of soldiers, urging on each man: "Come, good Achaeans, fight man against man and strive for victory in the struggle. I myself will go right through their battle lines, and I doubt that any one of the Trojans will be glad to come near my spear."

Thus he encouraged his men, but glorious Hector urged on his Trojans with a shout and vowed he would face Achilles himself. Then the Trojans raised up their spears against the enemy, and both sides joined in furious combat, and the cry of battle rose up. And just then Phoebus Apollo came and stood beside Hector, saying, "Hector, do not in any case go forth to fight with Achilles but wait in the crowd amid the roar of the battle, or he will strike you down with a throw of his spear or at close range with his sword." When he had said this, Hector sank back into the throng of warriors, alarmed when he heard the words of the god.

But Achilles, his heart clad in courage, sprang upon the Trojans with a fearful war cry. He went after godlike Polydorus, son of Priam, with his spear. Mighty Achilles, swift of foot, struck him full in the back with a thrust of his spear as he ran by, and Polydorus fell to his knees with a groan, and a dark cloud engulfed him.

When Hector saw his brother Polydorus fall to the ground, a mist spread over his eyes, and he could not bear to stay out of the fighting any longer; but he went at Achilles, flourishing his sharp sword, like a flash of flame. As soon as Achilles saw him, he sprang toward him at once, murmuring a prayer of thanks, "This is the man who wounded my heart deeply when he killed my good friend. Now we will no longer flee from each other in fear on the field of battle."

Fearlessly Hector of the gleaming helmet said to him, "Son of Peleus, I know that you are indeed a brave man and a far better man than I. But it lies, as all things do, in the laps of the gods whether I, even though I am weaker than you, shall take your life with a cast of my spear, since my weapon also has been known to be sharp before this."

As he spoke, he aimed his spear and hurled it, but Athena turned it away from noble Achilles with a light breath, and it came back to glorious Hector and fell before his feet. Then Achilles rushed at him furiously with a dreadful cry, ready to kill him, but Apollo snatched Hector up easily, as a god can, and hid him in a thick mist. Three times then, godlike Achilles of the swift feet sprang at Hector with his bronze spear, and three times he struck a dense mist. But when he rushed at him for the fourth time like a demon, he chided him fiercely with winged words: "You dog, now you have escaped death again, but indeed your doom came close to you! Now Phoebus Apollo has rescued you again. But, in truth, I will kill you when next we meet if there is some god somewhere who will help me too. Now I shall go after the others, anyone I can find."

Just as a furious fire rages through the deep valleys of a parched mountainside and the thick forest is consumed by flames and the driving wind whirls the fire in all directions, so Achilles rushed about everywhere with his spear, like a demon, and the black earth streamed with blood. But when they came to the ford of the full-flowing river, the eddying Xanthus, begotten of immortal Zeus, he cut the enemy in two. And he drove one part toward the city across the plain where the Achaeans had fled in terror on the day before, when glorious Hector raged in battle. They spread out over the plain in confused flight, and Hera laid a dense mist in front of them to hinder their escape.

Aged Priam was standing on the ramparts and saw mighty Achilles and the Trojans being driven in helpless confusion before him. Then with a cry of grief he climbed down from the fortifications, calling to the gatekeepers stationed along the wall, "Hold the gates open wide until our fleeing soldiers get to the city. Achilles is close behind them, driving them in rout, and now I fear disaster. But when they have come inside the walls and can breathe again, then close the double doors again at once, for I am afraid that deadly man may dash in after them."

At his command they unfastened the doors and thrust back the bars, and the wide-open gates brought a ray of hope. In addition, Apollo sprang forth to meet them so that he might avert disaster from the Trojans.

Then, gathered inside the city like frightened fawns, they were cooling off and drinking to quench their thirst as they leaned against the great battlements resting, while the Achaeans came toward the wall with their shields balanced on their shoulders. But vicious fate bound Hector to stay where he was, in front of Ilium before the Scaean Gate.

Achilles, with thoughts of great success in his mind, hurried on toward the city, running like a victorious horse before his chariot when he wins the prize. The aged Priam was the first to catch sight of him, shining as brightly as a star as he dashed across the plain. And he cried out in alarm, warning his dear son, who was standing in front of the gate firmly resolved to fight with Achilles, but he could not sway Hector in his determination. And Hector's mother also, in her turn, wept and mourned for him. Thus they both cried out to their dear son, pleading with him earnestly and tearfully, but they could not move him, and he stood firm as mighty Achilles approached.

Achilles came toward him as though he were Ares, the warrior with the waving helmet plume, brandishing the dread ashen spear over his shoulder. Hector, when he saw him, was seized with trembling, and he did not dare to keep his post. He left the gate and fled from it in terror. But the son of Peleus dashed after him, relying on his own swiftness of foot.

As Achilles raced after him, following close behind, Hector fled below the walls of Troy, running as fast as his legs would carry him. They sped along the wagon track, always staying some distance from the wall, past the watchtower and the windblown fig, and came at length to the two beautiful springs, the sources that feed the eddying Scamander. They ran right on by, Hector fleeing, Achilles pursuing him. A good man fled in front, but a far better one followed him in hot pursuit; and they were not racing for a sacrificial animal or a shield of oxhide, the prize of the foot-race, but they were running with the life of horse-taming Hector at stake. And thus they raced three times around Priam's city, their feet flying, and all the gods watched them.

Achilles followed after Hector in a steady chase, and Hector could not escape from the swift-footed son of Peleus. As often as he darted off toward the Dardanian gates, trying to reach the protection of the well-built walls in the hope that those on the wall above might come to his rescue with their arrows, his pursuer would forestall him and turn him away, forcing him toward the plain while he himself raced along close to the walls. Just as in a dream one can not catch up to the one he pursues, nor is the pursued able to move out and away from the pursuer, so Achilles could not overtake Hector in the chase, nor could Hector escape from him.

But when they came to the springs for the fourth time, then the Father lifted up his golden scales and placed upon them two lots marked with death—one on one side for Achilles, another on the other side for horse-taming Hector—and then he raised up the balance, holding it by the middle. And the day of death of Hector's fate sank down and vanished into Hades, and Phoebus Apollo abandoned him.

And when they came close to each other as they ran, great Hector of the gleaming helmet was the first to speak, saying to Achilles, "No longer, son of Peleus, will I run from you as I have been fleeing before you just now, running three times around the great city of Priam without daring to stop and face you. But now my heart tells me to take my stand against you, whether I kill you or am killed myself."

Achilles poised his long-shafted spear and hurled it. But glorious Hector, watching him carefully, avoided it, for he stooped quickly as he kept his eye on it, and the bronze spear flew over his head and went into the ground. But Pallas Athena snatched it out and gave it back to Achilles without being seen by Hector, shepherd of his people.

Then Hector poised his long-shafted spear and hurled it. And it struck the shield of Achilles, son of Peleus, squarely in the middle; nor did it miss its mark, but the spear bounced off the shield and fell away from it. And Hector was angered when he saw his swift throw had left his hand in vain, and he stood dumbfounded, for he had no second ashen spear.

He drew the sharp sword that hung at his side, a large and sturdy sword, and, getting himself ready, swooped like a soaring eagle that falls to the earth through the dark clouds to pounce on a tender lamb or a fearful hare. Thus Hector dashed forward, flourishing his sharp sword. And Achilles rushed at him, his heart filled with savage anger.

Light flashed from the sharp point of the spear that Achilles held poised in his right hand, while he planned death for noble Hector and scanned his fair skin for the best spot to strike. All of Hector's body was covered by the splendid bronze armor that he had stripped from Patroclus when he killed him except for an opening where the collarbone crosses from the shoulders to the neck, just at the gullet, where a person can be killed most quickly. As he came toward him, noble Achilles drove his spear into this spot, and the point pierced through the tender flesh of his neck. He fell in the dust, and noble Achilles rejoiced over him.

Death engulfed Hector, and his soul, taking wing from his

body, flew off to Hades. But noble Achilles spoke to him even though he was dead, saying, "Die, and I will accept my own fate when Zeus and the other deathless gods see fit to end my life."

Then, when swift-footed Achilles had stripped him, he contrived a shameful treatment for noble Hector. He pierced the tendons at the back of both feet between the heel and ankle, fastened straps of oxhide through them, tied them fast to his chariot, and left the head to drag behind. Then, getting into the chariot, he lifted the splendid armor up into it, touched the horses with his whip, and off they flew eagerly. And a cloud of dust rose up as Hector was dragged behind, and his dark hair flew out on both sides. The head that was once so fine lay deep in the dust, for now Zeus had given it up to his enemies to maltreat in his own native soil.

Thus was Hector's head completely covered with dust. And his mother tore her hair and cast off the bright veil from her head and cried aloud when she caught sight of her son. His father, too, groaned pitifully, and the people around them cried out in despair and grief throughout the whole city. It was just as if all of towering Ilium were being completely consumed by fire.

But Hector's wife did not yet know anything about this for no one had gone to her with the message that her husband had stayed outside the gates. She was busy at her loom in the inner hall of the lofty house, weaving a purple mantle of double fold and working a pattern of different colored flowers into it.

But she heard the sound of the shrieking and weeping coming from the walls, and she grew weak with trembling, and the shuttle fell from her hand to the floor. She rushed through the house like a madwoman, her heart pounding with fear, and her handmaidens went with her. But when she came to the battlements and the crowd of people gathered there, she went and stood on top of the wall, looking all around anxiously, and she caught sight of her husband being dragged in front of the city as the swift horses were pulling him along heedlessly toward the hollow ships of the Achaeans. Then the world went black before her eyes as Andromache fell over backward in a dead faint.

From *Iliad* II, VI, VII, XII and XV–XXII

The Trojan Horse

Although Homer is the main source for accounts of the Trojan War, the details and incidents of the stories of the war were altered and embellished by later writers. The youth Sinon (in the following account), for example, does not appear in the earlier legends.

The incident of the Trojan Horse took place in the tenth, and final, year of the war, after the death of the Greek leader Achilles. At a banquet Dido gave for Aeneas and his followers, and at her request, Aeneas related the adventures he and his followers experienced from the time of the downfall of Troy to their arrival at Carthage. The following narrative is from the first part of that account.

The Roman author Vergil used Odysseus' Latin name, Ulysses, and the Greek goddess Athena appears as her Roman counterpart, Minerva.

As told in Latin verse by Vergil

"THE LEADERS of the Greeks, since so many years had already passed, built a horse the size of a mountain, aided by the divine skill of Minerva, and interwove its ribs with planks cut from pine. They pretended it was an offering for their return, and that rumor was spread abroad. Inside it they secretly enclosed chosen heroes, and they filled the huge cavity with armed men.

"Tenedos, an island very well-known by reputation, lies within sight. The Greeks sailed out that far and hid on the deserted shore. The Trojans thought they had gone away and made for Greece with a favoring wind. Therefore, all Troy relaxed from its long suffering, and the gates were flung open.

"The Trojans were amazed at the fateful gift of the maiden

Minerva and wondered at the massive structure of the horse. Thymoetes was the first to urge that it be drawn inside the walls and placed on the citadel, but Capys* and others suggested that we either cast this treacherous and suspicious gift of the Greeks headlong into the sea, or burn it, or pierce and search its hollow hiding places. The wavering crowd was divided by opposing desires.

"Then, accompanied by a large crowd, Laocoön ran down from the top of the citadel and cried out as he ran, 'O unfortunate fellow citizens, what is this great madness? Do you believe the enemy has sailed off or that any gifts of the Greeks are free from tricks? Is this how well you know Ulysses? Either some of the Greeks are enclosed and hiding in this wooden structure, or this is a machine of war built to menace our walls and to look into our homes, or some other treachery lies hidden within. Do not trust the horse, Trojans. Whatever it is, I fear the Greeks even when they bear gifts.'

"Then he hurled a spear with great force into the body of the beast. It hung there trembling, and if the fates had not been opposed Laocoön would have urged us to cut open the Greek hiding places, and Troy would still be standing.

"Just then, however, Trojan shepherds dragged a youth, with his hands bound behind his back, to the king amid great commotion. From all sides the young Trojans rushed up and surrounded him in their eagerness to see him and mock him. As the young man stood there in the middle of the watching crowd he cried out, 'Alas, what is left for me now, since there is no place for me among the Greeks and the hostile Trojans demand my life's blood?'

"The Trojans urged him to say from what race he came and what mission he had. This is what he told us when his fear was finally laid aside: 'I shall not deny that I am of the Greek race. Even if evil fortune has made me, Sinon, wretched, she will not make me false and deceitful. I beg you through the gods above, have pity on my heavy trials, have pity on a soul bearing undeserved burdens.'

* Capys fled to Italy after the Trojan War and became the legendary founder of Capua.

"After these pleading words the Trojans granted him his life and even pitied him. King Priam ordered his chains to be removed and spoke to him kindly in this manner: 'Whoever you are, forget the Greeks, for they are lost to you. You will be ours. Now tell me the truth about the questions I ask. Why have they built this huge horse? What do they seek? What religious offering is it or what device of war?'

"Sinon answered, 'It is right for me to hate the Greeks and their sacred laws and to bring everything out into the open. May you only abide by your promises if I reveal the truth.

" 'All the hope of the Greeks and their faith in undertaking the war always rested in the help of Minerva. From the time, however, when Diomedes and Ulysses stole the sacred image of Minerva from its temple,* the hopes of the Greeks fell; their strength was broken, and the goddess's heart was hostile. Then the prophet Calchas proclaimed that Troy could not be destroyed by Greek weapons unless they returned to Greece and brought back the divine favor.

" 'Because of his warning they built this image of Minerva's statue to make up for the injury to her divine power and the wrong they had done. Calchas cautioned them to build this huge monster of interwoven oaken timbers up to the sky, lest it might be taken into the gates or brought inside the city walls or watch over the Trojans under the protection of their ancient religion.'

"Because of the craftiness of the deceitful Sinon, his story was believed, and men whom neither Achilles nor ten years of war nor a thousand ships had vanquished were deceived by his tricks and false tears. Then another and more dreadful portent was presented to the Trojan people and threw their hearts into confusion.

"Laocoön, Neptune's allotted priest, was sacrificing a great bull at the altars. Behold, however, two snakes with huge coils came through the sea from Tenedos, making for the shore side by side, their blazing eyes streaked with blood and fire, their darting tongues licking their hissing mouths.

---

* The image that Diomedes and Ulysses stole was called the Palladium, a statue identified with Pallas Athena (or Minerva). It was believed that Troy would be safe as long as the Palladium remained intact in the city.

"The Trojans fled in all directions, pale at the sight. The serpents made for Laocoön in a straight course. First they entwined themselves around his two small sons, enveloping them and devouring their poor bodies. Then they seized upon Laocoön himself as he came to their aid with uplifted weapon and bound him in their huge coils. Laocoön raised dreadful cries to the heavens, and the two serpents, gliding away, escaped to the lofty shrine of Minerva and hid themselves at the goddess's feet under the circle of her shield.

"Then truly a new terror crept through the trembling hearts of all, and they said Laocoön had paid for his crime deservedly—he who had struck at the sacred oak with his spear. They cried out in unison that the image should be taken into the city and the divine will of the goddess should be sought in prayer.

"They broke apart the city walls and laid the buildings of the city open to view. Everyone made ready for the task and placed smoothly rolling wheels under the feet and drew ropes of hemp tight around the neck. The fateful contrivance, filled with armed men, mounted the walls. It entered, then glided threateningly into the midst of the city. The people adorned the shrines of the gods with festive boughs throughout the city.

"Meanwhile, the sky revolved and night rushed forth from the ocean, wrapping the earth and heavens and the tricks of the Greeks in a great shadow. The Trojans, scattered throughout the city, became silent. Sleep embraced their weary limbs.

"Then the Greek army sailed from Tenedos, seeking the well-known shores of Troy through the friendly silence of the quiet moonlight. When the royal ship sent up a signal of flames, Sinon, secretly loosening the pine fastenings, released the imprisoned Greeks from the belly of the horse. They rushed out through the city buried in sleep. They cut down the guards and let all their comrades in through the opened gates and joined together in fighting bands.

"The city was thrown into confusion, the sounds grew louder, and the horrible din of fighting rolled on. Then in truth the proof was clear, and the deceits of the Greeks were disclosed. The towering horse, standing in the midst of the city, poured forth armed men, and the victorious Sinon, taunting us, spread fire in the confusion. Some were at the wide-open gates, as many thousands as ever came from great Mycenae. Others blocked the narrow parts of the streets with their weapons held in the way. The one safety for the vanquished lay in not hoping for any safety."

From *Aeneid* II, 14–354

The Cyclopes

The Greek word kuklōps, *meaning "round-eye," characterizes the giants who had a single, round eye in the middle of the forehead. They were believed to be assistants of Hephaestus at his forges below Mount Aetna, an explanation of the rumblings and eruptions of that volcano. They were also thought to have built many fortifications in the ancient world, among them the "cyclopean" walls of Mycenae and Tiryns.*

In Hesiod, the Cyclopes are the giant sons of Uranus and Gaea. They are three in number and are like gods in all respects except for their eyes and size. In Homer, they are giants but not godlike, and there are numerous Cyclopes living around Polyphemus on an island later associated with Sicily, or one in that vicinity.

The stories of the Cyclopes, Circe, the Sirens, and Scylla and Charybdis that follow formed a part of Odysseus' account of his adventures. These he related at the request of Alcinous, king of the Phaeacians, by whom he was received with hospitality.

As told in Greek verse by Homer

"WE CAME to the land of the Cyclopes, arrogant and lawless people who, relying on the gods, neither plant nor plough, for all their crops spring up without being sown or cultivated. They have no assemblies or fixed laws, but they live on the tops of lofty mountains in hollow caves, and each one makes the laws for his own children and wives and has no care for any other person.

"When we looked across at the land of the Cyclopes lying close by, we saw the smoke of their fires and even heard their voices and the sounds of their sheep and goats. But when the sun went down and darkness came on, then we fell asleep on the shore of the sea.

"As soon as the first light of rosy-fingered Dawn appeared, I gathered my men together and spoke to them all: 'All you others remain here now, my faithful companions, while I go with my ship and my own crew to find out about those men—to learn who they are and whether they are fierce savages without laws or whether they are hospitable to strangers and are god-fearing people.'

"When we approached the place, which lay close by, we saw there, near the edge of the sea, a lofty cave, overshadowed with laurel. There many flocks, both sheep and goats, spent the night, and round it a great courtyard had been built of stones set deep in the ground among tall pines and oaks of lofty foliage.

"A man was in the habit of sleeping inside this place—a giant who shepherded his flocks alone and far away. He did not mingle with the others, but lived a lawless life apart from them. He was, indeed, a wondrous monster, not at all like a man who eats bread but like the wooded peak of some lofty mountain that rises up solitary, apart from the others.

"Then I told the rest of my faithful companions to stay by the ship and guard it, but I picked out twelve of the best men among my comrades and started out. I took with me a great wineskin filled with wine and provisions of food in a sack of leather, for a sudden foreboding came into my manly heart that soon a man would appear before me wearing the protection of mighty physical strength—a savage being, one knowing nothing of either law or justice.

"In a short time we reached the cave, and we did not find him at home, but he was watching over his fat flocks in the pasture. So we went inside the cave and looked around at everything. There were baskets filled with cheeses, and pens crowded with lambs and kids.

"Then my comrades urged me first of all to take off some of the cheeses and come back again and then quickly drive the kids and lambs out of their pens down to the swift ship and set sail over the salt water. But I did not listen to them, although it would have been better if I had.

"Then, when we had kindled a fire we offered a sacrifice, and, taking some cheeses for ourselves, we ate them and remained in the cave and waited until he came back shepherding his flocks. He drove his fat animals into the wide cave—all those that he milked —but the males, the rams and he-goats, he left outside in the large courtyard. Then he lifted up a great stone, a mighty stone, and set it in place to close the entrance. Not even two and twenty heavy, four-wheeled wagons could have moved it from the ground, so huge was the rock he put in the entranceway.

"Then, as he kindled the fire again, he caught sight of us and asked, 'Strangers, who are you? From what place do you sail over the paths of the sea?'

"Thus he spoke, and our spirits were indeed broken by our fear of his deep voice and his monstrous body. Nevertheless I was able to answer him and speak to him thus: 'We are Greeks returning from Troy, driven from our course by all sorts of winds over the great expanse of the deep sea. Longing for our homes, we have come back by a different route, a different way.'

"Thus I answered him, but he made no reply from his pitiless heart. Instead he sprang forward and put his hands out toward my comrades and seized two of them, dashing them to the earth like puppies. We lifted up our hands in prayer to Zeus and wept as we looked upon the cruel deed and a helplessness grasped our spirits.

"When the Cyclops, however, had filled his huge stomach by devouring human flesh and then drinking fresh milk, he lay down to sleep inside the cave, stretching out among his flocks. Then I formed a plan within my bold heart to get quite close to him, draw my sharp sword from its scabbard at my side, and strike him in the chest.

"A second thought stopped me, however, since we would have perished there with him in utter destruction; for certainly we would not have been able to push away from the lofty entrance with our own hands the huge stone that he had placed there. For this reason then we waited in sadness for the blessed light of day.

"As soon as the early Dawn appeared, rosy-fingered, he kindled the fire again and milked his splendid flocks, all in due order, and placed under each mother her young offspring. Then, after he had worked hard to perform these tasks, he again snatched up two men together and prepared his meal. When he had finished his meal, he herded his fat flocks out of the cave, moving the great stone away from the entrance with ease. But then he put it back in place again.

"I was left there turning over evil plans deep in my heart, wondering how I might take revenge on him. This, according to my judgment, seemed the best plan: the Cyclops had a great staff lying beside a pen, a trunk of green olive, which he had cut down so that he might carry it after it had seasoned. As we looked at it, we thought it seemed as big as the mast of a black ship of twenty oars—so great was its length, so great its thickness to behold.

"From this staff I cut off a piece about a yard long and handed it to my companions, urging them to trim it down. They smoothed it off, and I took it and sharpened it to a good point. Next I put it into the blazing fire to harden it and then set it carefully aside, hiding it.

"I also told my comrades to cast lots among themselves to decide who would have the daring to lift the stake with me and drive it into his eye when sweet sleep came to him. The lot fell on the very ones I myself would have chosen, four men, and I made the fifth in the group with them.

"By evening he returned, shepherding his fine woolly flocks, and soon drove into the wide cave every one of the fat animals and did not leave any outside in the courtyard. Then he lifted up the great doorstone and set it in place and sat down to milk the ewes and bleating goats, all in due order, and placed under each mother her young offspring. Then, after he had worked hard to perform these tasks, he again snatched up two men together and prepared his supper.

"Then, holding a drinking cup of dark wine in my hands, I went over to the Cyclops and spoke to him: 'Cyclops, take this wine and drink it, now that you have eaten human flesh, so that you may know what sort of drinking wine was stored in our ship.'

"When I had spoken to him thus, he took the cup and drank it all. He thoroughly enjoyed the sweet wine as he drank it, and he even asked me for a second cupful: 'Kindly give me some more and tell me your name now without delay so that I may give you a gift of hospitality, for this is a taste of ambrosia and nectar.'

"Thus he spoke, and again I handed him a cupful of the fiery wine. Three times I filled the cup and gave it to him, three times he drained it in his foolishness. But when the wine had overcome the wits of the Cyclops, then I addressed him with soothing words: 'Cyclops, you ask me my splendid name, and I shall tell you. Then give me the gift of hospitality as you promised. Noman is my name, Noman they call me—my mother and father and all my friends also.'

"That is what I told him, and then he answered me directly with pitiless heart: 'I shall eat Noman the last of his comrades, and all the others first before him. That shall be your gift of hospitality.'

"As he finished speaking he sank down and fell on his back, lying there with his thick neck twisted to the side, and sleep, the conqueror of all, overcame him. Then I thrust the stake deep under the embers of the fire to get it glowing hot, and I encouraged all my comrades so that no one would become afraid and back away.

"Soon, when the stake of olive wood was on the point of catching fire in the embers, even though it was green, and was red-hot, I pulled it from the fire toward my comrades, who were standing about me. Indeed a god inspired them with high courage. They seized the stake of olive wood, sharpened at the end, and drove it into his eye, while I leaned my weight on it from above to twist it around.

"He gave a terrible cry, and the rock resounded with the echo. We fell back in terror as he pulled the stake from his eye, covered with blood. Then he hurled it away from him, waving his arms madly, and gave a loud shout for the other Cyclopes who lived around him in caves throughout the windy heights. They, hearing his shout, ran to him from every direction and, standing outside the cave, asked him what his trouble was.

" 'Why are you so distressed, Polyphemus? Why are you crying out in the quiet night and waking us out of our sleep? Is some mortal man driving off your flocks against your will? Or is someone murdering you by treachery or violence?'

"Then from the depths of the cave mighty Polyphemus answered them: 'O friends, Noman is murdering me by treachery, not by violence.'

"They answered him, speaking winged words: 'If, indeed, no man is using violence on you in your loneliness, then you may not in any way escape sickness that comes from all-powerful Zeus; but you can only pray to your father, the lord Poseidon.'

"That is how they answered him, and then they left him while my heart laughed within me at the way my name and clever craftiness had completely deceived him. The Cyclops, moaning in the agony of pain and feeling his way with his hands, pushed the stone away from the entrance and sat down at the mouth of the cave with both arms stretched out wide in the hope of catching anyone who might try to slip out with the sheep—for he hoped in his heart I might be that foolish.

"Then I turned over all kinds of tricks and plans in my mind, just as one will when it is a matter of life or death, for great was the danger that was upon us. And this, according to my mind, seemed the best plan: there were well-fed rams with thick fleeces, fine large animals whose wool was violet-dark. These I silently bound together with the tightly twisted willow twigs on which the Cyclops, a lawless creature, slept, taking them three at a time. The ram in the middle was to carry a man, and the other two on each side would keep my comrades safe. Thus every three sheep carried one man. But for me there was a ram, by far the best of all the flock. Grasping him by the back, I lay clinging upside down below his shaggy belly, holding firmly to his wonderful fleece with my hands and keeping patience in my heart.

"Their master, suffering greatly from severe pain, felt along the backs of all the sheep as they stopped before him, but in his ignorance he did not realize that my men were tied beneath his woolly sheep. The ram was the last of the flock to come to the cave's mouth, weighed down by his thick fleece and by me with my mind full of clever schemes.

"The mighty Polyphemus felt along his back with his hands and then sent the ram on out of the doorway. When we had gone a short distance from the cave and its courtyard, I first freed myself from under the ram and then untied my comrades. Next we drove these long-legged sheep, animals rich in fat, down to the ship, turning around often to look back. We were a welcome sight to our dear comrades. The men quickly went on board, took their places in order at the rowing benches, and struck the gray sea with their oars.

"But when I was as far away as a man can be heard when he shouts, then I called to the Cyclops, mocking him: 'Cyclops, that was not such a weak man then, was he—the one whose companions you intended to eat there in your hollow cave by brute force? Indeed your evil deeds were destined to fall back on you, you merciless monster who did not fear to devour the guests in your own home. Therefore Zeus and all the other gods have taken vengeance on you.'

"Thus I mocked him and his heart grew so much more angry that he tore off the top of a lofty mountain and hurled it down in front of the dark blue prow of our ship. And the sea rose up under the stone as it fell. I urged on my comrades to make haste and pull hard on their oars so we might escape from this disaster. They put their backs into it and rowed steadily.

"But when we had reached a distance twice as far out to sea I called out to him again from my angry heart: 'Cyclops, if any one of mortal men should ever happen to ask you about the awful blinding of your eye, tell him that it was blinded by Odysseus, the sacker of cities, the son of Laërtes, who has his home in Ithaca.'

"At last we sailed on from there sad at heart—glad we had escaped death, but grieving that we had lost our dear comrades."

From *Odyssey* IX, 106–566

Circe

Circe was a sister of King Aeëtes of Colchis. Like Aeëtes'
daughter Medea, she was an enchantress skilled in the use of
charms, herbs, and spells.

It has been conjectured that either of two islands might have
been believed to be Circe's home: one at the northern end of the
Adriatic, the other off the west coast of the Italian peninsula. The
latter came to be associated with a town and promontory called
Circei (or Cercei), now called Circeo, and was mentioned by
Vergil and Horace.

As told in Greek verse by Homer

"WE SAILED on and came to the island of Aeaea, where fair-haired
Circe lives. She is a dread goddess who speaks with a human voice
and is the sister of crafty Aeëtes—both were born of Helios, who
brings light to mortals, and their mother was Persa, the daughter
of Oceanus. We came into shore here and brought our ship to
anchor in the harbor in silence, and some god guided us in. Then,
when we had disembarked, we rested there for two days and two
nights, eating our hearts out from weariness and grief.

"But when fair-haired Dawn brought forth the beginning of the
third day, I then took my spear and sharp sword and climbed up
quickly from the ship to a spot commanding a wide view, thinking I might see signs of human habitation and hear the sounds of
mortal voices. As I stood on the rocky lookout point I could see
smoke rising up from the broad earth in the direction of Circe's
halls, through the dense oak woods. Then I pondered in my mind
and heart whether I should go over and find out about the glowing smoke I saw. After thinking it over, it seemed better to go
first to our swift ship and the shore of the sea and give my companions their meal, and then send them out to explore.

"But just as I was approaching the curved ship, some one of the gods felt pity for me, lonely as I was, and suddenly sent a great stag with lofty antlers directly into my path. I struck him across the spine in the middle of his back, and the bronze spear went straight through him. He fell in the dust groaning, and his spirit departed from him. Weaving a rope of twigs and twisting it tightly from end to end, I tied the feet of the mighty animal together and went on to the black ship, carrying him across my shoulders. I let him fall in front of the ship, and then I encouraged my companions with gentle words, stopping beside each man.

" 'O friends, indeed we shall not yet, no matter how distressed we are, go down into the house of Hades before the day appointed by fate comes to us. But come, as long as we have food and drink in our swift ship let us give our attention to eating, lest we be worn out by hunger.' Thus I spoke, and they quickly obeyed my words of advice. And so, in truth, we sat feasting on the good meat and sweet wine all day long until sunset. And when the sun had set and darkness fell upon us, we then fell asleep on the shore of the sea. But as soon as early rosy-fingered Dawn appeared, I assembled my men and spoke to them all.

" 'Listen to my words, my companions, even though you are undergoing difficulties. Let us quickly consider whether there is still any plan of action left for us. But I do not think there is, for I climbed up to a spot commanding a wide view and looked out over the island, around which the boundless sea lies like a crown. The island itself stretches out flat, and, in the middle of it, I could see smoke through the thick oak woods.' Thus I spoke, and their hearts were broken within them, remembering the violent deeds of the stout-hearted Cyclops, the eater of men, and they cried aloud but not any good came of their weeping.

"Then I counted off all my companions into two groups and named a leader for each. I myself led one, and godlike Eurylochus the other. We immediately shook lots in a bronze helmet, and the lot of great-hearted Eurylochus leaped out. And so he started out with two and twenty companions following him, lamenting their fate, while we were left behind, weeping with grief for them.

"In a wooded glen they found the house of Circe, built of

smooth stone, lying in a wide clearing. And all around it were mountain wolves and lions that she herself had charmed by giving them evil drugs. They, in truth, did not rush at the men, but instead they stood about them, jumping up and down fawningly and wagging their long tails. But the men were afraid when they saw the terrifying beasts. They stood still, therefore, before the doorway of the fair-haired goddess, and they heard Circe inside, singing with beautiful voice as she worked at her great immortal loom, weaving fine cloth—delicate and lovely handiwork such as that of the goddesses.

"Then Polites, a leader of men who was the most beloved and most valuable of my companions, addressed them: 'O friends, indeed there is someone inside who is singing a sweet song as she works her loom, and the whole room echoes her voice. She is a goddess or a woman. Come, let us call out to her.'

"Thus, then, he spoke to them, and they called out to her, summoning her. And she came out at once, opened the shining doors, and invited them in. They all, in their foolishness, followed her in —all but Eurylochus, who stayed behind, suspecting that there was treachery. When she had led them into the house, she seated them on couches and chairs and then made a mixture of cheese and barley cakes and golden honey with Pramnian wine* for them. And she mixed into their food potent drugs so that they would completely forget their native land. Moreover, when she had given them the food and they had eaten it all, she then straightway struck them with her wand and shut them up in the pigpens. And indeed they had the heads, the grunts and bristles, and the bodily shape of pigs, but their minds were unchanged and the same as they had been before.

"Eurylochus, however, came directly back to our swift black ship, bringing the news about his companions and their bitter fate. He was not able to utter a single word, much as he tried, so stricken with grief was his heart. But when we all questioned him in stunned curiosity, he then recounted the doom of the others.

" 'We went, as you instructed us, through the woods, glorious Odysseus, and in a glen we found a splendid house built of smooth

* A wine from the area of Smyrna and Ephesus, and named for Mount Pramne on Icaria.

stone. Inside there was someone singing sweetly as she worked back and forth on a great loom, either a goddess or a woman, and they called aloud to her. And she came out at once, opening the shining doors, and summoned us in. They, in their foolishness, entered the house with her, but I stayed behind, suspecting this was trickery. Then they all disappeared together, and not one of them could be seen again, although I sat there for a long time keeping watch.'

"So he spoke, and I then slung my silver-studded sword over my shoulder, a great bronze sword, and also my bow, and bid him lead me back with him by the same path. But he, however, clung to me with both arms around my knees, begging me to heed his entreaty: 'Pray, do not take me back there against my will, O favorite of Zeus, but leave me here. For I know that you yourself will neither return nor bring back any of your companions. But let us try to flee quickly with the men who are left here, for we may yet escape from this evil day.'

"Thus he spoke, and I, in truth, answered him, saying, 'Eurylochus, do you indeed stay right here by the hollow black ship, eating and drinking, but I am going since sheer necessity compels me to go.' Speaking thus, I started away from the ship and the sea. But when I was just about to come to the great house of Circe the enchantress as I went through the sacred glens, then Hermes of the golden wand, resembling a young man with the first signs of a beard, met me. He took my hand in greeting and spoke to me.

" 'Where indeed are you going now, unfortunate man, alone through the hills, when you know nothing about the countryside? Your companions in Circe's house are penned up, in truth, like pigs in crowded sties. Are you coming here to set them free? I assure you, you will not return in safety, but instead you will stay there with the others. But come now, I shall free you from danger and rescue you. Here, take this powerful herb and go on to Circe's house, and it will avert the day of evil from your head. I shall tell you, also, about all the deadly tricks of Circe. She will prepare a mixture for you and mix drugs in the food. But she will not be able to put you under her magic power, however, for the counteracting drug I am giving you will not permit it, and I shall tell you how to use it. When Circe strikes you with her long wand, then you must draw your sharp sword from your side and rush at her as though you intended to kill her. Then she will be afraid and will set your companions free and show you hospitality.'

"Then, when he had said this, the slayer of Argus gave me the herb, pulling it up from the ground, and pointed out to me its nature. At its root it was black indeed, but the blossom was like milk. The gods call this herb moly, and it is difficult for mortal men to dig up, but the gods are able to do all things. Then Hermes set out for lofty Olympus through the wooded island, while I walked on toward the house of Circe, deeply troubled in my heart as I went.

"Thus I arrived at the gates of the fair-haired goddess, and I called out as I stood there, and the goddess heard my voice. Then straightway she came out and opened up the shining doors and invited me in. I followed her in, distressed at heart. Then she seated me, when she had led me in, on a silver-studded chair, a chair skillfully made, and there was a footstool beneath it. Then she prepared a potion for me in a gold goblet so that I might drink it, and in it she put a drug, planning evil in her heart. But when she gave it to me and when I had drunk it down but was not affected by its magic power, she struck me with her wand and spoke to me, saying, 'Go now to the pigsty and lie there with the rest of your companions.'

"Thus she spoke, but I drew my sharp sword from my side and rushed at Circe as if I intended to kill her. Then she gave a loud cry and fell to the floor, clasping my knees, and addressed me with winged words as she wept: 'Who are you? Where in the world do you come from? Where is your native city, and where are your parents? Wonder grips me when I see you were not affected at all when you drank this charm, for no one, no other man has ever resisted this drug when he has drunk it and it has once passed beyond the barrier of his teeth. In truth, you must indeed be Odysseus, the man of many skills, who the slayer of Argus with the wand of gold always told me would come this way when he was returning home from Troy in his swift black ship. But come now, put your sword back in its sheath. Then let us go to my bedchamber, you and I, so that united in love we may come to trust each other.'

"Thus she spoke, but I, in truth, answered her, saying, 'Oh Circe, indeed how can you urge me to be gentle with you—you who changed my companions into pigs here in this house and now hold me also here? You, goddess, must swear a mighty oath that you will not plan any other evil for me to suffer.' Thus I spoke, and she at once took the oath as I had bidden her.

"Then she urged me to eat, but this did not please my heart, for I sat there with my mind on other problems, and my heart foreboded trouble. And when Circe saw me sitting thus without reaching out toward the food and gripped by some deep sorrow, she came and stood near me and spoke winged words: 'Why do you sit this way, Odysseus, like who is dumb, eating out your heart, and why do you not touch the food and drink? You do not, in truth, suspect another trick, do you? You do not need to fear, for I have sworn a solemn oath to you.'

"Thus she encouraged me, but I answered her, saying, 'Oh Circe, can any man indeed, if he is a righteous man, bring himself to taste food and drink before he has set his companions free and has seen them with his own eyes? But if you really want me to eat and drink, then free them so that I may see my faithful companions before me.'

"Thus I spoke, and Circe went directly through the hall, holding her wand in her hand, and opened up the gates of the pigsty and drove out the men, who looked just like nine-year-old pigs. Then, as they stood thus in front of her, she walked among them and rubbed each one with another magic drug. And then the bristles, which the dread drug that revered Circe had given them first had caused to grow, fell from their limbs, and straightway they became men again—younger than they had been before and far handsomer and taller to behold. Then they recognized me, and each one in turn came up and clasped my hands. And as tears of joy overcame us all, the house echoed and reechoed all around, and even the goddess herself felt pity for us."

From *Odyssey* X, 133–399

The Sirens

AND

Scylla and Charybdis

Odysseus returned to Aeaea after he had visited Tiresias in the lower world. Circe then warned him of what lay ahead.

Homer intertwines the accounts of the Sirens and of Scylla and Charybdis in such a manner that they are clearer when presented as a unit.

In the Odyssey *there are two Sirens, but in later mythology there were three, and sometimes more. They lived on an island between Aeaea, Circe's home, and Scylla and Charybdis. Scylla and Charybdis have been identified with the Straits of Messina.*

As told in Greek verse by Homer

"QUEENLY CIRCE led me by the hand apart from my dear companions, then sat down next to me and said, 'Listen closely to what I tell you, and indeed a god himself will help you to remember. First you will come to the Sirens, who in truth enchant with their magic powers all men who draw near them. If anyone approaches them and hears the voice of the Sirens, he never returns home again—never again do his wife and young children welcome him happily, but the Sirens, sitting in a meadow, hold him spellbound with their sweet song. And all about them is a great heap of men's bones and decaying bodies.

" 'But you must row past the Sirens and stop up the ears of your companions with wax that you have worked until it is soft, lest any one of the others hear their song. But you yourself, if you wish to listen, have your men bind you in the swift ship, tying you hand and foot straight to the base of the mast so that you may listen with pleasure to the song of the Sirens. And if you beg and command your comrades to unfasten your bonds, then they must bind you with still more ties.

" 'But when your companions have rowed beyond the Sirens, then—I shall not advise you definitely which of the two routes you should take—you must decide in your own mind, and I shall tell you about both routes. For on one side, in truth, are projecting ledges of rock, and upon them the mighty waves of dark-eyed Amphitrite dash with a roar. The blessed gods call these the Wandering Rocks. Not any birds fly past them—not even the shy doves that carry ambrosia to father Zeus—but that the bare rock always snatches up one of even these birds for itself, and then father Zeus sends another dove to complete their number.

" 'Also, not any ship of men, not any that has come there, has ever escaped, but indeed the timbers of the ships and the bodies of the men are tossed about indiscriminately by the waves of the sea and deadly lightning storms. Indeed, only one sea-faring ship alone has sailed past there—the *Argo*, well-known to all—when she was sailing back from the land of Aeëtes, and then the sea certainly would have quickly hurled her against the mighty rocks, but Hera sent the ship safely along because Jason was dear to her.

" 'On the other side there are two cliffs, one of which reaches to the wide vault of heaven with its pointed peak. A dark cloud covers it and indeed never leaves it, and never does a clear sky surround the summit either in the summertime or at the time of harvest. Certainly a mortal man could neither climb it nor reach the top, not even if he had twenty hands and feet, for the rock is smooth, just as though it had been polished all over. In the middle of this cliff is a dark cave, facing toward the west and Erebus, where indeed you will steer your ship, glorious Odysseus. Not even a stalwart man could shoot an arrow from his hollow ship that would reach into the high vault of the cave.

" 'There, within the cave, Scylla dwells, howling fearfully. Her voice, in truth, is as loud as the yelp of a young puppy, but she herself, however, is an evil monster, and indeed not anyone would be glad to look upon her, not even if he who met with her were a god. In truth, she has twelve feet, all of them hanging down, and six necks, all very long, and on each one is a terrible head with three rows of teeth that are crowded and thick and full of black death. She is hidden in the hollow cave up to her waist; but she stretches her heads out from the awful opening and fishes there, gazing eagerly around the rocky cliff in search of dolphins and sea lions, or any bigger sea monster that loud-moaning Amphitrite nourishes in countless numbers, which she might snatch up. Not any sailors, up to this time, can boast that they have fled past her in their ship without injury, since with each head she seizes a man, taking him off his dark-prowed ship.

" 'You will see, Odysseus, that the other cliff is low, however. They are close to each other, and you could certainly shoot an arrow between them. On this one there is a large wild fig tree, rich with foliage, and below this tree divine Charybdis gulps down the black water. Three times each day she sends the water forth and three times she swallows it again in a terrible manner. May you not be there by any chance when she swallows it down, for certainly no one would be able to rescue you, not even Poseidon the earth-shaker. But instead, when you have drawn near to Scylla's high rock, quickly sail your ship past that spot, since it is far better to mourn the loss of six companions from your ship than all of them at once.'

"Thus she spoke, but I answered her, saying, 'Come now, I beg you, goddess; tell me truly whether I may escape from deadly Charybdis by any means and also defend myself from Scylla when she does injury to my companions.'

"Thus I spoke, and the lovely goddess answered me forthwith: 'Stubborn man, now you are thinking again of deeds of war and action. Will you never submit to the immortal gods? She is indeed not mortal, but she is an immortal evil, terrible and grievous and fierce, and not a foe to be faced in battle. There is not any defense against her. The best thing is to flee from her, for if you delay beside the cliff to prepare to fight her, I am afraid she will stretch forth as many necks again and carry off as many men a second time. No, it is better to row on by, pulling hard, and to call on Crataeïs, the mother of Scylla, for aid. Then she herself will stop her from rushing forth again.'

"Thus she spoke, and before long Dawn came on her throne of gold. Then I went down to the ship and urged my companions to get aboard and to unfasten the ropes at the ship's stern. They quickly went on board and sat down at the rowing benches. Then indeed I spoke to my companions, troubled in my heart: 'O friends, since it is not right for only one or two to know the warnings that Circe, the lovely goddess, gave to me, I shall tell you all so that we may be aware of the dangers and either perish together or escape from death and destruction.

" 'She advised us first to avoid the divinely sweet song of the Sirens and their flowering meadow. She urged that I alone listen to their singing; but you must tie me with heavy bonds so that I will stay there, standing at the base of the mast. But if I beg and command you to untie me, then you must bind me with still more bonds.'

"In this way, therefore, I related all these problems to my companions. In the meantime, the well-built ship quickly reached the island of the Sirens, for a favorable breeze carried her forward. Then the wind fell, and all became still and calm, as a god lulled the waves to sleep.

"Then I cut a large round cake of wax into small pieces with my sharp sword and rolled it in my strong hands. The wax quickly became soft from the heat of the pressure and the rays of Helios, and I stopped up the ears of all my companions, one after another, with the wax. And they bound me hand and foot straight to the base of the mast, tying the ends of the ropes to the mast itself. Then they sat down at the rowing benches and lashed the gray sea with their oars.

"But when we were as far away as one can make himself heard by shouting, our ship, speeding over the sea, did not escape their notice as it came near, and they began their sweet song: 'Come here, steer this way, famous Odysseus, great pride of the Achaeans. Bring your ship to land so that you may listen to our song. For no one has ever passed by this island in his dark ship before he has heard the honey-voiced music of our voices; but instead he stops to enjoy it and then goes away with greater wisdom. For we know, in truth, of all the trials that the Argives and Trojans suffered at Troy by the will of the gods, and we know, also, all things that happen on the abundant earth.'

"Thus they sang as their beautiful melody rang out, and, indeed, my heart longed to listen to them, and I ordered my companions to untie me, making signs to them with my eyebrows. They, however, bent to the oars and rowed onward. And soon Perimedes and Eurylochus got up and bound me with more bonds and also pulled them tighter. But when we had passed beyond them and could no longer hear the voices of the Sirens or their song, my faithful companions immediately took out the wax with which I had stopped up their ears and released me from my bonds.

"But when we had left the island behind us, I soon saw spray ahead of us, and a great swelling wave and heard its roar. Then the oars fell from the hands of my terrified men, and our ship herself came to a standstill. But I went through the ship cheering up my companions with soothing words as I stood beside each man: 'O my friends, we have indeed experienced danger before this, and I believe that some day we shall recall this trouble also as a memory. Come now, therefore, and all obey my orders just as I give them to you. You must stay at your rowing benches and pull hard against the deep waves of the sea with your oars in the hope that Zeus may grant us the power to escape and avoid this disaster somehow. And you, helmsman, I order to keep the ship well out of reach of that spray and surf and to keep close to the cliff, or, before you know it, she will head over that way and you will hurl us all to ruin.'

"Thus I spoke, and they straightway obeyed my words. But I did not speak of Scylla, an unavoidable danger, lest my companions might stop rowing and close themselves up in the hold. And then I completely forgot Circe's troublesome command that I should not arm myself at all. But I put on my splendid armor and picked up two long spears, then went to the forecastle deck of the ship; for I hoped that from there I would have the first sight of Scylla, who lived among the rocks—she who was to bring such grief to my companions. But I could not see her anywhere, even though my eyes grew weary as I looked around everywhere in the direction of the dimly visible cliff.

"As we sailed on into the narrow strait, we groaned, for on one side was Scylla, and on the other side fearful Charybdis sucked down the salty water of the sea. Then, when she sent it forth again, she roared and foamed with great confusion like a cauldron on a hot fire, and high above her the spray fell down over the tops of both cliffs. But when she drew in the salty sea water, the swirling turbulence within could be seen, and the rocks roared dreadfully all about. And the earth beneath, dark with sand, came into sight, and pale terror gripped the men.

"While we gazed toward her, expecting destruction, Scylla at that same time grasped from my hollow ship six of my companions who were the most outstanding in strength and ability. As I looked around over the swift ship and examined my crew, I could also see their feet and arms dangling high in the air overhead. And they cried out to me, calling me by name, calling my name for the last time in agony of heart as they were pulled up toward the rocks, struggling desperately. She devoured them on her very threshold as they screamed and stretched their hands out toward me in their terrible, final struggle. Of all the trials I endured while I wandered across the paths of the sea, that was the most pitiable sight my eyes looked upon."

From *Odyssey* XII, 33–259

Aeneas and the Lower World

After they left Carthage, Aeneas and his followers returned to Sicily, where funeral games were held in honor of Anchises, Aeneas' father. The shade of Anchises, appearing to Aeneas, advised him to visit the lower world to consult with him about the future. Aeneas, therefore, went on to Cumae to seek the help of the Sibyl.

Cumae was not far from Lake Avernus, one of the legendary entrances to the lower world. Founded on an acropolis at least as early as the eighth century B.C., Cumae was one of the earliest of the Greek colonies on the southern Italian peninsula. Excavations at the foot of the acropolis have revealed an extensive vaulted grotto, as well as temples and numerous other remains.

Aeneas was leading his fellow Trojans to a new home after the fall of Troy. They settled at last in Italy—in a district later called Latium—and founded the town of Lavinium. According to legend, Rome was ultimately founded by the descendants of Aeneas and his followers.

As told in Latin verse by Vergil

THEN, AT last, Aeneas' fleet landed at the shores of Cumae. Aeneas sought out the citadel where Apollo presided, and the home of the awesome Sibyl nearby, a huge cave. The prophet Apollo inspires her with a great knowledge and reveals to her the events of the future.

Aeneas and his men made haste to carry out the sacred rites, and soon the priestess summoned the Trojans to her lofty temple. When they reached the threshold of her cave, she cried out, "Now is the time to consult the oracle. Behold, Apollo is at hand. The doors of this dwelling will not open until you offer vows and prayers." Then she fell silent.

Cold fear ran through the bones of the Trojans, and Aeneas, their king, began his earnest prayer: "Phoebus, grant that now, finally, ill fortune may follow us no farther, and may you, most respected prophetess, grant that the Trojans and their gods may settle in Latium. Then I shall build a marble temple to Phoebus and Diana and a great shrine to you, also, in my kingdom.

"I beg this one favor. Since the entrance to the kingdom of the ruler of the lower world is said to be near here at the marsh where the Acheron overflows, may I have the good fortune to enter and behold my dear father's face. And may you be my guide and open the sacred gates for me."

Then the prophetess answered him, saying, "Trojan Aeneas, son of Anchises, the descent to Avernus is easy, for Pluto's gates lie open night and day; but to retrace your steps and return to the upper world is a difficult task, a laborious task. But if you have such a desire to cross the Stygian lake twice and to behold Tartarus twice, hear what must be done first. There lies hidden in the shadows of a tree a golden bough, with golden leaves and golden stem, declared sacred to the queen of the lower world. No one may be granted the privilege of entering the secret places below unless he picks this golden-leaved bough, for the fair Proserpina has established this as a special offering to her.

"After one bough has been plucked off, another golden bough appears, and its stem sprouts golden leaves also. Look up high in the tree, and you will pick it easily when you have found it if the fates summon you. But if they do not call you, you will not be able to break it off by force nor cut it with a steel blade. In this way you will, at last, see the Stygian groves and the kingdom that has no paths for the living." When she had spoken thus, the Sibyl was silent.

They went into an ancient forest, and Aeneas pondered all this in his heart as he gazed into the vast woods, and by chance he began to pray, "If only the golden bough would reveal itself now to us!" He had scarcely said these words, when two doves flew out of the heavens before his very eyes and alighted on the green grass. The noble hero recognized his mother's birds at once and began to pray, "Be our guides, I beg you, if there is a way, and show us, by your flight, our course into the grove to the place where the golden branch casts its shadow on the earth. O Venus, my goddess mother, do not fail me in this crisis."

Aeneas stood still, watching for a sign, waiting to see where the doves might fly. As they fed, the doves kept flying forward, but no farther than the distance at which those following them could keep them in sight. When they came to the gates of Avernus, they suddenly flew upward and gently came to rest on a tree that had two kinds of foliage and from which many shades of gold shone among the branches. The metal leaves were crackling in the breeze as Aeneas broke off the clinging bough eagerly and carried it off to the dwelling of the prophetess Sibyl.

Aeneas hastened to carry out the Sibyl's bidding. There was a great cave with a huge gaping mouth, stony and rough and protected by a dark lake and a dark shadowy grove where no birds could fly in safety, so harmful was the breath pouring from its jaws and rising to the skies. The Greeks, therefore, called the place *Aörnos*, "Birdless."

Here the priestess placed four black bullocks for sacrifice, the first offerings, and called upon Hecate, who has power in heaven and Erebus alike. Aeneas offered the life of a lamb to Night, the mother of the Furies, and a heifer to you, Proserpina. Then he built altars to Pluto, the Stygian king, and set whole bulls on the flames. Just before the early light of sunrise, the earth began to rumble, and dogs howled in the shadows at the coming of the goddess. Then the priestess said, "Now you must have courage, Aeneas; now you must have a brave heart." Then they walked along, covered by the darkness of night, through the shadows and the empty, ghostly realm of Pluto.

In the very entrance gate of Hades, Grief and vengeful Care have their couches. And there also abide pale Diseases and sad Old Age, Fear and Hunger and Poverty—shapes dreadful to behold—and Death and Labor, also Sleep—Death's twin brother—and wicked Pleasures. War, the bringer of Death, is on the opposite threshold. There also are the iron chambers of the Furies, and wild Discord with bloody fillets binding her snaky hair.

In the center is a huge elm tree with its aged branches stretching wide, where it is said idle Dreams have their abode and cling beneath the leaves. Many monstrous wild beasts are stabled in the entrance—centaurs and Scyllas, and Briareus, the giant with a hundred hands, the Hydra of Lerna hissing fearfully, Chimaera breathing flame, Gorgons, Harpies, and Geryon, the giant with three bodies. In sudden fear and trembling, Aeneas pulled his sword, and had his knowing companion not warned him that these were ghosts without bodies, he would have rushed in and struck at them, though in vain, with his sword.

The way that leads to the waters of Acheron begins in this place. Here a stream, filled with mud from a great whirlpool, hurls forth its sand into Cocytus. The ferryman Charon, terrible with filth, stands guard over the waters of the river. His white beard is matted, his eyes flash fire, his dirty cloak hangs down from a knot at his shoulder. He guides his raft with a pole and minds the sails as he ferries the dead across in his boat, already an old man but with the vigorous old age of a god.

Here a crowd was milling about on the bank, mothers and soldiers and mighty heroes, and boys and maidens, and youths whose funeral pyres their parents have seen—their lives over. They were as numerous as the leaves of the woods that flutter down in the first chill of autumn, standing there and begging to be first to pass over the stream and stretching their arms toward the farther bank in longing. But the sorrowful ferryman takes now these and now those, driving others away and holding them away from the shore.

Aeneas, wondering at the confusion, said, "Tell me, O maiden, the meaning of this throng at the river's bank. What do these souls want? How is it decided who are to leave the shore and cross the dark waters?" Then the aged priestess answered, "You see here before you the deep waters of Cocytus and the Stygian marsh, by whose power the gods swear their oaths and are afraid to swear falsely. All this crowd are the poor, unburied spirits. Their boatman is Charon. These who are carried over the water have been buried, but he is not allowed to carry the spirits across before their bodies have been laid to rest in a burial place. They wander and flit about the banks for a hundred years, and then, finally, they may return to the pools they long for."

Anchises' son stood still, thinking over many things and pitying their unjust fate in his heart. They went on then with their journey and approached the river. The ferryman, looking across the Stygian waters and seeing them in the distance, spoke first, rebuking them, "Whoever you are, you who are coming armed to the river, come, tell why you are coming. Stand there and come no closer. This is the land of shades and sleep and night; it is not right for me to carry the living in my boat."

In reply the Sibyl, the prophetess of Apollo, answered, "Trojan Aeneas, renowned for his devotion to duty and his ability with arms, is descending to the deep shades of Erebus, seeking his father. If such devotion does not move you, then you must at least recognize the power of this branch." And she showed him the branch she had hidden in her robe. The anger in Charon's heart subsided at the sight of it, and he said no more, but, marveling at the sacred bough, he turned his boat toward them and came to the river's edge. He hurried the souls seated on the long benches out of the way and took Aeneas into his craft, which groaned under the weight. Finally, he landed the prophetess and the hero on the other shore amid the mud and marsh reeds.

Huge Cerberus makes these realms resound with the barking of his three throats as he lies sprawled out full length in the cavern opposite. The prophetess threw him a honey cake drugged with sleep. Opening up his three mouths hungrily, he seized the cake, and then relaxing, he stretched out at full length on the floor of the cavern. Aeneas grasped the chance to enter, as soon as the guard fell asleep, and quickly passed beyond the bank of the river that can not be crossed again.

Immediately loud cries were heard—the voices of infants crying at the very entrance, spirits torn from their mothers' breasts by a sorrowful day and plunged into an early death. Beside them were those doomed to die on false charges. But these dwelling places are not assigned without a jury or without a judge. Minos is the one who shakes the urn and calls a council of the silent to consider both their lives and the charges against them. Next are the sorrowful souls who brought death on themselves by their own hands and threw their lives away in hatred of life.

Near this place can be seen the Fields of Mourning, extending far in all directions. Here hidden paths conceal those who have wasted away for cruel love. Among them Aeneas saw Phoenician

Dido, still bearing her recent wound,* roaming in the vast woods. The Trojan hero tried to comfort her with his words, but she stood with her eyes downcast, and she was no more moved than if she were hard flint or Parian marble. Then, at length, she turned and fled into the shade of the grove where Sychaeus, her husband of old, equaled her love with his own. Aeneas, shaken by her bitter lot, followed her with tearful gaze as she went, and pitied her.

Then he pressed on along the appointed path. Soon they reached the farthest fields, a place apart, where those famous in war dwell. These spirits gathered around him in a throng, eager to walk with him and learn why he had come. But the Greek chiefs and Agamemnon's troops, seeing the hero with his armor flashing in the shadows, trembled with great fear.

Meanwhile Aurora, riding across the sky in her four-horse chariot, had passed the zenith, and the Sibyl spoke to him in warning, "Night is coming fast, Aeneas, while we linger weeping. Here the way splits into two roads. The one on the right leads to mighty Pluto's walls and is the path by which we go to Elysium; the one on the left inflicts punishment on the wicked and sends them to dread Tartarus."

Aeneas looked around suddenly and saw a great fortress encircled with three walls standing at the base of a cliff, and a river, Tartarean Phlegethon, raging round it in flames and hurling rocks along its course. Facing him was a huge gate with columns of adamant so strong that no human power, and not even the gods themselves, could break them. A lofty iron tower stood there, and Tisiphone sat there guarding the entranceway day and night. Groans were heard rising from there and the sound of fierce lashes and the grating of iron chains. Aeneas stood still, appalled at the noise.

"Tell me, O prophetess, what form of crime is here, what sort of punishment?" Then the Sibyl answered, "Famous leader of the Trojans, no innocent person may tread on that wicked threshold. But when Hecate placed me in charge of the groves of Avernus, she told me about the punishments the gods inflict there, and she

---

* Dido had taken her life by the sword when she learned Aeneas was going to leave Carthage to continue his journey in pursuit of his destiny.

took me through the whole region. Rhadamanthus of Cnossus rules over these realms and listens to their crimes and punishes them. The avenger Tisiphone, carrying her whip, drives the guilty before her. A Hydra, fierce with fifty gaping mouths, has her abode within. Tartarus itself stretches straight down into the shadows twice as far as the view upward through the sky to Olympus.

"In this place the ancient offspring of Earth, the Titans, struck by a thunderbolt, writhe in the deepest part. Here, also, I saw the giants who tried to pull down the sky with their hands and bring Jupiter down from his kingdom on high. Here are those who hated their brothers during life, or beat a parent, or planned fraud, or brooded alone over their riches and set none aside for their relatives. All are confined and awaiting punishment.

"Some roll a huge stone, others hang bound to the spokes of a wheel. There sits Theseus in misery, and he will sit there forever. They all dared monstrous evil and gained what they dared. Even if I had a hundred tongues and mouths and an iron voice, I could not relate all the crimes or punishments."

Then the aged priestess of Apollo cried, "Come now, let us make haste and carry out the duty you have undertaken. I see the walls that the Cyclopes' forges built and the arched gates where we are to place our offering." Side by side they hurried along the dark path and came to the gate. Aeneas sprinkled himself with fresh water and placed the bough on the gateway.

When the offering had been completed they came to the happy places, grassy regions, the home of the blessed. Here ample air covers the fields with bright light, and they have their own sun and stars. Some of the spirits were exercising on grassy wrestling grounds and yellow sand; some were dancing and singing. And there, too, the Thracian bard Orpheus played in accompaniment, striking the strings sometimes with his fingers, sometimes with his ivory pick. Here was Teucer's ancient race, famous offspring, great heroes of happier times.

The Sibyl addressed the throng gathered together, especially Musaeus, who stood in the midst, asking, "Tell us, blessed spirits, and you, greatest of bards, in what region is Anchises' dwelling place? It is because of him we have come here, traveling across

Erebus' mighty streams." The hero answered her briefly, "No one has a fixed dwelling, but we live in shady groves or upon the soft river banks or in meadows fresh with streams. But if you will but climb this ridge I shall start you on the path." So saying, he walked ahead, and from the ridge he pointed out the fields below. Then Aeneas and the Sibyl began their descent from the hilltop.

Father Anchises was watching the souls who were enclosed in the green valley and were going to pass from there to the world above. When he saw Aeneas coming toward him, he stretched forth his hands and cried out to him as tears began to roll down his cheeks: "Have you really come at last, and may I actually hear your familiar voice and converse with you?" Then Aeneas replied, "It was your spirit, father, your mournful spirit, often appearing before me, that urged me to come here. My fleet lies at anchor on the Tyrrhenian Sea. Let me take your hand, father, and do not leave me." And as he spoke his face became wet with tears.

Aeneas caught sight of a grove set apart in the valley, a rustling wood, and the river Lethe, gliding past the peaceful abodes, and the souls of countless peoples flying around it. Amazed at the sight, Aeneas inquired about the river and the people crowding its banks. His father then answered, "They are the souls for whom fate has destined new bodies and who drink forgetfulness and release from care from Lethe's waters. For some time now I have wanted to show these people to you and to tell you about these descendants of our race so we may be even more joyful now that Italy has been found." Then Anchises began his account, telling every detail in proper order.

There are twin gates of Sleep, one of which is said to be of horn and to grant an easy exit to true shades; and the other is of gleaming white ivory, by which the spirits send false visions to the light of the upper world. When he had finished his tale, Anchises accompanied his son and the Sibyl to these gates and sent them out through the ivory gate. Then Aeneas hastened on his way to the ships and rejoined his companions.

From *Aeneid* VI, 2–899

Cupid and Psyche

The story of Cupid and Psyche is an example of the combining of a folk tale with an allegorical and romantic fairy story. Apuleius took a tale that appeared first in Greek mythology and wove a love story around Cupid, the god of love and desire, and Psyche, the personification of the spirit or soul.

La Fontaine and others have used this story, but Apuleius' account is the only one we have from the literature of ancient times.

As told in Latin prose by Apuleius

THERE WERE once, in a certain kingdom, a king and queen who had three daughters of remarkable beauty. The two older girls, very beautiful in appearance, could be described with all the praise of mortal words; but the beauty and grace of the youngest girl were so exceptional, so unusual, that they could not be expressed by human speech. Indeed, many of the citizens of the kingdom, and a number of strangers whom the rumor of her loveliness had reached, used to come to admire and worship her as though she were the goddess Venus herself.

Soon the rumor spread to kingdoms nearby and to bordering lands that the goddess Venus, born of the deep blue sea and brought up by the spray of the foaming waves, was now mingling in the gatherings of the people, bestowing the favor of her divine power everywhere. Countless mortals, therefore, made long journeys by land and traveled far by sea to behold this glorious sight. No one sailed to Paphos, or to Cnidus, or even to Cythera to worship Venus as people once had. Her sacred rites were forgotten, her temples were disfigured, her shrines fell into decay.

The people offered prayers to the girl, and the divine power of the great goddess of beauty was worshiped in human form. When the girl came forth each morning, sacrifices and offerings were presented to her in the name of the deserted Venus, and when she walked on the streets all the people prayed to her and offered her garlands of flowers.

This unrestrained transfer of divine honors to the worship of a mortal girl greatly aroused the spirit of the true goddess Venus. She, unable to restrain her anger, shook her head in rage and reasoned thus to herself: "Surely, if I share my divine power with another and a mortal girl walks about with the appearance of my likeness, then in vain did the shepherd Paris, whose judgment and truthfulness the great Jupiter trusted, judge me to be of exceptional beauty, placing me before all other goddesses. But this girl, whoever she is, will not be happy at having stolen my honors but shall come to regret her unlawful beauty."

Then, without delay, the goddess called her winged and bold son Cupid to her. Venus urged him on with her words, even though he was naturally full of mischief, and brought him to the city where the maiden lived. Venus pointed out Psyche—for the girl was called by this name—to her son. After she had told him the whole story of the rivalry of Psyche's beauty, sighing and grumbling in anger, she said, "I beg you by the bonds of a mother's love, take full vengeance for your mother and severely punish the proud beauty of this girl.

"I wish you to accomplish this one thing above all else; namely, that this girl may be held by a most passionate love for the worst sort of man—one whom Fate has condemned to be without worth or money or wealth and so base that no one of similar wretchedness could be found in the whole world."

Thus she spoke, and, after she had kissed her son lovingly and had embraced him for a long time, she departed and sought the shore of the sea that lay nearby.

Meanwhile, Psyche, although she knew her beauty was outstanding, perceived no rewards from the honors paid her. She was looked at with wonder by all; she was praised by all; but no one, neither king nor prince nor even one of the common folk, came as a suitor seeking her hand in marriage. Soon her two older sisters, whose moderate beauty was not greatly admired by the people, were happily married to royal suitors; but the maiden

Psyche, remaining at home unwed, wept in her lonely solitude.

Thus the unhappy father of this most unfortunate girl, suspecting the envy of the gods and the anger of the immortals, consulted the very ancient oracle of Apollo of Miletus. With prayers and sacrifices, he sought from that mighty god a husband in marriage for his unwed daughter. Apollo gave his response in Latin thus:

> "On the rock of a mountain high, leave the girl.
> In the dress of the funeral couch clothe her now.
> Do not hope for a husband of mortals born,
> but one wild as a serpent, a savage one,
> who with fire and his darts can make each thing weak
> as he flies through the sky, and all things tires out;
> before whom even gods bow in frightened fear,
> and the dark lower world and the rivers quake."

When he heard the response of the oracle of Apollo, the once happy king returned home sad and downcast and explained to his wife the instructions of the unfortunate prophecy.

There was grief and weeping and sorrow for many days, but soon the time was at hand for the hateful fulfillment of the cruel fate and the tragic wedding of the unlucky Psyche. The joyful singing of the wedding song ended in mournful wailing, and the girl who was about to wed wiped away her tears with her bridal veil. But the necessity of obeying the divine commands demanded that the unhappy little Psyche be led to her appointed destiny.

With a firm step the girl joined the procession of people accompanying her. They proceeded to the appointed rock on the steep mountain, where all the people left the girl on the lofty summit and departed.

The gentle breeze of Zephyrus, the west wind, breathing softly, fell upon Psyche, however, as she lay pale and trembling and weeping on the very peak of the rock. The west wind slowly raised the girl on the peaceful air, carrying her little by little through the slopes of lofty rock, and laid her down as she slipped softly into a bed of grass and flowers in a valley lying nearby.

Psyche, lying pleasantly on her bed of dewy grass amid the tender herbs—now that her mind had been comforted of its great trouble—was sweetly quiet. And soon, refreshed by a long sleep, she awakened with a feeling of calm and saw a grove filled with tall and vast trees. She saw, too, in the very middle of the grove a spring shining bright with crystal water.

Near the source of the fountain was a royal palace, built not by human hands but by divine skill. You would know at the first glance that you were looking at the splendid and luxurious home of some one of the gods.

Psyche, invited by delight at what she saw, approached nearer and, becoming more courageous, crossed the threshold. Soon, lured on by eagerness at the beauty of the sight, she examined everything. There was nothing that could not be found there.

As she was looking at these things with the greatest of pleasure, a certain voice without any body made itself heard and said to her, "Why, mistress, are you amazed at such riches? All these things are yours. Go, therefore, to your own room and refresh yourself by resting on your bed and have a bath, as you choose. We, whose voices you hear, are your handmaidens. We shall wait upon you carefully, and a royal repast will await you when you have refreshed yourself."

Psyche felt the happiness and encouragement of divine providence when she heard the formless voices, and she drove away her weariness first with sleep and then with a bath.

Soon Psyche saw a rounded chair placed next to a table heaped with food, and judging it had been set there just for her, she gladly sat down to eat. After a splendid banquet, a certain one came in and sang but was unseen, and another played on the cithara, likewise invisible.

When these pleasures came to an end and night fell, Psyche fell happily into bed. And as the night went on, a certain gentle sound came to her ears. Then suddenly her unknown husband was at her side and made Psyche his wife, but before the beginning of dawn he departed quickly.

Meanwhile, Psyche's parents grew old with unwearied grief and mourning, and the report of their sorrow spread far and wide until her two sisters learned of her fate. Then, sad and sorrowful, they hastily left their own homes and hurried to see and speak with their parents.

That night her husband—but, in fact, she never saw him with her eyes but knew him only by touch and sound—spoke to Psyche thus: "Psyche, my very beloved and dear wife, a rather cruel fate threatens you with deadly danger that I advise you to watch out for with cautious care. Your sisters, disturbed now by the belief that you are dead, are seeking traces of you and will come to the mountain without delay. If by chance you hear their weeping, do not answer and do not even look at them at all."

Psyche agreed and answered that she would act according to the wishes of her husband. But when he slipped away with the night, the poor girl spent the whole day in tears and sorrow, repeating again and again that now she had utterly perished—she who was confined to the barrier of this splendid prison and was deprived of the comfort of human conversation.

Nor was there any delay before her husband, reaching her side a little earlier than usual and embracing her even as she wept, scolded her thus: "Is this what you promised me, my Psyche?"

Then she extracted an agreement from her husband, by entreaties and the threat that she would die, that she might see her sisters and soothe their grief and talk with them face to face. So at the prayers of his new bride, he granted the favor, but he warned her again and again that she was not at any time to seek out the appearance of her husband.

She thanked her husband and, happier now, said, "But I would die a hundred times rather than be denied this very sweet marriage with you. For I love you and value you without measure, whoever you are, as much as I would my own soul, nor could Cupid himself equal you."

By the force and power of her love, Psyche led her husband, although unwilling, to submit, and he promised he would do all she asked.

Meanwhile Psyche's sisters, persistently searching, came shortly to the very rock and spot where Psyche had been abandoned. And they called their poor sister by her name until she ran from the house and called, "Why do you destroy yourselves in vain with tormented weeping? I, the one you mourn, am here."

Then summoning Zephyrus, Psyche advised him of the instructions of her husband. Nor was there any delay; for he, obeying the command, lifted them up at once without harm on gentle breezes and carried them off. Presently they were enjoying each other's embraces and many kisses.

"Now," she said, "enter my house and home with joy and restore your shattered spirits with your Psyche." So saying, she pointed out the great riches of the golden house, and the voices of the numerous household servants serving her reached their ears.

Psyche, however, did not betray the command of her husband in any way or release it from the hidden places of her heart; but, rising to necessity, she pretended he was a certain handsome young man, frequently engaged in hunting in the country places and mountains. Then, lest by any slip of the tongue she should reveal her secret knowledge as she talked, she called Zephyrus to her and proposed that he should carry them away again at once, laden as they were with things made of gold and necklaces of jewels.

When this had been accomplished directly, the beautiful sisters returned to their homes, and because they were now feverish with the poison of growing envy, they chattered to each other, talking over many things between them.

Then one began to speak thus: "Behold an empty and cruel and unjust fate! She, the youngest, has gained possession of these great riches and has a god as her husband—she who does not know how to use such an abundance of possessions correctly. It may be that if their love continues and their affection grows firm, the god, her husband, may even make her a goddess. Thus it is, by Hercules; thus she acts and carries herself."

The other sister continued: "Neither am I a woman nor do I even breathe unless I cast her down from this great wealth into ruin. And if our disgrace has embittered you also, as is right, let us both together seek out a strong plan. Let her realize that she does not have us as slaves but as older sisters."

Thus filled with madness, they hurried to their own homes, devising a shameful crime, indeed even murder, against their innocent sister.

Meanwhile, Psyche's husband—her husband though she knew him not—again warned her thus as he spoke to her at night, saying, "Do you see how much danger there is for you? Fate threatens you from afar, and unless you take very firm precaution, it will soon be close upon you. Treacherous witches are, with determined effort, preparing a wicked trap for you, the main purpose of which is to persuade you to search out my face—which, as I have often told you before, you will not see again if once you have looked upon it. But soon you will bear an infant, a divine child if you cloak our secrets in silence, but, if you violate them, a mortal one."

At this news Psyche was filled with joy and was delighted by the comforting thought of a divine offspring. But already those destructive and shameful furies, breathing forth their snakelike poison and hurrying with wicked speed, were proceeding with their plot.

The two sisters, joined together in the plan they had agreed upon and not even visiting their parents, sought out the rock with headlong haste directly from the ship, and not waiting for the support of the wind to carry them, with abandoned rashness they leaped forth into space. Not unmindful of the royal command, Zephyrus—although unwilling—catching them up in the lap of a wafting breeze, carried them back again to earth. And they, not delaying, immediately entered Psyche's home with quick step.

With pretended affection they won over the confidence of their sister little by little. Straightway, when they had been refreshed from the weariness of their journey by sitting quietly and had been renewed by the warm waters of their baths, Psyche delighted them in the extreme by a dinner with all its wonderful and delicious foods and delicacies. She ordered the harp to play, and the music sang forth; the flutes to sound, and they were played; the chorus to sing, and there was song.

The wickedness of the plotting women was not put to rest, however, for they began deceitfully to try to learn what sort of man Psyche's husband was and from what place and lineage he came. Then Psyche, forgetting her previous answers in her excessive frankness, devised a new story—that her husband was from a neighboring province, dealt in great sums of money, and was of middle age with hair sprinkled with gray. Without lingering even for a short time over this conversation, Psyche sent them off again, loaded down with lavish gifts, to be carried away by the wind.

But while they were returning to their homes, carried on high by the gentle breeze of Zephyrus, they deliberated with each other thus: "You will find out nothing, my sister, other than the fact that either this very evil woman has fashioned a lie or she does not know the appearance of her husband. Whichever of these possibilities is true, she must be driven away from those riches as quickly as possible. And if she does not know the face of her husband, she has indeed been wed to a god."

Thus—after they had passed a disturbed night in wakefulness— inflamed and desperate, they dashed to the cliff early in the morning. From there, with the usual support of the wind, they hurried down quickly, and with tears forced by rubbing their eyelids, they addressed Psyche with this craftiness: "You, for- tunate indeed and happy in your ignorance of such great mis- fortune, remain careless of your danger. We, however, with ever watchful care keep guard over your affairs, tormented as we are with pity for the fate that awaits you. For we have learned as a certainty—nor can we hide it from you, we who are indeed the companions of your misfortune and fate—that a huge snake, a serpent with coils of many knots, comes to you secretly each night.

"Now remember the oracle of Apollo, who proclaimed that you were destined for marriage with a savage beast. Most of your neighbors have seen him returning in the evening. Everyone says that he will not feast you very long on pleasantries of food, but that, as soon as your child is ready to be born, he will devour you. Now the decision in regard to this situation is yours. And if the solitude of this voice-filled countryside, or marriage with a secret love and the embrace of a poisonous serpent delight you, certainly we have done our part as devoted sisters."

Then poor little Psyche, since she was simple and yielding in spirit, was caught up by the horror of these very gloomy words, and pushed beyond the limit of her courage, she utterly lost all memory of the admonitions of her husband and of her own promises to him. She answered them thus: "You, dearest sisters, as is right, have indeed remained fast in the kindness of your devotion. I have never seen the countenance of my husband nor do I know at all by sight what his appearance might be.

"I agree justly with you when you say rightly that he is some beast or other. He always terrifies me greatly in regard to his appearance and threatens great evil from my curiosity about his features."

Then one of her sisters spoke thus: "We shall point out to you the way that alone makes clear the road to safety. Conceal a very sharp knife, made razor-sharp by the whetting of its thin blade, in secret on that side of the bed where you are accustomed to sleep, and a lamp filled with oil, ready and gleaming with a clear light.

"When all this provision has been hidden most securely, and after he has come to bed as usual and lies stretched out full in his accustomed place and, enveloped by the beginning of a sound sleep, has begun to breathe in deep slumber, slip out of bed. With bare feet, taking small quick steps on tiptoe, and with the lamp freed from the prison of its dark hiding place, make use of the opportunity for your brilliant deed afforded by the helping glow of your lamp. With that dangerous sharp weapon raised high in your right hand, sever the poisonous serpent's head from the joint of his neck.

"Nor will you lack our help, for when you have made yourself safe by his death and have hastily carried away all your possessions with you, we shall join you as a wife in solemn marriage to a human husband."

When their sister's heart—already in fact aglow—had been inflamed by the fire of these words, they left her. Psyche, being left alone, was tossed about by her sadness like the tides of the sea. Although she was firm in plan and resolute in spirit, she wavered, torn in her feelings toward this calamity.

She hurried, she delayed. She dared, she trembled. She was diffident, she was angered. Worst of all, she hated the beast, but loved the husband. When evening was already ushering in the night, however, with headlong haste she gathered together the materials for the wicked crime.

Night was at hand, and her husband came and showed her his love. After he fell into a deep sleep, Psyche, although she was not strong in body or bold in spirit, nevertheless acquired strength and force from the fierceness furnished by fate.

Under the glow of the lamp, Psyche saw the gentlest and sweetest beast of all wild creatures—that very Cupid himself, a handsome god, lying in the bed gracefully. Frightened at such a countenance and losing her courage, Psyche sank down weak and trembling to her knees. She sought to hide the knife even in her own heart, which she certainly would have done if the weapon had not slipped and dropped from her heedless hands at the horror of such a shameful deed. But as she gazed upon the beauty of the divine expression, she was restored in spirit.

Over the shoulders of the winged god, feathers were dewy white with gleaming down, and although his wings now lay quiet, the soft and delicate little outer feathers, quivering tremulously, were moving to and fro restlessly. His body was glowing, and such as Venus would not have been ashamed to have given birth to him.

At the foot of the bed lay his bow and quiver of arrows, the gracious weapons of this great god. While Psyche, quite curious, was examining these with eagerness, she drew out one of the arrows from the quiver. Then, when she was trying out the sharpness of the point on the tip of her trembling finger, even then, pressing too hard, she pricked herself so deeply that tiny drops of rosy blood trickled through the surface of her skin. Thus, all unknowing, Psyche by her own action fell in love with Love.

While Psyche was moved thus, excited by such good fortune and smitten by love, there fell from the top of the lamp onto the right shoulder of the god a drop of burning oil. Burned thus, the god jumped up. When he saw the sorrowful evidence of betrayed faith, he promptly flew from the kisses and arms of his most unhappy wife without a word.

Psyche, quickly clasping his right leg with both hands as he rose up, wearied at last, lost her grip, and fell to the ground. Nor did the god of love desert Psyche as she lay on the ground, but he flew into the nearest cypress tree, and from its high top, deeply disturbed, he spoke to her thus:

"You very simple girl. Disregarding the instructions of my

mother, Venus, who ordered that you, helpless in your desire for the most miserable and lowly sort of man, be wedded in the basest of marriages, I flew to you myself instead. I did this without thought, I know, and I, that famous archer, wounded myself with my own weapon and made you my wife.

"I kept repeating that you must always beware of this; I kept warning you kindly of this. But certainly those fine advisers and so dangerous counselors of yours shall straightway pay me for their offenses. You, in truth, I shall punish only by my flight." And with these words he took wing and flew off into the sky.

Psyche was indeed cast down into the utmost grief of spirit. When the great expanse of space had taken her husband, snatched away on flying wings, from her sight, she threw herself headlong into the edge of the river nearby. But the gentle stream, fearing for itself, without delay carried her on a harmless eddy and placed her upon the bank, flowering with herbs.

At that moment by chance, Pan, the rustic god, was sitting next to the river's shore, embracing Echo and teaching that mountain goddess to sing and repeat soft notes of all kinds. The goatlike god, noticing her plight and calling the stricken and deserted Psyche gently toward him, thus soothed her with kind words: "Pretty girl, I may be a rustic shepherd, but I am wise and full of experience by virtue of great age. Truly, if I conclude correctly from the excessive pallor of your skin and your constant sighing and indeed from your sorrowful eyes, you are afflicted by a powerful love. Therefore, give heed to me and do not try to destroy yourself again. Cease your grief and hold Cupid, the greatest of the gods, in reverence, and since he is a pleasure-loving and exuberant young man, win over his love with charming indulgences."

When Psyche, plodding with weary step, had made her way over a considerable distance, as the day was just fading, she came to a certain city in which the husband of one of her sisters held the throne. When she realized this, Psyche was eager to have her presence made known to her sister.

Psyche was soon guided to her sister, and when they had exchanged embraces and finished their greetings to each other, in answer to her sister's questions Psyche began thus to tell the circumstances of her coming: "Do you remember your advice by which you know you persuaded me that I should slay the beast who, falsely calling himself my husband, came to lie with me at night, before he might devour me in ravenous gluttony? As soon as I looked upon his countenance with the aid of the lamp, as I had also been told to do, I beheld a wonderful and utterly divine sight. He was the very son of the goddess Venus, even Cupid himself, I say, lying at rest in gentle sleep.

"While I was struggling with the helplessness of my enjoyment, by the worst misfortune indeed, burning oil bubbled forth from the lamp onto his shoulder. Aroused from sleep at once, when he saw me armed with knife and lamp he said, 'Leave straightway because of this dreadful, evil deed and take your things with you, for in truth I shall join your sister'—and he spoke the name by which you are known—'to me in solemn marriage at once,' and forthwith he instructed Zephyrus to bear me off beyond the limits of his house."

Psyche had hardly finished her story before her sister, driven by the goads of fierce desire and wicked envy, at once took ship and proceeded directly to the cliff. Although an unfavorable wind was blowing, she was nevertheless panting with blind hope, and as she said, "Take me, Cupid, as a wife worthy of you, and you, Zephyrus, lift me, your mistress, up!" she threw herself headlong with a mighty leap. As her limbs were tossed and scattered through the jagged crags and torn apart in the manner they deserved, she perished.

Nor was the punishment of her next victim delayed, for Psyche, again with roving step, came to another city, where this sister was treated in the same manner as the other had been. No less was she led into Psyche's trap, and in jealousy over the infamous marriage of the first sister, she hurried to the cliff and fell to the same kind of death.

Meanwhile, Cupid, while Psyche was traveling around among the people intent on her search for him, afflicted by his wound from the lamp and resting in his mother's bed, was moaning in pain. Then that very white bird, the sea gull, which skims over the waves of the sea in its flight, plunged quickly toward the bottomless depths of Oceanus. There, standing near fair Venus, who was bathing and swimming, the gull revealed to her that her son had been burned and was lying moaning in great pain from the wound, with his life in danger.

And Venus, thoroughly angered, suddenly cried out, "Then does that fine son of mine now have some girl he loves! Come now, you who alone do loving service to me, tell me the name of the one who has tempted my innocent and boyish son; tell me whether she is of the host of Nymphs, or of the number of the Hours, or of the band of the Muses, or of the train of my Graces."

And that talkative bird was not silent but said, "I know not, Mistress, but I think he is desperately in love with a girl—if I remember correctly—called by the name of Psyche."

Venus rose up quickly from the sea and at once went to her golden bedchamber. When she found her son injured just as she had been told, crying out in a loud voice, she said, "Is this either honorable to your parents or in harmony with your reputation that you have scorned the commands of the one who is indeed first your mother and also even your queen? You have not afflicted my foe with a lowly love, and I must evidently endure my enemy as a daughter-in-law! Now I shall make you have cause to repent this sort of play and feel that this marriage of yours is bitter and distasteful.

"How I am held in ridicule now! What shall I do? Where shall I go? In what way shall I hold this crafty friend of yours in check? I should not, however, reject the solace of Vengeance. By all means, I must summon her and not any other for advice. It is she who may punish this worthless fellow most harshly, may unroll his quiver and deprive him of his arrows of power, unstring his bow, and extinguish his torch."

When she had spoken thus, Venus hurried forth from her bedchamber, outraged and angered. At once Ceres and Juno came up to her and, seeing her face filled with anger, asked why she overshadowed the great beauty of her shining eyes with a frowning brow.

Venus then answered, "You have come, surely, to carry through the fury of my utterly inflamed heart. In fact, I beg you, search out for me that elusive fugitive, Psyche, with all your powers."

Then they, not ignorant of what had happened, undertook to soften the savage wrath of Venus thus: "What great fault has your son committed that you should attack his pleasure with such a determined spirit and that you should delight also in destroying the one who gives him pleasure?"

Thus they, since they were in fear of his arrows, tried to defend Cupid, although he was absent, with flattering protection. But Venus, angered that they were intent on treating her injuries jokingly, turned from them and made her way with quick steps to the sea.

Meanwhile, Psyche was driven hither and thither as she searched night and day for traces of her husband. And when she saw a temple on the top of a certain lofty mountain she said, "How do I know, in fact, whether my lord and master might not be there?" Swiftly she directed toward that place her faltering footsteps, which hope and prayerful determination soon aroused to the demanding labor.

At length, when she had crossed over the towering ridges, she drew near to the sacred inner places of the temple. She saw sheaves of grain in a great pile and others twisted into wreaths, and she saw tufts of barley. There were also scythes and all the implements for the work of harvest, but everything was lying scattered without order in careless confusion and, as is usual in the heat of summer, simply dropped from the hands of the workers. Psyche diligently picked up each one of these things and, when she had sorted them, arranged them in their proper places, thinking that she should indeed not neglect the temples and sacred rites of any god but should seek to win the kind favor of all the gods.

Bountiful Ceres discovered her as she was carefully and busily attending to this task and called to her directly from afar: "Is it you indeed, Psyche—you who are to be pitied? Venus, raging in spirit, is searching through the whole world for you and demands revenge with all the powers of her divine force. Do you take care of these things that are mine and think of everything else but your own safety?"

Then Psyche, falling on her knees before Ceres and uttering a succession of prayers, begged for pardon: "By that fruit-bearing right hand of yours, by the joyous ceremonies of harvest time, I entreat you to support the soul of pitiable Psyche, your suppliant. Permit me to conceal myself, even for a few short days, in that mass of corn stalks until the savage anger of that mighty goddess is tamed by the passage of time, or at least until my strength, sapped by long labor, may be renewed by an interval of quiet."

Ceres answered her: "Indeed I am both moved by your tearful entreaties and also wish to assist you, but I cannot subject myself to the ill will of my sister goddess. And so depart from this temple directly and consider yourself very fortunate that you have not been held and kept in custody here."

Psyche, driven away contrary to her hopes, set forth again on her search. She caught sight of a temple built with skillful art and set in the glimmering grove of a valley lying below. Not wishing to overlook any opportunity for hope and desiring to gain pardon from some one of the gods, she drew near to the sacred doors.

Psyche saw precious gifts and garments embroidered with gold hanging from the doorposts, which, offered in gratitude, gave witness to the name of the goddess to whom they had been dedicated. Then, falling upon her knees, she prayed thus: "Sister and wife of great Jupiter, whether you abide at the ancient shrine of Samos or whether you linger among the joyful crowds at lofty Carthage, may you be Juno the deliverer in my extreme misfortune. Free me, weary with the great trials I have suffered, from the fear of threatening danger. For I know it is you who comes to the aid of women who are pregnant and in danger."

At once Juno appeared before the girl in the majestic dignity of all her divinity and straightway said, "How I should like in faith to answer your prayers. But shame does not allow me to take any action contrary to the will of Venus. Then, also, I am restrained by the laws that forbid the fugitive servants of others to be taken if their masters are unwilling."

Psyche, thoroughly frightened by this added shipwreck of her fate and not able now to catch up with her winged husband, thus took counsel in her own thoughts: "Now what other place of refuge can be tried or what help can be summoned in my tribulation, when my petitions have not been able to win over even one of the goddesses, even though they are willing? And so to what place shall I direct my step—I, who am caught in these great snares? Why do I not, therefore, take firm courage and surrender myself to my mistress of my own will? How do I know whether I might not find the one for whom I have searched for so long even there in the house of his mother?"

Thus, preparing for doubtful obedience—nay, rather for certain destruction—Psyche thought over to herself the beginning of the supplication she was about to make.

Venus, rejecting earthly aids in her search, returned to the heavens. She ordered her chariot, the one that Vulcan, the goldsmith of the gods, had devotedly adorned with delicate workmanship and had presented to her as a wedding gift, to be brought to her. Out of the many that roosted near the bedchamber of their mistress, four white doves flew forward and, bending their necks of many hues to the gem-studded yoke, flew off with her happily.

The clouds withdrew, and the sky was laid open to its daughter, and the upper air received the goddess with joy. Then straightway Venus steered her chariot toward the royal citadels of Jupiter and, petitioning proudly, demanded the service of Mercury, the messenger god. Nor did the azure brow of Jupiter deny her.

Then, rejoicing, Venus descended quickly from the heavens, accompanied even by Mercury, and she anxiously phrased her instructions to him: "O brother, Arcadian born, it has not escaped you that for a long time now I have been unable to find that maidservant who lies in hiding. Nothing is left, therefore, but to announce to the people, with you proclaiming it aloud, a reward for her discovery. See to it, then, that you hasten to do my bidding, and point out her description clearly so that she may be recognized."

As Venus said this she handed him a little note on which Psyche's name and other information were written. Having done this, she set out for home immediately.

Mercury did not neglect his duty; for, hurrying to and fro in every direction to all the people, he carried out his task of making the public proclamation as he had been commanded, thus: "If anyone can bring her back from flight or point out the hidden fugitive, the daughter of a king, the maidservant of Venus, Psyche by name, he will receive as an informer's reward seven sweet kisses from Venus herself and one honey-sweet from the tip of the goddess's tongue."

As Mercury delivered his message in this manner, the desire for so great a reward excited the zeal of all mortal men in rivalry. This fact now most definitely took away all Psyche's hesitation, and just as she was approaching the gates of the court of her mistress, one of the attendants of Venus, by the name of Custom, ran up to her and exclaimed, "Have you finally, most worthless maidservant, begun to realize that you have a mistress? You are about to pay, you may be sure, the penalty for such obstinacy." Then, grasping her firmly by the hair, she pulled Psyche off without a struggle.

As soon as Venus saw Psyche brought in and thrust before her, she began to laugh very happily and loudly and then she said, "Have you at last condescended to pay your respects to your mother-in-law? Or rather, have you come to pay a visit to your husband, who is in danger from the wound you inflicted?"

Then Venus, beginning to laugh again, said, "Just look how she stirs up pity in us at the thought of her unborn child, by which she may certainly make me a happy grandmother to her splendid offspring! In truth, I am fortunate—I, who, in the very flowering of my life, shall be called a grandmother and shall hear that the son of a common maidservant is the grandson of Venus!"

With these words, Venus flew at Psyche and tore apart her clothing everywhere. Clutching her hair and shaking her by the head, she threw her violently to the ground. Then, when she had taken wheat and barley and millet and poppy seeds and chick peas and lentils and beans and had mixed them together in heaps confused into one little hill, she spoke to her thus: "You seem to me such a loathsome maidservant that I myself shall put your value to the test. Separate the confused pile of those seeds and, setting the individual grains in order and dividing them properly, finish the task for my approval before this very evening."

When she had thus assigned to Psyche the task of sorting out the great pile of seeds, Venus herself departed. Nor did Psyche bring her hands to that hopelessly disordered mass of grain, but, thoroughly dismayed at the cruelty of the command, she sat silent and stunned.

Then an ant, a very small and country-dwelling ant, well aware of the great difficulty of the task, pitied her. Running to and fro, he eagerly called together and collected the entire army of ants living in the neighborhood, saying, "Take pity, take pity now on the wife of Love, and hurry to the aid of this charming girl, who is in great trouble."

The ants rushed forth and with the greatest zeal they separated the whole heap, grain by grain, one at a time. When the different kinds had been divided and set in order separately, the ants swiftly disappeared from sight.

With the beginning of night, Venus saw the industry of the remarkable labor and said, "This is not your work, most worthless girl, nor the work of your own hands, but the work of him who is enamored of you to his own harm." And she tossed her a scrap of coarse bread.

Meanwhile, Cupid, closed up alone in the fastness of a single little room in the interior of the house, was strictly confined, partly lest he aggravate his wound by riotous frolic, partly lest he meet with his love. But when Dawn was just crossing the sky, Venus called Psyche to her and spoke thus: "Do you see the grove that stretches along the length of the banks of that river? Sheep, shining and bright with the color of gold, wander there at pasture untended. I expect you to bring to me without delay a handful of the wool of that precious fleece, obtaining it in whatever way you can."

Psyche went off willingly, not indeed to perform this duty, but to seek rest from her misfortunes by falling headlong onto the rocks of the river. But then a green reed sang thus from the river in prophecy: "Psyche, burdened as you are by such tasks, do not dishonor my sacred waters by your miserable death. Nor, indeed, should you propose to approach those terrifying sheep at this hour because, deriving heat from the glow of the sun, they are wont to be carried away by fierce madness and to become violent. When the midday heat of the sun has subsided and the flock has become still in the quiet of the river breeze, by shaking the leafy branches of the bordering grove you may find the golden wool, which will have stuck everywhere on the arching branches."

Thus the simple and gentle reed showed the despondent Psyche the way to her preservation. Complying with everything and easily gathering up soft masses of the yellow gold, she carried it clutched in her arms to Venus.

Psyche did not, however, prove herself worthy of her mistress even after the danger of this second task, for Venus said, "It has not escaped me that the person responsible for this deed also is someone who has taken your place. Even now I shall carefully put you to the test. Do you see the peak of the steep mountain that stands on that very lofty cliff, from which the dark waters of a black spring flow down and, caught up and received in the valley nearby, pour into the Stygian swamps and nourish the deep-sounding stream of Cocytus? From that very source, and without delay, bring me in this little pitcher some frozen drops drawn from the bubbling water in the very heart of the top of the spring." So saying, she handed Psyche a small vessel inlaid with crystal.

Then Psyche, eagerly quickening her pace, sought the highest part of the mountain, most assuredly to find the end of her most miserable life there. But, as soon as she approached the area adjoining the prescribed ridge, she saw the fatal difficulty of the enormous task. For a high rock of immense size, and hazardous because of its unapproachable roughness, threw forth terrible fountains from openings in the midst of the rock.

On the right and on the left, fierce dragons were crawling out of the hollow rocks and stretching forth their long necks. Moreover, even the very waters themselves protected themselves as they resounded, for they repeatedly cried out: "Depart," and "What are you doing? Look out," and "What are you thinking of? Beware," and "Flee" and "You will perish."

Thus Psyche, utterly overwhelmed by the weight of her indescribable peril, lacked even the final solace of tears. Nor did the distress of this innocent soul lie hidden from the grave eyes of good Providence, for that regal bird of mighty Jupiter, the grasping eagle, suddenly swooped down with wings spread out at full length.

Flying before Psyche's very face, the eagle said, "Surely you are indeed simple and inexperienced in such matters if you hope that you can draw one drop of this most sacred and very wild water or even touch it at all! But give me that water pitcher——"

Grasping the pitcher suddenly and clasping it in his beak, the bird hung poised in flight on the balancing strength of his fluttering wings between the dragons' mouths of savage teeth and their three-forked quivering fangs. He gathered up the willing drops of water—under the pretence that he was doing so by the command of Venus and would carry it back to her—and they allowed him to get away unharmed. When, to her joy, she had received the full pitcher, Psyche quickly took it back to Venus.

Psyche was not, however, even able to win the approval of the angered goddess; for Venus, threatening her with even greater and worse shame, spoke to her thus: "Now indeed you seem to me to be some kind of enchantress, since you have complied so zealously to all these commands of mine. You must, however, carry out still this one more task. Take this small box and go straight to the lower world and the deadly dwelling of Orcus himself. Then, taking the little chest to Proserpina, say that Venus requests her to send a little of her beauty, at least enough for one brief day. Tell her that Venus has used up and entirely destroyed the beauty she once had, while she has been caring for her invalid son."

Then Psyche felt most strongly that her fortunes were at an end, and she clearly understood she was being driven to a quick death. She did not delay any longer but went to a certain very high tower, intending to throw herself headlong from the top—for thus she thought she could get down to the world of the dead most easily and most directly.

The tower suddenly burst forth into speech and said, "Why do you, O wretched girl, seek to destroy yourself so hastily? Why do you now surrender rashly to this last danger and task? Listen to me with attention. Sparta, a noble city, is located not far from here. Near this city is Taenarum, the breathing-hole of the lower world, and through its yawning gates a pathless way is made known, on which you will enter at once when you have crossed over the threshold. You will then come to the very palace of Pluto by a straight path.

"You ought not to go far through those lower regions with empty hands, but you should carry in both hands morsels of pearly barley rolled in honey wine. Also, carry two pieces of money in your mouth.

"Before long you will come to the river of the dead, on which Charon is the ferryman. He demands the passage money on the spot, before he carries the newly arrived dead to the far bank of the river in his patched boat. A very powerful dog, possessed of a three-fold and quite huge head, immense and terrible, barking with thundering jaws at the dead to whom he can now do no harm, lying always before the very threshold of the gloomy palace of Proserpina, guards the deserted house of Pluto. You will easily pass by him if you have tamed him with the reward of one of your little cakes.

"Next, you will go directly in to Proserpina herself, who will receive you courteously and kindly. Then, when you have told why you have come to her and have taken what she gives to you, as you pass the dog again on your return, ward off his savageness with your remaining cake. At last, after you have given to the greedy ferryman the coin that you have saved for him and have again crossed his river, retracing your former course, you will return to that heavenly host of the stars.

"I urge you that, during all this, you must watch out especially for one thing; namely, that you are not to open or to look into that little box that you will be carrying, or even to be too curious about the treasure chamber devoted to divine beauty."

Thus did that lofty tower unfold its gift of prophecy. Not delaying, Psyche set out for Taenarum and when those small coins and little cakes had been duly acquired, she ran down along the path to the lower world. And when she had given her passage money to the ferryman and had quieted the horrendous fierceness of the dog by the taste of one of the little cakes, she entered into the palace of Proserpina. Falling down in humility before the goddess's feet, she carried out her mission for Venus.

As soon as Psyche had received the little chest, secretly filled and closed, and when she had stopped the barking of the dog by the trick of a second barley cake and had paid the remaining coin to the ferryman, she ran back out of the lower regions.

When she again viewed with reverence that bright light of day—although she was in haste to bring her task to an end—Psyche's mind was seized by rash curiosity, and she said, "Behold, I am the foolish bearer of divine beauty if I do not take for myself even a small part of it or improve my own beauty by this means."

As she spoke, Psyche opened up the little box, but there was not anything there and no beauty at all—only sleep, deathlike and truly Stygian. As soon as it was freed from under the cover, it fell upon her and poured through all her limbs in a heavy cloud of slumber and took possession of her as she crumbled in her very tracks and fell to the path.

Cupid, however, now wholly recovered from his wound and not able to endure the absence of his Psyche any longer, slipped out through the very high window of the bedchamber in which he was confined and hastened to his Psyche. When he had wiped away the sleep carefully and had again enclosed it in its former place in the little chest, he aroused Psyche with a harmless little prick of his arrow and said, "Behold, wretched little one, again you almost met death, and by a similar curiosity. But, meanwhile, you must indeed carefully carry out the duty that has been entrusted to you according to the command of my mother. I myself shall see to everything else."

With these words, he lifted himself lightly on his wings. Psyche, in truth, quickly carried the gift of Proserpina to Venus.

Then Cupid, consumed by his excessive love and dejected in appearance, and fearing the quick anger of his mother, returned to his old tricks. When he had pierced the summit of the sky on swift wings, he knelt down before great Jupiter to plead his case.

Then Jupiter kissed him affectionately and said to him, "You, my masterful son, have never observed the respect due me according to the laws of the gods. You have wounded this heart of mine, by which the laws of the elements and the rotations of the stars are set in order, with continual blows. In spite of this and because you have been raised by these very hands of mine, I shall do everything you ask, provided, however, you take care to beware of your rivals."

When Jupiter had spoken thus, he ordered Mercury to call together an assembly of the gods immediately. The theater of the gods was filled at once. Sitting on high, Jupiter spoke out thus from his lofty throne: "O gods, you who are registered in the roll of the Muses, you certainly all know this young man whose impetuous youth, I believe, should be curbed by some kind of bridle. He has chosen a girl and has made her his wife. Let him keep her and possess her, and as he embraces Psyche may he always enjoy his love."

Then, turning his eyes toward Venus, Jupiter said, "And you, my daughter, must not be saddened at all nor have any fear because of this marriage with a mortal."

At once he ordered Psyche to be snatched up by Mercury and brought safely into the heavens. He held forth a cup of ambrosia, saying, "Take this, Psyche, and be immortal. Cupid will never depart from your embrace, but instead your marriage will be everlasting."

Nor was there any delay before a plentiful wedding feast was brought forth. Then indeed, Jupiter's own cupbearer, that country boy, poured a cup of nectar, which is the wine of the gods, for him, and Bacchus served the others. Vulcan prepared the dinner; the Hours adorned everything with roses and other flowers; the Graces sprinkled fragrant balsam about. The Muses, too, filled the hall with melody, and Apollo played on the cithara. Venus danced, entering beautifully into the sweet music.

The scene was thus set in such a way that the Muses sang in chorus and played upon their flutes as a satyr and little Pan made music on their reed pipes. Thus was Psyche wed to Cupid with proper ceremony, and a daughter, whom we call Pleasure, was born to them in due time.

From *Metamorphoses* IV, 28–VI, 24

Pyramus and Thisbe

The story of Pyramus and Thisbe is perhaps the most appealing love story of all time. Shakespeare satirized the story in A Midsummer Night's Dream *and many elements in the plot of* Romeo and Juliet *are reminiscent of Ovid's moving tale.*

Semiramis was the legendary founder and queen of Babylon. The legends surrounding her may have some basis in the historical facts in the life of an actual Assyrian queen by the name of Sammuramat who ruled in the ninth century B.C.

As told in Latin verse by Ovid

PYRAMUS AND Thisbe—he the most handsome of youths, she surpassing all the girls to be found in the East—lived in neighboring houses in the city of Babylon, which Semiramis is said to have surrounded with lofty walls of brick. Their closeness brought them to the first steps of intimacy.

Their love grew with time, and they would have been united in marriage, but their parents forbade it. But, a thing that they could not forbid, the two young people loved each other with an equal and ardent love. No one knew of their secret. They conversed by nods and signs, and the more it was covered, the more the hidden fire of their love burned.

A common wall between the two houses had been split by a thin crack that had formed in the past when the wall was being built. This defect, which had been noticed by no one during all that time, these lovers first saw—what does love not notice?—and they made it the passage for their voices, and their words of endearment used to pass safely through it in a soft whisper.

Often, when they stood there, Thisbe on this side, Pyramus on that, and when each in turn had listened for the sound of the other's breathing, they used to say, "Envious wall, why do you stand in the way of us who love each other? How great a task would it be for you to allow us to be joined in a real embrace, or, if that is too much, to stretch open so we can at least exchange kisses? Yet we are not ungrateful. We confess we owe it to you that a passage has been given for our words to reach each other's loving ears."

When they had spoken in this manner, separated to no purpose, as night fell they would say "Farewell," and they would plant kisses on their own sides of the wall—kisses that did not reach the other side.

When the following dawn had taken away the stars of the night and the sun had dried the dewy grasses with its rays, they met at their usual place. Then in a low whisper, after they had first uttered many complaints, they decided that in the silence of the night they would try to escape from their guardians and steal from their homes, and that when they got away from home they would leave the city and its houses far behind. And, so that they might not wander about in the open spaces of the wide country-side, they agreed to meet at the tomb of Ninus and lie hidden under the shadow of the tree that stood there full of snowy berries—it was a tall mulberry tree—beside an ice-cold spring.

Their plan seemed good to them, and the day seemed to pass slowly. At last the sun rushed headlong into the ocean's waves, and the night rose up from the same waters.

Quietly opening the door, Thisbe stole out of the house and went out through the darkness with her face covered by a veil. When she arrived at the tomb, she sat down under the appointed tree. Love gave her daring.

But behold, a lioness, her jaws covered with foaming blood from cattle she had just slain, came to quench her thirst in the pool of the spring nearby. Thisbe of Babylon saw the beast in the distance under the light of the moon and fled with timid step into the darkness of a cave. But as she fled her veil fell from her and was left behind.

When the savage lioness had checked her thirst with great drinks of water, by chance, as she turned back to the forest, she found the thin covering but not the girl herself, and she tore it to pieces with her bloody mouth.

Arriving just a bit later, Pyramus saw the clear tracks of the beast in the heavy dust and turned pale with dread. When, indeed, he discovered the veil and saw that it was stained with blood, he exclaimed, "A single night shall destroy two lovers. She was the one most worthy of a long life. My soul is the guilty one. I have brought you to your death, O pitiable girl, I who urged that you come at night to this place so full of danger and did not get here first myself. Tear my body to pieces and consume my accursed flesh with your savage bite, O whatever lions dwell below this cliff. But it is cowardly simply to wish for death."

He picked up Thisbe's veil and carried it over to the shade of the tree where they had agreed to meet, and as the tears fell and as he kissed the familiar covering, he cried out, "Now take the stream of my blood also." Drawing his sword from its sheath, he plunged it into his side and quickly pulled it from his burning wound as he fell dying.

As he lay fallen on the ground, his blood spurted high, not otherwise than when a pipe bursts open where the lead is faulty and, from a little hissing opening, shoots forth long sprays of water and pierces the air with its streams. The tree's fruit was turned by the sprinkling of blood to a dark red hue, and its roots, soaked with his life's blood, colored the hanging mulberries with a reddish-purple tint.

And behold, although her fear was not yet forgotten, but fearing more lest she fail her lover, Thisbe returned and searched for Pyramus, anxiously looking everywhere and eager to tell him what great dangers she had escaped. And even though she recognized the spot and the shape of the tree she had seen there, yet the color of the berries made her uncertain. She was puzzled, wondering whether this was the same tree. While she hesitated she saw human limbs tremble and beat the bloodstained soil. She turned back, her face paler than boxwood, and she shuddered in dread, just as the sea quivers when its surface is ruffled by a slight breeze.

But when, bending over him, she recognized her love, she beat her innocent arms with loud lamentations and tore her hair. Then, embracing his beloved body, she filled his wounds with her tears, and the tears mingled with his blood.

And as she pressed her kisses on his lips, now cold, the girl cried out, "Pyramus, what tragedy has taken you from me? Pyramus, answer me! Your dearest Thisbe is calling your name. Hear me, and raise your fallen head from the ground!"

At the name of Thisbe, Pyramus opened his eyes, heavy with death, and when he had looked upon her once more, closed them forever.

When Thisbe caught sight of her own veil and the ivory sheath empty of its sword, she murmured, "Your own hand and your love destroyed you, unlucky one. I also have a hand brave enough for this one act; I too have a love deep enough. This will give me strength for my death wound. I shall follow you into death, and I shall be called both the very pitiable cause and the companion of your death. And you who could be taken from me, alas, by death alone, you can not be torn from me even by death.

"May you, O my most unhappy parents, and his also, nevertheless be asked this favor by the entreaties of both of us. Do not begrudge that we, whom a perfect love, whom our final hour has joined together, be laid to rest in the same tomb. And you, O tree, who now cover the wretched body of one of us with your shading branches and who will soon protect the bodies of two, as a symbol of our death may you always have fruit that is dark and appropriate to grief, an eternal monument of double bloodshed."

Even as she spoke she placed the sword, still warm with her lover's blood, just below her breast and fell forward on it. Her prayers, indeed, touched the gods and moved the lovers' parents; for the color of the mulberry, when it is ripe, is deep red, and the ashes from their two funeral pyres rest in one urn.

From *Metamorphoses* IV, 55–166

Pygmalion

The Pygmalion of the following myth was a king of Cyprus. It will be noticed that Pygmalion's statue remained nameless in Ovid's version. It was only as the story came down through the years in many different versions and types of presentations that the name Galatea was applied to the maiden.

As told in Latin verse by Ovid

PYGMALION, DISPLEASED with the faults that nature had given the female sex in such abundance, remained a bachelor and lived for a long time removed from the company of women. Then, with remarkable artistic skill, he carved a statue of snowy ivory and gave it form and beauty such as no woman born could equal, and he fell in love with the girl he had made.

The face of the girl was so lifelike you could almost believe it was alive. Pygmalion gazed upon her in awe, and his heart drank in the fire of a burning love for the statue he created. Often he touched his work to test whether flesh or ivory was beneath his hand. He kissed her, he imagined she returned his kisses. He spoke to her, held her. At times he caressed and flattered her, then he gave her the little gifts that please girls so much—shells and shining stones, small birds, and flowers of a thousand colors, lilies and painted balls, and beads of amber. He dressed her in embroidered garments, put jewels on her fingers, necklaces about her neck, and pearls on her ears. All these adornments made her beautiful, but the unadorned statue seemed no less beautiful.

Soon the day of the festival of Venus arrived, and all the people of Cyprus gathered to celebrate it. Heifers were sacrificed to the goddess, and incense smoked on the altars. But Pygmalion, who had come to the altar with a gift, stood there and prayed timidly,

"If, O deities, if you can grant all desires, I pray that as my wife I may have——" But, afraid to say "this ivory maiden," Pygmalion said instead, "one like my ivory maiden." The goddess—indeed golden Venus herself was attending the festival—realized the meaning of his prayer, and three times the flames of the altar burned brighter and leaped up, an omen of her kindly favor.

When he returned home, Pygmalion sought out his statue of the maiden and kissed her. She seemed warm to his caress. He kissed her again, and at his touch the ivory grew warm and its stiffness disappeared, yielding to the touch of his fingers, as the wax of honey from Hymettus softens in the sun and can be molded into many different shapes.

Pygmalion was struck with amazement and wavered between doubt and joy, fearing he was deceived. Again and again the lover stroked his creation with his fingers. It was living flesh! Blood was coursing beneath his fingertips!

Then, in truth, Pygmalion poured forth his heartfelt thanks to Venus as he pressed his lips to lips that were real at last. And the maiden felt the touch of his lips and blushed. Then she raised her eyes timidly, and at one and the same time she beheld the light of the sky and her lover. The goddess Venus blessed the marriage she had bestowed, and in due time there was born to them a son, Paphos, who gave his name to the island.

From *Metamorphoses* X, 243–297

Bibliography

Atlas of the Classical World. Camden, N. J.: Thomas Nelson, 1959.

Bulfinch, Thomas. *Age of Fable.* New York: Harper, 1966.

Finley, M. I. *The World of Odysseus.* New York: Viking, revised, 1965.

Fox, William S. *Greek and Roman Mythology.* New York: Cooper, 1964.

Frazer, James G. *Golden Bough.* New York: Macmillan, 1951.

Gayley, Charles M. *Classic Myths in English Literature and in Art.* Waltham, Mass.: Blaisdell, 1968.

Grant, Michael. *Myths of the Greeks and Romans.* Cleveland: World, 1965.

Graves, Robert. *Greek Myths.* New York: Braziller, 1959.

Guthrie, W. K. C. *Religion and Mythology of the Greeks.* New York: Cambridge University Press, 1964.

—— *The Greeks and Their Gods.* Boston: Beacon, 1955.

Hutchinson, Richard W. *Prehistoric Crete.* Baltimore: Penguin, 1963.

Kitto, H. D. F. *The Greeks.* Chicago: Aldine Pub. Co., 1964.

Larousse. *Encyclopedia of Mythology.* New York: Putnam, 1959.

MacKendrick, Paul. *The Greek Stones Speak.* New York: St. Martin's, 1962.

Nilsson, Martin P. *Mycenaean Origin of Greek Mythology.* New York: Norton, 1963.

Robinson, Cyril E. *History of Greece.* New York: Crowell, 1965.

Rose, Herbert J. *Gods and Heroes of the Greeks.* Cleveland: World, 1958.

—— *Handbook of Greek Mythology.* New York: Dutton, 1959.

Schefold, Karl. *Myth and Legend in Early Greek Art.* New York: Abrams, 1966.

Glossary

ABAE   A town in Phocis; site of a temple and oracle of Apollo.

ABAS, MOUNT   A mountain on the island of Erythea.

ABDERA   A city on the coast of Thrace named for Abderus, a son of Hermes who was killed by the mares of Diomedes.

ACASTUS   The son of Pelias who went with Jason on the expedition of the Argonauts.

ACHAEA (or ACHAIA)   (1.) A region in southern Thessaly. (2.) A district on the north coast of the Peloponnesus.

ACHAEANS   The inhabitants of Achaea. In Homer, the name refers to the followers of Achilles and Agamemnon, or to the Greek army in general.

ACHERON   The river of woe, one of the rivers of the lower world. Also a term for the lower world in general.

ACHILLES   The son of Peleus and Thetis; a Greek hero and leader of the Myrmidons in the Trojan War.

ACROPOLIS   A high fortified place serving as the citadel of a Greek city. The Acropolis, in particular, refers to the citadel of Athens.

ADMETE   A daughter of Eurystheus.

ADONIS   A youth loved by Venus.

ADRASTEA   A nymph of Crete who nurtured the infant Zeus.

AEA   A city on the Phasis River in Colchis.

AEACUS   The son of Zeus and the nymph Aegina; father of Peleus and Telamon, and grandfather of Achilles.

AEAEA   The legendary island home of Circe.

AEËTES   A king of Aea, and the father of Medea, Chalciope, and Absyrtus (or Apsyrtus). Aeëtes was a son of Helios and Persa, and the brother of Circe and Pasiphaë.

AEGEAN SEA   That part of the Mediterranean Sea lying between Greece and Asia Minor.

AEGEUM, MOUNT   A mountain on the island of Crete.

AEGEUS   A king of Athens, and the husband of Aethra, the

295

mother of Theseus, and of Medea. His earlier wives were Meta and Chalciope. Aegeus was a son of Pandion.

AEGINA   The daughter of Asopus, a river god, and Metope. She was the mother of Aeacus by Zeus.

AEGLE   One of the Hesperides.

AENEAS   The son of Aphrodite and Anchises, and hero of Vergil's *Aeneid*.

AEOLIA   The island kingdom of Aeolus.

AEOLUS   (1.) The ruler of the winds. (2.) A king of Thessaly.

AESON   The half brother of Pelias, and the father of Jason.

AETHER   A son of Erebus and Nyx. Also, a name for the heavens.

AETHRA   The daughter of King Pittheus of Troezen, the wife of Aegeus, and the mother of Theseus.

AGAMEMNON   King of Mycenae, brother of Menelaus, and husband of Clytemnestra.

AGENOR   A son of Poseidon, a king of Tyre (or of Sidon), and the father of Cadmus and Europa.

AÏDONEUS   A name sometimes used in poetry for Hades.

AJAX   A son of Telamon, and one of the great Greek heroes.

ALCIMEDE   One of several who were said to be Jason's mother.

ALCMENE   Granddaughter of Perseus and Andromeda, the wife of King Amphitryon, and the mother of Heracles by Zeus.

ALCYONE   One of the Pleiades.

ALPHEUS   A river in the western Peloponnesus, and the name of the god of that river.

AMAZONS   A tribe of female warriors who lived in the Black Sea area.

AMMON   The Greek and Roman name for Amon or Amen, the Egyptian god of the sun; identified with Zeus (or Jupiter).

AMOR   Amor, the Latin word for "love," was another name for Cupid.

AMPHION   A king of Thebes and the husband of Niobe.

AMPHITRITE   A sea goddess, daughter of Nereus and wife of Poseidon.

AMPHITRYON   The husband of Alcmene, mother of Heracles.

AMYMONE   (1.) A Danaid loved by Poseidon. (2.) A spring that was the source of the river Lerna in Argolis.

ANCAEUS The helmsman of Jason's ship, the *Argo,* after the death of Tiphys.

ANCHISES A Trojan and the father of Aeneas.

ANDROGEUS A son of King Minos and Pasiphaë.

ANDROMACHE Daughter of Eëtion, wife of Hector, and mother of Astyanax.

ANDROMEDA The daughter of King Cepheus of Ethiopia and Cassiopeia.

ANTAEUS A giant, son of Poseidon and Gaea.

ANTHEMUS RIVER A river on the island of Erythea.

ANTIGONE The daughter of Oedipus and Jocasta and sister of Ismene, Eteocles, and Polynices.

ANTILOCHUS A son of King Nestor of Pylos and close friend to Achilles.

APHRODITE The Greek goddess of love and beauty, born from the waves; the mother of Eros. In Roman mythology, Aphrodite's counterpart is Venus.

APOLLO In both Greek and Roman mythology Apollo is the god of light, music, poetry, healing, and prophecy. He was the son of Zeus (Jupiter) and Leto (Latona), and the twin of Artemis (Diana). In later mythology he was also known as Phoebus Apollo and sometimes (as in Ovid) simply as Phoebus.

AQUILO In Roman mythology, the north wind, the counterpart of the Greek Boreas.

ARACHNE The daughter of Idmon of Lydia who challenged Athena to a contest of weaving.

ARCADIA A region in the central Peloponnesus noted for its mountains, springs, caves, and beautiful pastoral setting.

ARES A son of Zeus and Hera, he was the Greek god of war; identified by the Romans with Mars.

ARGES One of the Cyclopes; according to Hesiod, a son of Uranus and Gaea.

ARGIVES The Greeks of Argolis, a district in the northeastern Peloponnesus; used by Homer to refer to the Greeks as a whole.

ARGO The ship Argus built for Jason and the Argonauts.

ARGONAUTS Those who accompanied Jason in the *Argo* on his expedition to recover the golden fleece from Colchis.

ARGOS A city in Argolis that was sacred to Hera.

ARGUS (1.) The 100-eyed guardian of Io, he was slain by Hermes. (2.) The builder of the *Argo*. (3.) One of the four sons of Phrixus and Chalciope, daughter of King Aeëtes of Colchis.

ARIADNE The daughter of King Minos of Crete and Pasiphaë.

ARTEMIS The daughter of Zeus and Leto, and twin sister of Apollo. Artemis was the Greek goddess of the hunt and of light. Her Roman counterpart was Diana.

ARTEMISIUS, MOUNT A mountain lying between Arcadia and Argolis that was named for Artemis and sacred to her.

ASIUS The brother of Hecuba and uncle of Hector.

ASTEROPE (or STEROPE) One of the Pleiades.

ASTRAEA (or ASTREA) A goddess of purity and justice in classical mythology; daughter of Zeus and Themis.

ASTYANAX The son of Hector and Andromache; also called Scamandrius.

ATALANTA A swift-footed maiden, daughter of Iasus of Arcadia or of Schoeneus of Boeotia.

ATHENA (or ATHENE) The Greek goddess of wisdom and the womanly arts, daughter of Zeus and Metis or of Zeus alone. Also known as Pallas Athena, she was identified by the Romans with Minerva.

ATHENS The chief city of Attica.

ATLAS The Titan son of Iapetus and Clymene, he was the father of the Hesperides, the Hyades, and the Pleiades. According to Homer, Atlas was the father of the nymph Calypso.

ATTICA A district in eastern central Greece. Its chief city is Athens.

AUGEAS (or AUGEIAS) A king of Elis who had a large herd of cattle; one of the Argonauts.

AURORA The Roman goddess of the dawn; identified with the Greek goddess Eos.

AVERNUS A lake near Naples that was believed to be an entrance to the lower world.

BABYLON The chief city and capital of Babylonia; located on the Euphrates River.

BACCHANTES Female attendants and worshipers of Dionysus (Bacchus); also called maenads.

BACCHUS A name, probably of Lydian origin, for Dionysus; also known as Bacchic Dionysus, the name by which the Romans called him.

BALEARIC ISLANDS A group of islands in the Mediterranean near Spain.

BAUCIS The wife of Philemon.

BEBRYCES A group of people of Bithynia.

BELLEROPHON A grandson of Sisyphus and son of Glaucus of Corinth.

BELLONA The Roman goddess of war.

BERECYNTIA A name for Cybele, who was worshiped in the area of Mount Berecyntus in Phrygia.

BISTONES A Thracian tribe whose king was Diomedes.

BITHYNIA A district in northwestern Asia Minor adjacent to Phrygia. The name was used interchangeably with Phrygia.

BLACK SEA The Black Sea was known in ancient times as the Euxine Sea.

BOEOTIA A district in eastern Greece lying northwest of Attica. Its chief city was Thebes.

BOREAS In Greek mythology, the north wind; identified with Aquilo by the Romans.

BRIAREUS One of the Hecatonchires, children of Uranus and Gaea.

BRONTES One of the Cyclopes; according to Hesiod, a son of Uranus and Gaea.

CADMUS The son of King Agenor of Phoenicia and Telephassa, and brother of Europa. He was the legendary founder of Cadmea, the citadel of the city later called Thebes.

CALCHAS A Greek prophet who went with the Greeks to the Trojan War.

CALLIOPE The Muse of epic poetry.

CALLIRRHOË. (1.) The mother of the monster Geryon. (2.) The wife of Tros, and mother of Ganymede.

CALYMNE One of the Dodecanese Islands of the Aegean Sea.

CARTHAGE A city on the north coast of Africa, opposite Sicily. Dido of Phoenicia was its legendary founder.

CASSIOPEIA (also CASSIEPEIA, CASSIOPE, CASSIOPEA) The wife of King Cepheus of Ethiopia and mother of Andromeda.

CASTOR The son of Leda and Tyndareus or Zeus, and the twin brother of Pollux.

CATREUS A son of King Minos of Cnossus and Pasiphaë, and the grandfather of Agamemnon and Menelaus.

CECROPS The legendary first king of Athens.

CELAENO One of the Pleiades.

CELEUS A king of Eleusis who welcomed Demeter to his home.

CENTAURS A race of creatures, half man and half horse, who lived mainly in Thessaly.

CEPHEUS A king of Ethiopia; husband of Cassiopeia and father of Andromeda.

CERBERUS A three-headed dog that guarded the entrance to the lower world.

CERCYON A king of Arcadia who challenged passers-by to wrestle with him.

CERES An Italian goddess of grain, identified by the Romans with the Greek goddess Demeter.

CERYNEAN HIND A swift hind with horns of gold and hoofs of bronze that was sacred to Artemis.

CHALCIOPE (1.) A daughter of King Aeëtes of Colchis, and the wife of Phrixus. (2.) A daughter of Rhexenor, and the second wife of Aegeus.

CHAOS Infinite space; the shapeless condition of the universe before it took form and shape; the deity ruling over it.

CHARON The ferryman of the river Styx.

CHARYBDIS A monster, daughter of Poseidon and Gaea; she came to be identified with the Strait of Messina.

CHIMAERA A monster with a goat's body, serpent's tail, and lion's head; offspring of Echidna and Typhon.

CHIRON A wise centaur who taught a number of Greek heroes, including Achilles and Jason.

CHRYSAOR A son of Poseidon and father of the monster Geryon.

CILICIA A district on the south coast of Asia Minor.

CIRCE A daughter of Helios who was an enchantress living on the island of Aeaea. She was the sister of King Aeëtes of Colchis and of Pasiphaë.

CITHAERON   A mountain range lying between Attica and Boeotia and sacred to Dionysus and Zeus.

CLIO   The Muse of history.

CLYMENE   (1.) The mother by Helios of Phaëthon. (2.) A daughter of Oceanus, and the mother by Iapetus of Atlas, Prometheus, and Epimetheus.

CNIDUS   A city on the southwest coast of Asia Minor that was sacred to Aphrodite.

CNOSSUS (or KNOSSOS)   A city near the north coast of Crete; site of the palace of Minos.

COCYTUS   The river of wailing, one of the rivers of the lower world.

COLCHIS   A land at the eastern end of the Black Sea.

CORINTH   A city in the northern Peloponnesus at the Isthmus of Corinth.

COTTUS   One of the Hecatonchires, children of Uranus and Gaea.

CRATAEÏS   Named by Homer as the mother of Scylla.

CREON   Son of Menoeceus of Thebes and brother of Jocasta.

CRETE   A large island between Greece and Africa; the seat of the Minoan civilization.

CROMMYON   A village near Megara and the Isthmus of Corinth.

CRONUS (or KRONOS)   A son of Uranus and Gaea; leader of the Titans and early ruler of the universe; father of Zeus.

CUMAE   A city north of Naples where the Sibyl revealed the prophecies of Apollo.

CUPID   The Roman god of love, son of Venus and Mercury. He was the counterpart of the Greek god Eros.

CYBELE   A goddess of Asia Minor, especially of Lydia and Phrygia, whom the Greeks identified with Rhea and the Romans with Ops, the Great Mother.

CYCLADES   A group of islands, including Delos, Paros, and Naxos, lying in the southern part of the Aegean Sea.

CYCLOPES   One-eyed giants. According to Hesiod, they were the sons of Uranus and Gaea, named Brontes, Steropes, and Arges. According to Homer, there were numerous Cyclopes living on an island.

CYLLENE, MOUNT   The mountain in Arcadia where Hermes was said to have been born.

CYNTHUS, MOUNT   The highest point on the island Delos, the birthplace of Apollo and Artemis.

CYPRUS   An island in the northeast corner of the Mediterranean that was sacred to Aphrodite.

CYRENE   The mother by Ares of Diomedes of Thrace.

CYTHERA   An island off the southeastern coast of the Peloponnesus, where Aphrodite was said to have been born from the sea.

CYTHEREA   An epithet of Aphrodite.

DAEDALUS   The son of Metion and a descendant of Erechtheus who built the labyrinth for King Minos.

DAMASTES   A highwayman whom Theseus killed on his way to Athens; also called Polypemon or Procrustes.

DANAANS   The descendants of Danaus, a king of Argos, and his fifty daughters. Also, a term used for the Argives or for all the Greeks.

DANAË   The daughter of King Acrisius of Argos, she was the mother of Perseus by Zeus.

DAPHNE   A nymph loved by Apollo. She was the daughter of the river god Peneus.

DARDANIANS   The inhabitants of Dardania, which later became Troy.

DARDANUS   A son of Zeus and the Pleiad Electra from whom the Trojans were descended.

DAULIA (or DAULIS)   A town in Phocis near Delphi.

DELOS   One of the Cyclades Islands and the birthplace of Apollo and Artemis.

DELPHI   A town located in Phocis on the slopes of Mount Parnassus; the site of a temple and an oracle of Apollo.

DEMETER   The Greek goddess of the fruits of the earth, especially corn. She was the daughter of Cronus and Rhea, and the mother by Zeus of Persephone. The Romans identified her with Ceres.

DEMOPHOÖN   The son of King Celeus of Eleusis and Metaneira who was nursed by Demeter.

Deucalion   A son of Prometheus; he was the husband of Pyrrha.

Dexamenus   A centaur who was the king of Olenus in the northern Peloponnesus.

Dia   (1.) The early name of Naxos. (2.) The wife of Ixion.

Diana   An Italian goddess of the woods and fertility and, by her identification with Artemis, of the moon and hunting.

Dido   The legendary founder and queen of Carthage.

Diomedes   (1.) A king of the Bistones of Thrace who owned man-eating mares; son of Cyrene and Ares. (2.) A king of Argos who fought in the Trojan War.

Dionysus   The son of Zeus and Semele, and the Greek god of the vine and wine; identified by the Romans with Bacchus.

Dorians   Invaders who entered Greece from the north about the twelfth century B.C. They settled mainly near the Isthmus and in the Peloponnesus, and they migrated to Crete and Asia Minor.

Doris   The daughter of Oceanus and Tethys, and the wife of Nereus.

Dryads (or Hamadryads)   Nymphs of the trees and woodlands.

Dryops   The ancestor of the Dryopians, who lived around Mount Parnassus and in the Peloponnesus; the father of Dryope.

Dulichium   An island in the Ionian Sea near Ithaca, the home of Odysseus.

Echidna   A monster, half woman and half serpent, and the mother of Orthrus, the Hydra, Cerberus, the Chimaera, the Nemean Lion, and the Theban Sphinx.

Echion   The husband of Cadmus' daughter Agave who helped Cadmus in the building of Thebes.

Echo   A wood nymph who lost her power of speech except for the repetition of the words of others. Echo was the mother of Iynx by Pan, and she loved Narcissus.

Eëtion   A king of Cilicia; he was the father of Andromache.

Electra   (1.) One of the Pleiades; she was the mother by Zeus of Dardanus. (2.) Mother of the Harpies.

Eleusis   A town near Athens that was sacred to Demeter.

Elis   A district and city in the western Peloponnesus. The Olympic Games of ancient times were held in Elis at Olympia.

ELYSIUM   In classical mythology, the home of the good, the blessed, and the heroes after death; sometimes called the Islands of the Blessed.

Eos   The Greek goddess of the dawn; identified by the Romans with Aurora.

EPAPHUS   The son of Io and Zeus. He became king of Egypt and was an ancestor of Danaus.

EPIDAURUS   A city in eastern Argolis; site of a large sanctuary of Asclepius.

EPIMETHEUS   The son of Iapetus and Clymene; brother of Prometheus and Atlas; and husband of Pandora.

ERATO   The Muse of lyric and love poetry.

EREBUS   (1.) The son of Chaos, and the brother and husband of Nyx. (2.) The personification of darkness and the unknown. (3.) A region of darkness in the lower world; the lower world in general.

ERECHTHEUS   A legendary king of Athens.

ERGINUS   A son of Poseidon, he was the king of Orchomenus in Boeotia.

ERIDANUS RIVER   A mythical river generally identified with the Po.

ERINYES   In Greek mythology, avenging spirits who pursued the guilty; also known as the Eumenides. The Romans called them Furiae (Furies).

ERIS   The Greek goddess of strife or discord. Her Roman counterpart was Discordia.

EROS   (1.) An elemental force and, according to Hesiod, one of the first of the gods to come into being. (2.) The Greek god of love, and, in later mythology, the son of Aphrodite; identified by the Romans with Cupid.

ERYMANTHUS, MOUNT   A mountain sacred to Artemis; located between Achaea and Arcadia.

ERYTHEA (or ERYTHEIA)   A legendary island in the far west; the home of Geryon.

ERYTHEIA (or ERYTHIA)   One of the Hesperides.

ERYX   (1.) A son of the Argonaut Butes (or of Poseidon in some accounts) and Aphrodite. He lived on Sicily. (2) A mountain on Sicily.

EUROPA   The daughter of King Agenor of Tyre and Telephassa, she was the sister of Cadmus. Homer and Moschus, however, name Phoenix as the father of Europa. She was the mother by Zeus of Minos and Rhadamanthus.

EURUS   The east wind.

EURYDICE   The bride of Orpheus.

EURYLOCHUS   One of Odysseus' companions.

EURYPYLUS   A Thessalian leader in the Trojan War.

EURYSTHEUS   The king of Mycenae who imposed the labors upon Heracles.

EURYTION   (1.) The herdsman of Geryon's cattle. (2.) A centaur who was slain by Heracles.

EUTERPE   The Muse of flutes and music.

EVENUS RIVER   A river in the northern Peloponnesus.

FAVONIUS   In Roman mythology, the west wind personified; identified with the Greek Zephyrus.

FURIES (Latin, Furiae)   Roman goddesses of vengeance, the counterparts of the Greek Erinyes.

GAEA (or GE)   The personification of the earth, and the mother and wife of Uranus; mother by Uranus of the Titans, the Cyclopes, and the Hecatonchires.

GANYMEDE (or GANYMEDES)   A son of Tros and Callirrhoë who was carried off to Olympus to be cupbearer to the gods.

GERYON   A three-headed (in some accounts, three-bodied) monster of Erythea slain by Heracles.

GIANTS   The monstrous offspring of Uranus and Gaea, they were defeated by the Olympian deities with the help of Heracles.

GORGONS   Stheno, Euryale, and Medusa; three beautiful daughters of the sea deities Phorcys and Ceto, they were changed into snake-haired monsters.

GRACES   The Graces, called Charites by the Greeks and Gratiae by the Romans, were the personification of grace and beauty.

GYGES (or GYES)   One of the Hecatonchires, children of Uranus and Gaea.

HADES   A son of Cronus and Rhea, and the husband of Persephone; the Greek god and ruler of the lower world. Hades was also known as Pluto and was called Dis by the Romans.

HAMADRYADS See Dryads.

HARPIES Monstrous winged creatures, daughters of Thaumas and Electra, who plagued people or snatched them up and carried them off.

HEBE A daughter of Zeus and Hera, she was cupbearer to the gods and represented eternal youth. After Heracles took his place on Olympus, Hebe became his wife.

HECATE A Greek goddess associated with the moon, crossroads, and the lower world. Hecate was connected with the number three and the powers of witchcraft and magic. The Romans called her Trivia, meaning "triple way."

HECATONCHIRES (or HECATONCHEIRES) Briareus, Cottus, and Gyges (or Gyes), monstrous sons of Uranus and Gaea; each had 100 arms.

HECTOR A son of King Priam of Troy and Hecuba; the husband of Andromache, father of Astyanax, and a hero of the *Iliad*.

HECUBA Wife of King Priam and the mother of Hector, Paris, and Polydorus, among others.

HELEN The beautiful daughter of Zeus and Leda, and the sister of Castor, Pollux, and Clytemnestra. Helen was the wife of Menelaus of Sparta, and the mother of Hermione.

HELIOS (or HELIUS) The son of Titans Hyperion and Theia, and the father of Phaëthon, Aeëtes, Circe, and Pasiphaë. Helios was the Greek god of the sun, and in later times was often confused with Apollo. (*See also* Phoebus.)

HELLAS Originally the name of a town and district in southern Thessaly; later the term was used to denote all of Greece.

HELLENES The name by which the ancient Greeks were known; originally the name of a tribe in Thessaly.

HELLESPONT The strait between the Aegean Sea and the Propontis; now called the Dardanelles.

HEMERA A daughter of Erebus and Nyx; later identified with the dawn or day.

HEPHAESTUS The Greek god of fire and of forges and smiths; the husband of Aphrodite and the son of Hera and Zeus. Hephaestus was identified by the Romans with Vulcan.

HERA   Daughter of Cronus and Rhea, she was the sister and wife of Zeus; queen of the Olympian deities, and the mother of Ares, Hebe, and Hephaestus. She was identified by the Romans with Juno.

HERACLEA   A city of Bithynia in northwestern Asia Minor; according to legend, named for Heracles.

HERACLES (or HERCULES)   The son of Zeus and Alcmene, and the most famous of the Greek heroes. His Latin name is Hercules.

HERMES   In Greek mythology the messenger of the gods and the god of travelers, commerce, flocks, and dreams; the son of Zeus and Maia. Hermes was identified by the Romans with Mercury.

HERMIONE   The daughter of King Menelaus of Sparta and Helen.

HESIONE   A daughter of King Laomedon of Troy.

HESPERE   One of the Hesperides.

HESPERIA   A name applied by the Greeks to the west in general and Italy in particular.

HESPERIDES   According to Hesiod, the daughters of Erebus and Nyx, or of Atlas and Hesperis, or of Phorcys and Ceto, in later accounts; guardians of the golden apples. They are variously said to be three, four, or seven in number.

HESPERUS   In Greek mythology, the evening star; called Vesper by the Romans.

HESTIA   A daughter of Cronus and Rhea, and the Greek goddess of the hearth and family life; identified by the Romans with Vesta.

HIPPOLYTE (or HIPPOLYTA)   A daughter of Ares, and the queen of the Amazons.

HIPPOMENES   A grandson of Poseidon, he won Atalanta's hand by defeating her in a footrace.

HOURS (HORAE)   The Hours were goddesses of nature and agriculture and the seasons of the year.

HYDRA   A dragon with nine heads that lived in the marshy region of Lerna in Argolis.

HYLAS   The young follower and companion of Heracles on the expedition of the Argonauts.

HYMEN (or HYMENAEUS)   Originally a Greek marriage song. In later classical mythology the name became the personification of the marriage song as the god of marriage.

HYMETTUS, MOUNT   A mountain near Athens noted for its honey as well as its marble.

HYPERBOREANS   In Greek mythology a race living in the far north in a land of abundance and sunshine.

HYPERION   A Titan and father by his sister Theia of Helios, Eos, and Selene. Hyperion was sometimes identified with Helios and Apollo.

IAMBE   A daughter of King Celeus of Eleusis and Metaneira.

IAPETUS   A Titan and father of Prometheus, Epimetheus, and Atlas by Clymene, daughter of Oceanus.

ICARIA   An island west of Samos in the Aegean Sea and named for Icarus.

ICARIAN SEA   In ancient times, that part of the Aegean Sea in the vicinity of Samos.

ICARUS   The son of Daedalus who was drowned in their flight from Crete.

IDA, MOUNT   (1.) A mountain in northwestern Asia Minor. (2.) A mountain in Crete on which the infant Zeus was cared for.

IDAS   The brother of Lynceus, and one of the Argonauts.

ILIUM   The Latinized form of the Greek word Ilion or Ilios, a name for Troy.

ILLYRIA (or ILLYRICUM)   A region on the Adriatic Sea north of Greece.

INACHUS   A river in Argolis and the god of that river; the son of Oceanus and Tethys, and the father of Io.

IO   The daughter of the river god Inachus, and the mother by Zeus of Epaphus; later identified with the Egyptian goddess Isis.

IOLAUS   The son of Heracles' brother Iphicles, and the loyal companion of Heracles.

IONIAN SEA   The waters between Italy and Greece; the southern part of the Adriatic Sea.

IPHICLES   The son of Amphitryon and Alcmene, and the twin brother of Heracles.

IRIS   The goddess of the rainbow, she was a messenger of the gods, especially of Zeus and Hera.

ISMENE   A daughter of Oedipus and Jocasta, and the sister of Antigone, Eteocles, and Polynices.

ISMENUS (1.) One of the seven sons of Amphion and Niobe. (2.) A river near Thebes.

ISTER RIVER The modern Danube.

ISTHMUS OF CORINTH The isthmus that connects the Peloponnesus and the central part of Greece.

ITHACA An island in the Ionian Sea near the Gulf of Corinth; the home of Odysseus.

IXION A king of the Lapithae, he was punished in Tartarus by being bound to a revolving wheel.

JASON The son of Aeson and leader of the Argonauts.

JOCASTA The wife of King Laius of Thebes, mother and wife of Oedipus, sister of Creon, and daughter of Menoeceus. She was the mother by Oedipus of Antigone, Ismene, Eteocles, and Polynices.

JUNO In Roman mythology the sister and wife of Jupiter, and the queen of the gods. Juno was identified with the Greek goddess Hera.

JUPITER The chief deity of the Romans, he was the son of Saturn and Ops, and husband of Juno; identified with the Greek god Zeus.

LABDACUS A king of Thebes, and the father of Laius.

LACONIA A district in the southeastern Peloponnesus. Sparta was its largest city.

LADON RIVER A river of Arcadia flowing into the Alpheus River.

LAËRTES The husband of Anticlea, who was the mother of Odysseus. In Homer, Laërtes is Odysseus' father, but in some later accounts Odysseus is the son of Sisyphus of Corinth.

LAIUS A king of Thebes, and the great-grandson of Cadmus; the husband of Jocasta, and the father of Oedipus.

LAOCOÖN A Trojan priest of Apollo or, according to some accounts, of Poseidon.

LAOMEDON A king of Troy, and the father of Priam and Hesione.

LAPITHAE A people of Thessaly who were attacked by the centaurs at the wedding of their king, Pirithous, and Hippodamia.

LATIUM A district on the west coast of Italy lying south of the Tiber River.

LATONA   The Latin name for Leto.

LEBINTHOS   One of the Dodecanese Islands, lying in the southeastern part of the Aegean Sea.

LEDA   The wife of King Tyndareus of Sparta, and the mother of Castor, Pollux, Helen, and Clytemnestra.

LEMNOS   An island in the northeastern Aegean Sea.

LENAEUS   An epithet of Dionysus, who was honored by the Lenaea, a festival celebrated in a sanctuary near the Acropolis.

LERNA   A marshy section in Argolis that was the haunt of the Hydra.

LETHE   The river of forgetfulness in the lower world.

LETO   The mother by Zeus of the twins Apollo and Artemis. Her Roman name was Latona.

LIBYA   A name used in ancient times for Africa or, more specifically, north of the equator, often excluding Egypt and Ethiopia.

LIRIOPE   A river nymph, she was the mother of Narcissus.

LOXIAS   An epithet of Apollo referring to him as a god of prophecy.

LUCIFER   The morning star. The name means "light-bearer" or "light-bringer."

LUNA   The Roman goddess of the moon; sometimes identified with the goddess Diana.

LYCAEUS, MOUNT   A mountain in Arcadia sacred to Zeus and Pan. Lycaeus was also an epithet of Zeus.

LYCIUS (or LYCEUS)   An epithet of Apollo, it was of uncertain origin, but possibly used in connection with the district of Lycia in Asia Minor.

LYCUS   (1.) One of the four sons of King Pandion of Athens. (2.) A king of Mysia who entertained Heracles.

LYDIA   A district in the western part of Asia Minor.

LYNCEUS   The brother of Idas, he was one of the Argonauts and was noted for his sharp sight.

LYRCEA   The name of a town and its environs in Argolis.

MACEDONIA   A country lying north of Thessaly and west of Thrace.

MAENADS   Female worshipers of Dionysus; also called bacchantes.

MAEONIA   An early name for Lydia.

MAIA   One of the Pleiades—daughters of Atlas and Pleione—and the mother of Hermes by Zeus.

MALEA   The southeastern promontory of the Peloponnesus where Chiron lived in a cave.

MANTO   The daughter of Tiresias.

MARATHON   A plain located at the edge of the sea on the northeast coast of Attica.

MEDEA   An enchantress, the daughter of King Aeëtes of Colchis; wife first of Jason and then of King Aegeus of Athens; a niece of Circe.

MEDUSA   A daughter of the sea deities Phorcys and Ceto. She was a monster with wings, snakes in place of hair, and the power to turn people to stone with her glance.

MEGARA   The chief city of Megaris, a district lying west of Attica at the Isthmus of Corinth.

MELEAGER   A son of King Oeneus of Calydon; one of the Argonauts and a member of the Calydonian Boar Hunt.

MELIAE   The nymphs of the ash trees. The name is derived from the Greek word *melia*, "ash."

MELPOMENE   The Muse of tragedy.

MENELAUS   A son of Atreus, and the brother of Agamemnon; husband of Helen, he was the king of Sparta at the time of the Trojan War.

MENOECEUS   (1.) The father of Creon and Jocasta. (2.) The son of Creon.

MERCURY   The Roman god of commerce, the protector of travelers, and the messenger of the gods; son of Jupiter and Maia. Mercury was the Roman counterpart of the Greek god Hermes.

MEROPE   (1.) A Pleiad and the wife of Sisyphus. (2.) The wife of King Polybus of Corinth.

METANEIRA (or METANIRA)   The wife of King Celeus of Eleusis.

METION   According to Diodorus, he was the grandson of Erechtheus, a legendary king of Athens, and the son of Eupalamus. In most accounts, however, he was the son of Erechtheus.

METIS   The daughter of Oceanus and Tethys, and the first wife of Zeus; Athena was their daughter. Metis means "counsel," "wisdom," or "thought" in Greek.

MIDAS   A king of Phrygia, and the son of King Gordius.

MILETUS   A son of Apollo who founded the city Miletus in southwestern Asia Minor.

MINERVA   An Italian goddess of the womanly arts and of artisans; identified by the Romans with Athena.

MINOS   A son of Zeus and Europa, and the brother of Rhadamanthus. Minos was king of Cnossus, the husband of Pasiphaë, and the father of Ariadne and Androgeus. After his death, Minos was made a judge of the lower world.

MINOTAUR   The monster, half man and half bull, born to Pasiphaë, wife of King Minos. The name Minotaur comes from the Greek words for "Minos" and "bull."

MNEMOSYNE   A Titan, the daughter of Uranus and Gaea, and the personification of memory. She was the mother of the Muses by Zeus.

MOPSUS   A Lapith who sailed with Jason and the Argonauts.

MUSAEUS   A legendary Greek poet and prophet whose name was often linked with that of Orpheus.

MUSES   The nine daughters of Mnemosyne and Zeus, they were goddesses of the arts and sciences, and poetry and song. The Muses were Calliope, Clio, Euterpe, Thalia, Melpomene, Terpsichore, Erato, Polyhymnia, and Urania. Roman mythology assigned to them their functions (*see* each individual Muse by name).

MYCENAE   An ancient city on the Argive plain. Agamemnon was king of Mycenae at the time of the Trojan War.

MYGDON   A king of the Bebryces in Bithynia, he was slain by Heracles.

MYRMIDONS   The subjects of King Aeacus of Aegina and, later, subjects of his son Peleus and grandson Achilles.

MYSIA   A district in northwestern Asia Minor.

NAIADS   Nymphs of the streams, rivers, springs, and fountains.

NARCISSUS   The handsome son of the river god Cephisus and the nymph Liriope; he was loved by Echo.

NAXOS   The largest of the Cyclades Islands. Also known as Dia, it was sacred to Dionysus.

NEMEA   A valley in Argolis, and the haunt of the Nemean Lion.

NEMESIS A goddess of order and balance who exacted just retribution from mortals on behalf of the gods.

NEPTUNE An Italian deity of water, identified by the Romans with Poseidon.

NEREIDS Sea nymphs, the fifty daughters of Nereus and the Oceanid Doris.

NEREUS A sea god, the son of Pontus and Gaea, husband of Doris, and father of the Nereids.

NESSUS A centaur killed by Heracles.

NESTOR A king of Pylos who was highly respected by the Greeks for his wisdom and sound advice; father of Antilochus.

NINUS A king of Assyria and husband of Semiramis.

NIOBE The daughter of Tantalus, sister of Pelops, and wife of King Amphion of Thebes.

NOTUS The south wind.

NYMPHS Maidens who were protective deities; spirits of various places and of nature, especially rivers, streams, fountains, mountains, and woods.

NYX The personification and goddess of night. She was the daughter of Chaos and sister and wife of Erebus.

OCEANUS A Titan son of Uranus and Gaea. Oceanus and his wife Tethys bore the river gods and the nymphs of the seas and rivers. According to Homer, Oceanus was the river that encircled the earth.

ODYSSEUS A king of Ithaca, husband of Penelope, father of Telemachus, and, in Homer, son of Laërtes. Odysseus was a leader in the Trojan War and is the hero of the *Odyssey.*

OEDIPUS The son of King Laius of Thebes and Jocasta, and a descendant of Cadmus; also the husband of Jocasta, and father of Antigone, Ismene, Eteocles, and Polynices.

OLENUS A town on the coast of Achaea where Dexamenus was king.

OLYMPUS, MOUNT A lofty mountain (about 9700 ft.) in northern Thessaly; considered to be the home of the gods.

ONCHESTUS A city near Thebes, in Boeotia, that was sacred to Poseidon.

ORCUS   A Roman god of the lower world who was later identified with Hades or Pluto.

ORION   A hunter of gigantic size who became a constellation in the southern skies after his death.

ORPHEUS   A son of King Oeagrus of Thrace or, in some accounts, of Apollo and Calliope; the husband of Eurydice. Orpheus was noted as a musician and poet.

ORTHRUS (or ORTHUS)   The two-headed dog that guarded the cattle of Geryon.

OSSA, MOUNT   A high mountain (about 6500 ft.) near Mount Pelion in eastern Thessaly.

OTHRYS, MOUNT   A mountain in southern Thessaly.

PACTOLUS RIVER   A small branch of the Hermus River in Lydia.

PALLAS   (1.) A giant son of Gaea, sprung from the blood of Uranus. (2.) A son of Pandion. (3.) A giant killed by Athena. (4.) A title of Athena, who was often called Pallas Athena.

PAN   According to most accounts, including Homer and Plato, the son of Hermes (some give Zeus as his father); the god of pastures and woodlands.

PANATHENAEA   The annual festival held at Athens in honor of Athena. The Great Panathenaea was held every fourth year.

PANDION   The father of Aegeus, Pallas, Nisus, and Lycus. When his nephews drove him from Athens, Pandion went to Megara in exile.

PANDORA   The first woman, she was created by Hephaestus at the command of Zeus. She became the wife of Epimetheus in spite of Prometheus' warnings to his brother.

PANTHOUS   A priest of Apollo who counseled the Greeks during the Trojan War; father of Euphorbus.

PAPHOS   (1.) A city near the southwest coast of Cyprus that was sacred to Aphrodite. (2.) The son of Pygmalion.

PARIS   A son of King Priam of Troy and Hecuba; also called Alexander or Alexandros.

PARNASSUS, MOUNT   A lofty mountain (about 8000 ft.) in Phocis that was sacred to Apollo and the Muses. Delphi is located on its lower slopes.

PAROS   One of the Cyclades Islands. Parian marble was famous for its fine quality and whiteness.

PASIPHAË   The wife of King Minos of Crete, and the mother of Ariadne and the Minotaur.

PATROCLUS   A son of Menoetius, and a close friend of Achilles. He was a hero in the Trojan War.

PEGASUS   A winged horse, son of Poseidon, born from the blood of Medusa.

PELASGUS   The legendary ancestor of the Pelasgians, the early, pre-Hellenic inhabitants of Greece.

PELEUS   A son of King Aeacus, the husband of Thetis, and the father of Achilles.

PELIAS   A king of Thessaly and half brother of Aeson, Jason's father.

PELION, MOUNT   A mountain (about 5000 ft.) near the east coast of Thessaly; the home of the centaurs.

PELOPONNESUS   The "island of Pelops," the large peninsula that forms the southern part of Greece.

PELOPS   The son of Tantalus and brother of Niobe. Pelops was the father of Atreus, whose sons were Agamemnon and Menelaus; according to some, he was the father of Sciron.

PENEUS   The god of the Peneus River, a river flowing through the Vale of Tempe in Thessaly.

PERIMEDES   One of Odysseus' companions on his voyage.

PERIPHETES   A son of Hephaestus and Anticleia, or of Poseidon, according to some.

PERSA (or PERSEÏS)   A daughter of Oceanus and Tethys, and the mother by Helios of Aeëtes, Circe, and Pasiphaë.

PERSEPHONE   The daughter of Zeus and Demeter, and the wife of Hades. Her Latin name was Proserpina, a corruption and perhaps the name of an early Italian goddess who became associated with her.

PERSEUS   The son of Zeus and Danaë, and the slayer of Medusa.

PHAEA   The name of a sow, killed by Theseus, and of the old woman who kept it.

PHAËTHON   A son of Helios and Clymene.

PHASIS RIVER   A river in Colchis that flowed into the Black Sea.

PHILEMON   The husband of Baucis. Philemon and Baucis were a kindly old couple who were devoted to the gods.

PHILOCTETES   The son of a king of Thessaly; a Greek hero and one of Helen's suitors.

PHLEGETHON   The river of fire in the lower world.

PHOCIS   A district of central Greece lying north of the Corinthian Gulf and west of Boeotia. Delphi was located in Phocis.

PHOEBE   A Titan and the mother of Leto. Phoebe, whose name means "bright one," was later identified with the moon and with Artemis and Diana.

PHOEBUS   In later mythology Apollo had the epithet Phoebus, meaning "light" or "bright," and was often identified with the sun god Helios.

PHOENICIA   A narrow land at the eastern end of the Mediterranean. Tyre and Sidon were located in Phoenicia.

PHOENIX   The son of King Agenor of Tyre and Telephassa; the brother of Europa and Cadmus. He was the legendary founder of Phoenicia. According to some accounts Phoenix was Europa's father.

PHOLUS   A centaur who lived in a cave in the southern Peloponnesus and was visited by Heracles.

PHRIXUS   The brother of Helle, she who fled to Colchis on the ram with the golden fleece. He married Chalciope, a daughter of King Aeëtes, and they had four sons.

PHRONTIS   One of the four sons of Phrixus and Chalciope.

PHRYGIA   A country in central and western Asia Minor with boundaries that varied at different periods.

PHTHIA   A district in southeastern Thessaly; also, a town in that district.

PIERIA   An idyllic district in northern Thessaly where Mount Olympus was located; birthplace of the Muses.

PINDUS MOUNTAINS   A mountain range in northern Greece, it lies between Epirus and Thessaly.

PIRENE   A fountain at Corinth where Bellerophon found Pegasus.

PIRITHOUS   The son of Zeus and Ixion's wife Dia; a king of the Lapithae and a close friend of Theseus. Hippodamia was his wife.

PISCES   The Fishes, the twelfth sign of the zodiac, February 19–March 20.

PITTHEUS   A son of Pelops, and a king of Troezen.

PLEIADES   The seven daughters of Atlas and Pleione, a daughter of Oceanus and Tethys.

PLUTO (or PLUTON)   A name or title of Hades; it means the "wealthy one" or the "wealth-giver."

POLLUX (Greek, POLYDEUCES)   The son of Zeus and Leda, he was the twin brother of Castor, as well as the brother of Helen and Clytemnestra.

POLYBUS   A king of Corinth, he was the husband of Merope. Polybus and Merope adopted the infant Oedipus and reared him as their son.

POLYDORUS   (1.) The youngest son of Hecuba and King Priam of Troy. (2.) A son of Cadmus and Harmonia, and the father of Labdacus.

POLYHYMNIA   The Muse of sacred poetry and song, and of pantomime.

POLYIDUS (or POLYEIDUS)   A seer of Corinth.

POLYPEMON   The father of Sinis; also called Damastes or Procrustes.

POLYPHEMUS   A Cyclops and son of Poseidon; he was outwitted by Odysseus.

PONTUS   (1.) The sea personified; son of Gaea, and the father of Nereus. (2.) A district in northern Asia Minor.

POSEIDON   The Greek god of earthquakes and the sea; also a deity of horses. He was the son of Cronus and Rhea, and the husband of Amphitrite. Poseidon became the father of Pegasus by Medusa. The Romans identified him with Neptune.

PRIAM   A son of Laomedon, and the king of Troy at the time of the Trojan War; husband of Hecuba and father of Hector, Paris, Polydorus, and many others.

PROMETHEUS   The son of Iapetus and Clymene, and the brother of Epimetheus and Atlas. His name means "forethought" or "forethinker."

PROSERPINA   The Latin name for Persephone.

PROTEUS   A sea deity with the power to change form; he lived on the island of Pharos and was often confused with a king of Egypt of the same name.

Psyche   The human representation of the soul, she was loved by Cupid and became his wife.

Pygmalion   (1.) A king of Tyre, and the brother of Dido. (2.) A king of Cyprus who fell in love with a statue he carved.

Pylos   A town, in the southwestern Peloponnesus, of which Nestor was king at the time of the Trojan War.

Pyramus   A Babylonian youth, Thisbe's lover.

Pyrrha   The daughter of Epimetheus, and the wife of Deucalion.

Pythia   The priestess of Apollo at Delphi.

Rhadamanthus   A son of Zeus and Europa, and a judge of the lower world.

Rhea   A Titan, the daughter of Uranus and Gaea, and the sister and wife of Cronus; the mother of Demeter, Hades, Hera, Hestia, Poseidon, and Zeus. She was the Great Mother goddess and was identified with Cybele.

Rhegium   A city in Italy at the Strait of Messina.

Rhodope Mountains   A mountain range in northern Thrace.

Samos   An island in the Aegean Sea off the southwestern coast of Asia Minor.

Sardis (or Sardes)   The chief city and capital of Lydia.

Saturn   The Roman god of agriculture; identified with the Greek god Cronus. Saturn was the husband of Ops and the father of Jupiter.

Satyr   A goatlike spirit of the hills and woods, an attendant of Dionysus.

Scaean Gate   The main gate of Troy, located on the northwest side of the city.

Scamander   The name of a river at Troy; called Xanthus by the gods.

Scamandrius   A name for Astyanax, son of Hector and Andromache.

Sciron   A highwayman slain by Theseus near Megara; a son of Pelops, or, in some accounts, of Poseidon.

Scylla   A sea nymph who was transformed into a monster and later identified with the Strait of Messina.

Scyros (or Skyros)   One of the Northern Sporades islands in the western Aegean.

Selene   According to Hesiod, the daughter of Hyperion and
Theia; elsewhere, the daughter or wife of Helios. Selene was the
Greek goddess of the moon, associated with Artemis.

Semele   The daughter of Harmonia and King Cadmus of Thebes
and the mother of Dionysus by Zeus.

Semiramis   The legendary founder and queen of Babylon.

Sibyl   A prophetess who had the ability to know the will of the
gods. One of the most famous was the Cumaean Sibyl, who wrote
the prophecies of Apollo on leaves.

Sidon   A city in Phoenicia north of Tyre; an important center of
commerce.

Silenus   A satyr who was associated with Dionysus. The plural,
Sileni, was sometimes used in poetry to refer to them as wise,
elderly, and drunken merrymakers.

Sinis   A highwayman who haunted the Isthmus of Corinth and
was slain by Theseus; son of Polypemon and Sylea.

Sinon   A Greek youth who deceived the Trojans into accepting
the wooden horse.

Sipylus   (1.) A town and a mountain in Lydia associated with
Tantalus and Niobe. (2.) One of the seven sons of Amphion and
Niobe, and a grandson of Tantalus.

Sirens   Creatures, half maiden and half bird, who lured sailors to
their island with their song.

Sisyphus   A son of Aeolus, and a king of Corinth; condemned
forever to roll a stone up a hill in the lower world.

Sparta   The chief city and capital of Laconia, a district in the
southern Peloponnesus.

Sphinx   A monster with the body of a lion and the head of a
woman who watched over the road near Thebes and killed all
passers-by who could not answer the riddle she set.

Steropes   Named by Hesiod as one of the Cyclopes.

Stymphalus   The name of a region, a lake, and a town in Arcadia.

Styx   One of the rivers of the lower world, often identified with
a small river that flowed from a high cliff in Arcadia. The gods
swore binding oaths by the Styx.

Sychaeus   Dido's husband, who was murdered by her brother
Pygmalion.

Syrinx   A nymph of Arcadia loved by Pan.

TAENARUM   A peninsula and cape in the southern Peloponnesus, and the site of one of the entrances to the lower world.

TAMASUS   A city on Cyprus.

TANTALUS   (1.) The father of Pelops and Niobe. (2.) One of the seven sons of Amphion and Niobe.

TARTARUS   A dark abyss in the lower world where the wicked were punished. The name Tartarus was often used to refer to the lower world in general.

TARTESSUS   A city and a region in southwestern Iberia, the modern Spain.

TAYGETE   One of the Pleiades.

TELAMON   The brother of Peleus, and the father of Teucer and Ajax. He was a Greek hero and one of the Argonauts.

TEMPE, VALE OF   A lovely valley in Thessaly, lying between Mount Olympus and Mount Ossa.

TENEDOS   An Aegean island off the coast of Asia Minor near Troy.

TERPSICHORE   The Muse of the dance.

TETHYS   A Titan and the wife of Oceanus.

TEUCER   (1.) A legendary king of Troy. The Trojans were often called Teucri, or Teucrians. (2.) The son of Telamon and Hesione.

THALIA   The Muse of comedy.

THEBES   The chief city of Boeotia. Cadmus, son of King Agenor of Tyre, was the legendary founder of Thebes.

THEIA (or THIA)   A Titan and the mother of Helios, Eos, and Selene by her brother Hyperion.

THEMIS   A Titan and the mother of the Fates and the Seasons; she was a prophetess and represented justice.

THEMISCYRA   A city on the southeast coast of the Black Sea.

THERMODON RIVER   A river in northern Asia Minor.

THESEUS   The son of King Aegeus of Athens or, by some accounts, of Poseidon and Aethra; one of the great legendary heroes of the Greeks.

THESSALY   A large district in the northeastern part of Greece.

THETIS   A Nereid; the wife of Peleus, and the mother of Achilles.

THISBE   A Babylonian maiden loved by Pyramus.

THORICUS   A town in southeastern Attica on the Aegean Sea.

THRACE   A region lying to the northeast of Macedonia.

THYMOETES   A Trojan who urged that the Trojan Horse be brought inside the walls of Troy.

TIBER RIVER   A river flowing through the central part of Italy and into the Tyrrhenian Sea.

TIPHYS   The helmsman of the *Argo*.

TIRESIAS   A long-lived, blind prophet of Thebes whom Oedipus and many others consulted for advice.

TIRYNS   A city in Argolis near Mycenae.

TISIPHONE   One of the Furies.

TITANS   Children of Uranus and Gaea: the Titans were Coeus, Crius, Cronus, Hyperion, Iapetus, and Oceanus; the Titanesses were Mnemosyne, Phoebe, Rhea, Tethys, Themis, and Theia. In later mythology Helios was sometimes called Titan.

TMOLUS   A mountain in Lydia, and the deity of that mountain.

TRITONIS   A lake in Libya associated with Athena.

TROEZEN   A city in Argolis near Mycenae and Tiryns.

TROS   The grandson of Dardanus for whom the Troad, the region of Troy, and the Trojans were named. His grandson was Laomedon, the father of Priam.

TROY   A city in northwestern Asia Minor; the scene of the Trojan War.

TYDEUS   A son of King Oeneus of Calydon.

TYNDAREUS   A king of Sparta, and the husband of Leda.

TYPHON (or TYPHOEUS)   A monstrous son of Gaea and Tartarus, and the father by Echidna of the Hydra, Orthrus, Cerberus, and the Chimaera.

TYRE   A city of Phoenicia noted for its prosperity and luxury.

TYRRHENIAN SEA   That part of the Mediterranean lying west of Italy and bounded by the islands of Sardinia, Corsica, and Sicily.

ULYSSES (or ULIXES)   The Latin name for Odysseus.

URANIA   The Muse of astronomy.

URANUS   The Greek god who was the personification of the sky and heavens; the son of Gaea and father by her of the Titans, Cyclopes, and Hecatonchires.

VENUS   An Italian goddess who was identified by the Romans with Aphrodite, the Greek goddess of love and beauty.

VULCAN   The Roman god of fire; later identified with the Greek god Hephaestus.

XANTHUS   (1.) The name by which the gods called the river at Troy which mortals called the Scamander; the god of that river. (2.) A city in southwestern Asia Minor.

ZEPHYRUS (or ZEPHYR)   The personification of the west wind.
ZEUS   Known as the father of gods and men, Zeus, the son of Cronus and Rhea, was the ruler of the Olympian deities.